HEIRS OF AMBITION

For my parents.

HEIRS OF AMBITION

AMBITION

The Making of the Boleyns

CLAIRE MARTIN

First published 2023
Reprinted 2023

The History Press
97 St George's Place, Cheltenham,
Gloucestershire, GL50 3QB
www.thehistorypress.co.uk

British Library Cataloguing in Publication Data.
A catalogue record for this book is available from the British Library.

ISBN 978 0 7509 9998 4

Typesetting and origination by The History Press
Printed and bound in Great Britain by TJ Books Limited, Padstow, Cornwall.

Trees for Life

Contents

Abbreviations

BL	British Library
Blomefield	Francis Blomefield, *An Essay Towards A Topographical History of the County of Norfolk*, 11 vols (London, 1805–10), www.british-history.ac.uk
CCR	Calendar of Close Rolls
CFR	Calendar of Fine Rolls
CPMR	*Calendar of Plea & Memoranda Rolls of the City of London 1323–1482*, ed. A.H. Thomas & Philip E. Jones, 6 vols (Cambridge, 1926–61)
CPR	Calendar of Patent Rolls
Davis	*Paston Letters and Papers of the Fifteenth Century*, ed. Norman Davis, 2 vols (Oxford, 1971)
GEC	*The Complete Peerage of England, Scotland, Ireland, Great Britain and the United Kingdom*, ed. George Edward Cockayne, 13 vols (Gloucester, 1910–59)
LBA–L	*Calendar of Letter Books of the City of London: Letter Books A–L*, ed. Reginald R. Sharpe (London, 1899–1912)
LCA	*The London Customs Accounts*, ed. Stuart Jenks, Hanseatic History Association (Lübeck, 2016–19), www.hansischergeschichtsverein.de/london-customs-accounts
LMA	London Metropolitan Archives

LP	Letters and Papers, Foreign and Domestic, of the Reign of Henry VIII, ed. J.S. Brewer, J. Gairdner & R.H. Brodie, 21 vols (London, 1862–1932)
LPRH	*Letters and Papers Illustrative of the Reigns of Richard III and Henry VII*, ed. James Gairdner, 2 vols (London, 1861–63)
MA	*The Medieval Account Books of the Mercers of London: An Edition and Translation*, ed. Lisa Jefferson, 2 vols (Farnham, 2009)
NRO	Norfolk Record Office
TNA	The National Archives

Acknowledgements

No book, particularly a first book, can get itself born without the aid of many helping hands. I am grateful to Simon Thurley for sight of his report on Hever Castle and to Henry Summerson for his advice on the legal position of Nicholas Boleyn. I also wish to extend special thanks to Richard Asquith for the Boleyn references from Ralph Verney's executors' accounts and to all members of the Medieval London seminar group (you know who you are). Our fascinating discussions, your wide-ranging knowledge and your invaluable pointers have helped to make this project better than I could ever have managed alone. Particular thanks must go to Nick Holder, and to Christian Steer and posthumously to the much-missed Clive Burgess for help with and discussion of Geoffrey Boleyn's memorial provision.

I am grateful to Prof. Tom Dening for his advice on a possible diagnosis of Margaret Boleyn's mental disorder and for his willingness to engage with a random request for help from a historian with peculiar questions. I also wish to thank Graham Dudley of Kentish Photography for supplying the photographs of Wickham Court and with them the evidence for Anne Boleyn and Henry Heydon's apparently happy union.

Archivists from around the country have made valuable contributions but I particularly wish to thank Gudrun Warren, Librarian and Curator of Norwich Cathedral, for discussion of William Boleyn's tomb and the vital information she provided that put me on the right track. I am also grateful for the generosity of staff at the Norfolk Record Office for photographing Salle's manor court rolls for almost the entire fourteenth century when minor flooding nearly ruined a research trip.

As always, I am particularly grateful to Caroline Barron, in this case for her meticulous edit of the final draft and for her excellent ideas and suggestions, but even more importantly, for being the best PhD supervisor any fledgling historian could hope for. I thank her for the inspiration, skills and love of Medieval London, without which this book would never have been written, and for her unwavering support. I also wish to thank Christine Fox for tirelessly reading endless drafts of the same early chapters while apparently remaining engaged and enthusiastic. Your dedication to our friendship knows no bounds.

Last but certainly not least, I am grateful for all my friends and family, who have learnt to politely enquire after Geoffrey Boleyn, and I would like to thank my parents. Your continued support and belief in everything I do have made this possible.

A Note on Money and Language

For ease of understanding, Latin and archaic English have been translated or rendered into modern spelling, except where the original serves to illustrate a point, and here explanation is provided as necessary.

Sums of money are given both in pounds, shillings and pence and in marks. The mark was never a physical amount of money represented by a coin but was commonly used for accounting purposes. It was equivalent to two thirds of a pound or 13s. 4d.

Where it serves to provide context, some sums of money are additionally translated into their modern-day equivalent with the assistance of The National Archives currency converter at www.nationalarchives.gov.uk/currency-converter/. This employs data from the royal household and Exchequer but such comparisons are an inexact science and other interpretations will always be possible.

Boleyn Family

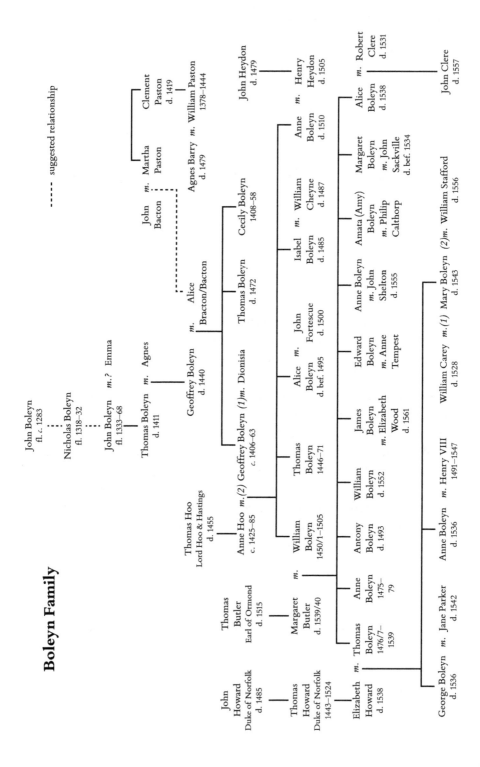

Hoo Family

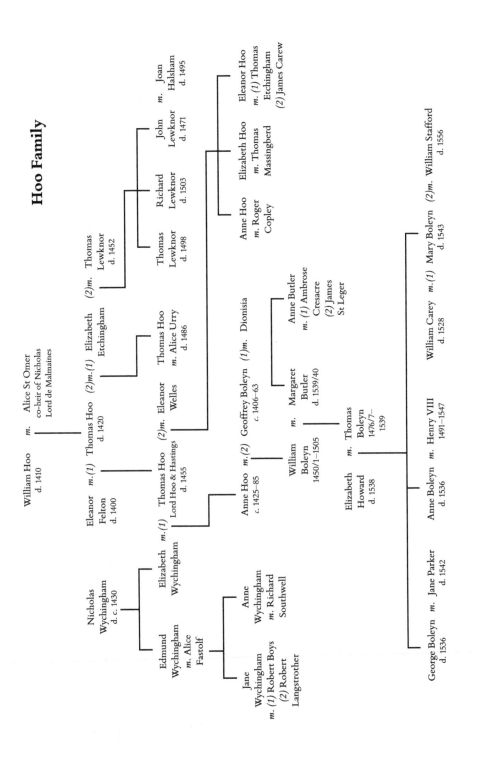

The Boleyns' London

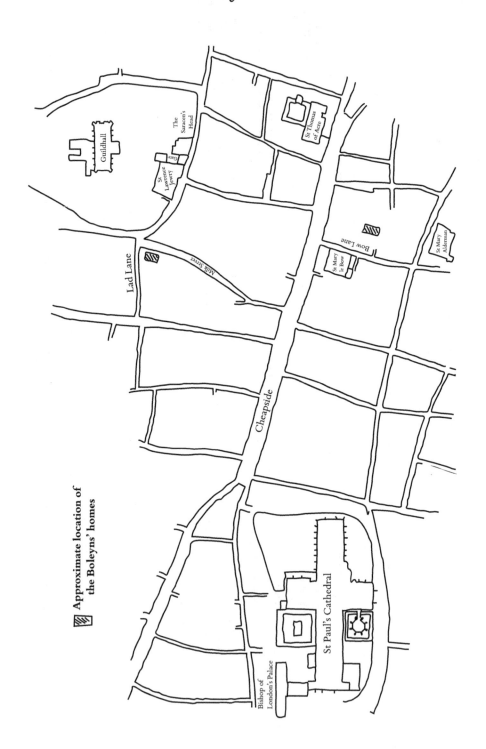

Guildhall

St Lawrence Jewry

Gate

The Saracen's Head

St Thomas of Acre

Lad Lane

Milk Street

Bow Lane

St Mary le Bow

St Mary Aldermary

Cheapside

Approximate location of the Boleyns' homes

Bishop of London's Palace

St Paul's Cathedral

Norwich, Salle, Blickling and the Boleyns' Norfolk

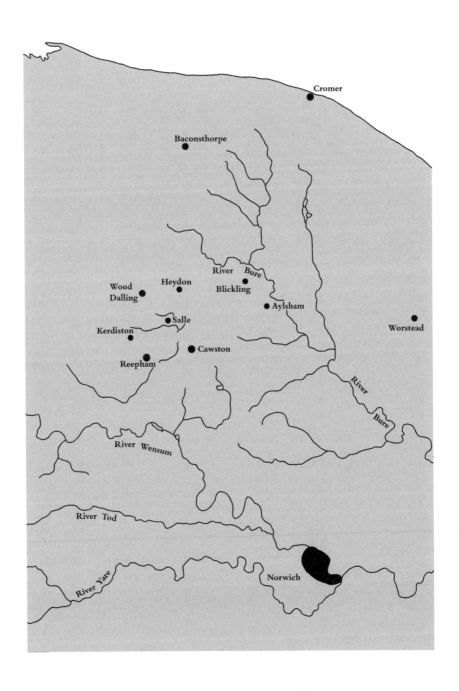

Cromer

Baconsthorpe

River Bure

Wood Dalling

Heydon

Blickling

Aylsham

Worstead

Kerdiston

Salle

Reepham

Cawston

River Bure

River Wensum

River Tod

River Yare

Norwich

Introduction

The Name of the Game

'It is always seen now a days
That money maketh the man'[1]

Late fifteenth-century ballad

The name of Boleyn is set in stone, carved deep into the heart of British history, but the labels the family took as their own have been numerous and wide-ranging. Nicholas Boleyn of Salle; Thomas Boleyn, 'donsel'; Geoffrey Boleyn, yeoman; Geoffrey Boleyn, citizen, hatter, mercer, merchant, sheriff, alderman, mayor; Master Thomas Boleyn, clerk; Lady Boleyn, widow; William Boleyn, esquire, knight; Thomas Boleyn, esquire, knight, viscount, earl; George Boleyn, esquire, knight, viscount; Anne Boleyn, marquess, queen.[2] Together they tell a story of lives well lived, fortunes changed and sons who surpassed the ambition of their fathers. But was fifteenth-century England really the open, mobile society their story suggests? Wasn't this a time of all-powerful kings and grovelling peasants where a few reclined in silken splendour while the many were enjoined 'to keep their own estate'?

The answer is, as always, rather more complex, but it is an important one. For this was the world in which the Boleyns played the game so well. The rules, the economy, the society, the prejudice through which they forged a path that began in the sheepfold and ended on the scaffold. While their ascent was not commonplace, neither was it unique, for the medieval elites had never been an impregnable fortress. Here and there, other families had breached the walls. But as long as their numbers were few and their ascent slow and limited, they did not disturb the peace of the residents within.[3] Change, however, was in the air. In the century and a half after the Black Death left straying livestock the only residents of some villages, a 'brave and ruthless new world' emerged.[4] Ordinary people were more prosperous, more free and more aspirational. Now when they approached the door to gentility they found it ajar.[5]

In 1500 a Yorkshire knight with a grudge against a city alderman wrote of him to the mayor as 'a churl which ye know is come lightly up and of small substance'.[6] With supreme arrogance of rank and title, he thought he knew exactly where he stood in relation to his upstart enemy. However, the insulted alderman, and the mayor who defended him, were equally assured of their position as leaders of York's society. For hundreds of years, rich and poor had similarly assessed those around them, although usually more quietly. They noted subtle signs like dress and speech, or more obvious indicators such as wealth or title, and positioned themselves accordingly. This impulse to define categories and apply names to people who are 'like me' or 'not like me' was, and always has been, irresistible. Before England was England, when Mercia fought Northumbria and Alfred was not yet Great, kings and ealdormen looked down long, Anglo-Saxon noses on thegns and churls. But for every individual, and for wider society, these relationships of precedence went far beyond mere dominance or deference. To 'lord it' over your dependants certainly could mean fiscal exploitation and flamboyant display but it also meant protecting those who looked to you for justice, good governance or patronage. When you, in turn, looked up at the royalty or nobility who 'lorded it' over you, it was with the same expectations. This was the chivalric ideal of good lordship, the two-way street where men knew what they were required to do for their lord or master but also what he was expected to do for them. Even when it failed (and it did) the emphasis was on improving the system, removing or reforming the bad apples, rather than upending the applecart. While individuals could and did climb around the many layered branches of medieval society, no one was looking to fell the tree.[7]

As far as medieval thinkers were concerned, the God-given order of society could be described in two complementary, hierarchical forms. There was the Body Politic, with the king as the head, the peasants as the feet and all other essential functions spread out in between. Alternatively, there was the tripartite doctrine of the Three Estates. Preachers from York to Yarmouth would remind their Sunday flock that 'there be in this world three manner of men, clerks, knights and commonalty', or those who prayed, those who fought (and governed) and everyone else.[8] The hierarchy of men who prayed stood separate from the rest, crowned by noble prelates who may wield both sword and political might. It was amongst the fighters and the toilers that generation after future generation would devote countless hours and lines of text to naming, defining and distinguishing themselves. The names and categories would change countless times and long chains of precedence would give way to greater class consciousness and group identity but the irresistible urge to name ourselves remains.

Most of the words we now find ourselves compelled to use in any such discussion would have been alien to our medieval ancestors. 'Class' in the sense of social groupings did not arrive until the seventeenth century, although it quickly caught on and out-classed older terms such as 'order' or 'degree' and new interlopers such as 'sort'.[9] 'Aristocracy' put in an early appearance but was not widely used until the sixteenth century. More familiar to earlier generations was 'noble', from the Latin *nobilis*, which originally meant well known or famous but quickly came to denote good birth or family connections and implied moral superiority. Historically it aligned with the second estate of men who fought, and those who laid claim to nobility often came from families whose origins were clad in armour. With the ability to pull together and lead a body of fighting men, such families had proved useful to rulers and they had been rewarded accordingly. That world, however, was becoming an ever more distant memory. From the fifteenth century, 'gentle' became the term of choice and the word that nobles used to describe themselves. Its connotations of refinement, manners and honourable behaviour suited an age in which elite identity was expanding to encompass more than just knightly prowess.[10]

Noble or gentle, for hundreds of years these men saw themselves as one, from the baron with the ear of the king to the poor knight worth little more than his horse, harness and £20 per year. The range of wealth and power was vast but they were united in a common culture of military skill, chivalric honour, service and landed property. With ease they could distinguish themselves from those who had to earn their bread by the labour of their hands or the dexterity of their minds. But time's winged chariot is apt to crush the comfortable constructs that men hold dear. The changes began in the thirteenth century but quickly gathered pace. Small landowners, who should have been knights, no longer wanted to shoulder the burden of military service or the growing expense of shield, spurs and other knightly superfluities. Instead they took an ever more active role in the Crown's administration of the realm until the leading men in a county could no longer be easily identified as the knights while, conversely, those who had been 'girt with the sword' on the battlefield might be relatively impoverished.[11] The confusion was insidious and would only get worse.

In the changed economic world after the Black Death, it was ever more difficult to ignore those who had never had a niche in the doctrine of the Three Estates or who were flying out of their convenient pigeon holes. The glut of available land, tumbling rents and rocketing wages spelled a boom in real income for the 'vulgar', 'simple' peasantry.[12] But they were not the only group on the march. Growing urban mercantile populations, particularly in London, were flexing their social and fiscal muscles while the growing professionalism of the law and civil service produced men who challenged the old boundaries of gentility. Newly aspirational rustics, urbane merchants and educated lawyers could now afford the outward furs and finery of their betters, and the ability of gentle men or women confidently to draw a line between themselves and the uncomfortable masses below seemed to be under threat.

The answer was more precision, more names, more boundaries and more rules. In the countryside the prospering 'yeoman', with his extensive acres, was distinguished from the smaller 'husbandman' below him and from 'farmers' who leased or 'farmed' former demesne estates. Many could clearly be separated from the gentle folk above by the dirt beneath their finger nails but the yeomanry pressed hard against the rickety boundary fence, and they were not the only ones. Much angst and insecurity would be directed towards this contested frontier in search of a new accord. 'Esquires', who originally served and bore the arms of their knightly masters, were sucked upwards to the bottom rungs of the nobility and became an independent, non-military social rank.[13] In 1363, sumptuary legislation against the 'outrageous and excessive apparel of divers people against their estate and degree' lumped esquires worth £100 a year in with merchants and artificers worth £500.[14] Yet despite these vastly differing sums, rich London merchants knew that city wealth must be exchanged for both manors and manners to smooth out those disparities.

Further efforts to treat this outbreak of social anxiety with more precise definitions came with the Statute of Additions of 1413, which required a man's 'estate, degree or trade' to be specified in all legal documents. 'Gentlemen', as a group distinct from the larger mass of the well-to-do but below the rank of 'esquire', were given formal recognition, either as landowners or for professional administrative service, although it was some time before the term was generally accepted. With upwardly mobile lawyers grudgingly accorded the rank of gentleman by the end of the fifteenth century, efforts towards realignment seemed complete.[15] The new names were not rigid classes – one man may be termed 'esquire' on Monday and 'gentleman' on Tuesday – but the new ways of defining self-identity were an attempt to quell the fears or aspirations of those who sat near contested boundaries. In the process, however, something new had emerged. A striving, energetic, innovative something that the pioneering social historian Sylvia Thrupp termed the 'middle strata'.

This elusive, indefinable middle strata has long perplexed historians and contemporaries alike. In one sense they were not really new at all. England had never been a land without middling people, of middling wealth and middling status, but something undoubtedly changed in the century or so before Henry Tudor seized the throne. The sharp canon of Leicester, who observed, in 1388, that 'one person cannot be discerned from another in splendour of dress or belongings, neither poor from rich, nor servant from master', knew it and he was not alone.[16] In 1970, the historian F.R.H. Du Boulay broke new ground, branding the post-Black Death period an Age of Ambition.[17] He saw the birth of a new middle class, enriched by the wealth of a struggling ancient nobility. But this alleged realignment of riches was not as extensive, permanent or novel as it may, at first, appear. Yes, the brave new economic world was real. Some yeomen enjoyed twice the annual income of gentlemen or esquires while, from the other direction, hard-pressed sons of gentility were driven to poach on the territory of their inferiors, engaging in trade or even the law. Such anomalies of the purse, however, were not what alarmed contemporaries or marked out the middle strata. It was the way that flourishing yeomen, merchants, lawyers or administrators demanded such facts be recognised. With newly purchased gowns and hastily learnt manners, they crowded around the door to gentility and expected to be admitted, not by right of birth but by right of worth.

As Chaucer's Wife of Bath argued, it was virtuous living and gentle deeds that made 'the grettest gentil man', not ancestry, and Chaucer knew his audience well. Such a doctrine of learned or earned, rather than inherited, gentility was popular with the aspirational middle who thenceforth set out on a wholesale appropriation of the behaviours that made the nobility distinct. Wealthy London merchants widely assumed heraldic arms, making them their own with symbols of their trade, while the knighting of the city's mayors was routine by the end of the fifteenth century. Courtesy books, dubbed 'manuals of social mobility', taught the habits, behaviours and traditions of the elite, and were the must-have reading of the age. By careful study of the advice therein the gauche merchant might avoid embarrassment when at table with his betters and 'by fair manners ... may be advanced'. The writer and printer William Caxton dedicated his hugely successful *Book of Courtesy* to 'great lords, gentlemen' and, crucially, 'merchants'. Along with similar, older works, it was enthusiastically devoured by aspiring Londoners, civil servants and small landowners alike.[18]

What all this jockeying for position failed to create, however, was a cohesive group identity or any real sense of a middle class amongst the men and women who were, undeniably, in the middle. Despite gentle and non-gentle drawing closer together in wealth, interests and outward appearance, they did not yet see themselves as one body of men distinct from those above or below. The land-poor esquire still had no desire to be in the same club with the merchant or the prosperous yeoman. Despite convenient use of the term by medieval historians, including myself, the 'gentry' were not formally divorced from the greater aristocracy until the seventeenth century, but in the meantime what the middling sort did have in common was something that would become the core doctrine of a future middle class. Individualism. From the younger sons of nobility, cast onto their own resources by primogeniture, to aspirational yeomen, they, like the Boleyns, were driven to shape their lives by their own efforts.[19] In commerce, the legal profession, the Church or whatever opportunities came their way, they lived and died by their own ambition. The middle class as we know it may not have been named in the late Middle Ages but it was, nevertheless, alive and well.

Today we no longer write our social rank after our name and yet we remain fascinated with it. When the Great British Class Survey coined seven new social classes, in 2013, seven million people logged on to find out what they should call themselves. On the one hand it is novelty and entertainment, the rules of a game that no longer exists. It is doubtful that many participants lost sleep on finding themselves to be a 'new affluent worker' or 'technical middle class' but this game is still not played on a level field. Enthusiasm for the Great British Class Survey was disproportionately weighted towards professionals from the south-east, Oxford and Cambridge. Those who feared they might be consigned to the 'precariat' declined to get involved.[20] For the Boleyns an awareness of rank and position would have been all too familiar as they elbowed their way through the hustling middle strata. From Norwich Gaol to Hampton Court, they scrambled upwards, sometimes in great leaps and bounds, adopting and shedding rank and title as they went. The names they called themselves were there, in black and white, on every document to which they set seal and they spoke a truth that could not be ignored.

PART I

Welcome to Norfolk

1283–1440

Meet the Boleyns

London, 14 June 1463

Beyond the window, tucked under London's closely packed eaves, the city's sparrows were busy tending late summer broods. Their chirping and cheeping was a dawn-to-dusk soundtrack of courtship and new life but inside the house on London's Milk Street it was the end of life that occupied every mind. Geoffrey Boleyn, mercer, merchant, mayor, one of the richest men in England's richest city, son of a Norfolk yeoman and future great-grandfather of a queen, was dying. At his bedside friends, family and parish priest drew close to whisper prayers or last goodbyes and standing beside him in the final days, just as she had through a lifetime together, was his wife, Anne.

Since he slipped that gold band onto her finger around eighteen years ago, her hand in his had changed. More lines for both of them and, he knew, a few grey hairs under her headdress but together they had made a fortune and built a family to carry it forward. Now, for Geoffrey, it was time to let go of both, but before he drew his final breath there were arrangements to be made, and a hastily summoned scribe was already hard at work.

Under his ink-stained fingers Geoffrey's last will was taking shape.[21] Vast sums, great houses and numerous country estates handed down to children who were just that, children. Thomas, his eldest, was not yet 17, his brother, William, no more than 12 and their sisters all still unwed maidens. Never a man to leave matters to chance, Geoffrey had tried to make plans. Young Thomas Fastolf would have been a fine match for one of his girls but that wardship had slipped through his fingers years ago and now there was no time left.[22] So he was writing a will to shield his fortune and protect his family. It would prevent Thomas or William from blowing the lot at 21 and reduce the risk of Anne, Isabel or Alice running off with a tradesman, but Geoffrey's greatest trust lay with their mother. Anne, he knew, would set the right course.

These five young Boleyns were the future but under the hand of the labouring scribe the ink was still wet on thoughts of the past, as with masses and prayers Geoffrey dutifully remembered his parents. Geoffrey and Alice may have been many years dead, their souls long since departed, but in their sons, Geoffrey and Thomas, their legacy lived on. Thomas had been sent to climb the career ladder in the Church, Geoffrey dispatched to earn a fortune in London, and both men had travelled far in their new careers. Behind them stood not just their parents but their grandparents, Thomas and Agnes, and the many other Boleyns who had made the road over which they walked. They too had done all they could to build better lives for their children and although, to Geoffrey, they were no more than names, memories recently dusted off by his brother, Thomas, for some legal matter of his own, as he contemplated joining their number, those long-dead Boleyns perhaps seemed closer than ever.[23]

Geoffrey knew his body would never walk from that room again. It would be carried just a few yards down Catte Street to his London parish church, although once he had planned for a final resting place that was miles, not yards, away. Once he had hoped that he would lie, at last, in the soil of his birth, under boundless Norfolk skies.

Norwich, 3 May 1318

Tucked behind the imposing walls of Norwich Castle, the chamber may have been shrouded in shadows but the prisoner still flinched from the light as he emerged blinking from the cells. Foot followed foot followed foot across the expanse of floor towards two grave faces and a jury. He would exit this room to freedom, to further incarceration or to his death. He had entered it because, in this case, his own family were not to be trusted.

It had been a month since the last gaol delivery brought the latest batch of prisoners to trial and it is unclear whether Nicholas Boleyn had spent four hours or four weeks in the bowels of Norwich Castle but on 3 May 1318 his life hung in the balance. On his charge sheet was the theft of 40s. worth of cloth from an unnamed man of Lincoln, in league with his kinsman, Benedict Boleyn of Wood Dalling, and the value of the goods made his case a capital crime. Imprisoned and indicted, Benedict had sought to save his own skin by turning approver or king's evidence, admitting his guilt and naming an alleged accomplice.[24] It was a common and often cynical ploy. The subsequent prosecution usually failed but if it was successful the approver's sentence of death would be commuted to exile. At best it bought him time, a chance at escape or hope of a pardon. At worst it meant longer in the harsh conditions of Norwich Castle and death by disease. In May alone three inmates died in the castle prison, but Benedict had confessed so he was a dead man walking anyway. Approvers certainly had every reason to accuse innocent men, and prison guards were not averse to forcing prisoners to turn approver so they could extort money from alleged accomplices.[25] But if Benedict was buying time by accusing a blameless man, why choose a relative? If both really were guilty, then he was trying to condemn a kinsman to death in order to save himself. In either case it was treacherous behaviour.

Fortunately for Nicholas there seems to have been little evidence against him and jury problems further hindered his prosecution. Since he was found to be of 'good repute' and could provide sureties, he was released until the next session, two months later, when the need to produce twelve good men of Lincoln proved tricky in Norwich and he was returned to prison. Here the trail goes cold but if there was no other evidence and he was of confirmed good character he could expect to be acquitted and it appears he was.[26] Benedict's fate, however, was already sealed, and although no record can be found, it probably involved a short walk and a sharp drop. Minus a kinsman but with his reputation and neck intact, Nicholas would have been free to get out of Norwich, heading 15 miles north towards home and the small village of Salle.

With perhaps as many as 500 men, women and children bedding down each night beneath Salle's cluster of thatched roofs, Nicholas Boleyn's home village was, like the rest of England, at the height of its population.[27] Sitting on what in Norfolk passes for high ground between the valleys of the rivers Bure and Wensum, with the sheep-grazing expanse of Cawston Heath to the east, Salle could not escape the wider problems gripping the realm but the region also enjoyed unique advantages. As Nicholas set out from Norwich he was leaving behind one of England's leading provincial cities, with a population of around 18,000, set in the country's most heavily populated county, but everywhere from Devon to Durham people were feeling the strain.[28] Around three quarters of English men and women were peasant farmers or rural labourers but despite reclamation efforts, productive land to sustain all those souls could not be found, resulting in a shortage of food and driving up rents. Work was hard to come by, wages stagnated and prices rose, spelling hardship for many. As Nicholas headed north, England was three years into a series of bad harvests that had another four years to run and famine was filling the graveyards.[29]

While there is little evidence that Norfolk suffered the wholesale harvest failures that destroyed lives in other communities, the county's high population density produced other extremes.[30] The simple equation of acres divided by people, combined with inheritance customs that dispersed land between heirs, led to an average peasant holding of less than 3 acres. In Norfolk, manors often stretched over parish boundaries and villages were fractured into multiple manors. Peasants might hold land from more than one lord but families were still commonly living on tiny holdings that could not sustain them. On the Salle manor of Kirkhall, 81 per cent of the holdings that were passed to heirs or returned to the lord at the Black Death in 1349 were of less than 4 acres.[31] Not all the news, however, was bad. Nicholas lived in a region where manorial lords exercised relatively relaxed control over those who held by villein tenure, where peasants enjoyed a lively market in land and where a greater than average number of families, including the Boleyns, were free rather than unfree by birth.[32] While their neighbours the Briggs were, in the early fourteenth century, regularly described as *nativi* or servile by birth and were repeatedly censured for buying freehold land contrary to custom, the Boleyns never were.[33] Necessity also fostered enterprise. Those without sufficient land to grow their food had to earn the money to buy it, which in Salle and the surrounding villages gave rise to a flourishing textile industry.

In the thirteenth century it was linen cloth known as Aylsham that kept the spindles turning. Named for a village east of Salle, it was a fine cloth made of flax, although a coarser cloth was also produced from hemp. By 1300 this industry was already in decline, hit by stiff competition from Flanders, but the looms were yet in motion and Salle would still be known for the specialist production of fine linen coverchiefs until at least the mid-fourteenth century. Meanwhile, innovators, inspired perhaps by Flemish weavers, switched their raw material to wool, and worsted was born.[34] A cloth that would become the pride of Norfolk. By the fifteenth century, John Paston, of the self-made gentry family, was keen to source the 'worsted which is almost like silk' that he might make his doublet 'all worsted for worship of Norfolk'.[35] Piece goods were also made in Salle, including woollen caps and hats, and the village's Cappes Bridge may have derived its name from the scouring process that was part of hat manufacture.[36]

This cradle of enterprise, individualism and personal success that the Boleyns called home would one day provide the contacts that Geoffrey needed to take him to London as an apprentice hatter but he was far from being the only young lad who was dispatched carrying family ambition. Fuelled by the domestic labour of countless women working drop spindles, families from the Norfolk textile villages sent promising young men into the London cloth trades, where it was hoped their mercantile connections would advance the industry of those left behind. Some became aldermen or even mayors. Their surnames, derived from the villages of their birth, march through London's records in the hundreds: Aylsham and Cawston, Dalling and Elsing, Reepham and Salle marking the way.[37] For the Boleyns it would just be a matter of time.

An accurate assessment of the life Nicholas Boleyn was heading home to does, however, face some fundamental hurdles. Salle comprised all or part of six different manors. The largest by far was Kirkhall, owned since the late thirteenth century by the Mautby family, but there was also Nugoun's, named for its owner; Stinton, which extended into Heydon and was owned by the Brews family; Hawes, owed in the early thirteenth century by the Attehawes; Moor Hall, held by Walsingham Abbey; and Bagerhall, which was part of Kerdiston. Any individual villager might hold land in any or all of these manors but records survive for just a few, allowing only a partial view of the Boleyns' lives.[38] Nevertheless, the family's changing fortunes are clear to see.

The family name Boleyn, or Bulen, may be geographical in origin, referencing the French seaport of Boulogne, but it is doubtful that any of the Salle Boleyns originated in Boulogne. French immigrant to manorial tenant would be an unusual trajectory. The alternative spelling of Bolling or Bollen derives from Middle English, *bolling*, meaning 'something swollen', and may have been a nickname for a fat person, but the same root also provided other words for round forms. Middle English *bolle* was both a bowl and other spherical structures such as bubbles, balls or the globular seed pods of flax. Recorded examples of its use as a word for a seed pod date from the mid-fifteenth century but if it was in use earlier it might explain the large number of Boleyns from the linen-producing areas of Norfolk.[39] Whether they had connections to Boulogne or an ancestor who simply ate too many pies, the Boleyns abounded not only in Salle but in several of the surrounding villages. Doubtless many were related, aunts, uncles or distant cousins, but no direct evidence can link them to the family from Salle.

The earliest recorded resident of Salle with the surname Boleyn was John, who before 1283 held a house and lands from the Abbey of Walsingham, but Nicholas's court appearance in 1318 is the first evidence of John's descendants.[40] The survival of manorial court rolls from 1327 makes the family less elusive and Nicholas reappears in 1332 when his straying sheep caused damage to crops and pasture belonging to John de Mautby, the lord of Kirkhall.[41] He was ordered to make repairs to the boundary, and to ensure his compliance he was 'distrained' to the tune of twelve sheep, which would be returned when the work was done.[42] This is the only reference to Nicholas, and twelve sheep is very little on which to assess a life, but these sheep have much to tell us. A better-off peasant with 30 acres of land and right of common pasture might be expected to keep around thirty sheep, his neighbour with half the land could maintain considerably fewer and those with just 3 acres little more than one cow.[43] Such calculations varied from county to county and from arable to pastoral areas, but it can be assumed that with at least a dozen sheep, Nicholas was somewhere in the middle of any village economic hierarchy, and possibly higher.

As Nicholas disappears from sight, having probably reached the end of his life, a John Boleyn emerges in a minor dispute with a neighbour in

1333.[44] He was certainly a young man, as his activities are recorded until 1368, and he was probably Nicholas's son. Over the next sixteen years John seems to have made few waves in the community of Kirkhall. He was involved in a number of the petty suits that were the fabric of village life and he acquired the lease of a small plot of land but his name was not among the Briggs, Baldwynes and Blodleters whose actions fill the court rolls.[45] Salle seemed peaceful, immutable and secure.

It came from the east, riding the silk roads to southern Europe. Sliding into merchants' bales and fleeing with the terrified. When it scuttled into ships' holds it could fly for miles on a friendly wind, before creeping backward into the beds of mothers sleeping soundly, thinking Death had passed their children by. At Siena in the spring of 1348, pits 'were piled deep with the multitude of dead' but still it came and came fast. Remorseless and insatiable. By summer it had sailed into Melcombe Regis in Dorset and probably many other ports.[46] Plague had reached England.

By November the dying had begun in London and by January Norwich was being consumed. There could be no sanctuary, no point in flight, nowhere to go and no remedy but prayer. In Salle, at the manor court session on 25 March 1349, it was business as usual: Robert Godyng transfers half an acre and sixteen perches to Thomas and Emma Martyn; John Ancy proceeds against Benedict Ancy in a plea of trespass. Four deaths were recorded but it had been a month since the last court so that was unremarkable.[47] The following session starts with the comforting routine of land transfers but degenerates halfway down the page into a new hand and hastily inserted text as the spinning wheels of bureaucracy struggled to keep up with rapidly changing reality. Eleven dead. By the next court on 17 July normality and procedure were a distant memory. There is no business beyond recording the deceased. *Obiit*, died, *morte*, death, pockmark the page like a disease. Thirty-nine dead. In October the names of those in freshly dug graves are still the first item on the agenda but there is space for some customary business. Ten fines for those young men and women who had failed to take a husband or wife as those around them perished. Eleven dead. By November the horror had passed, routine easily restored to written record but less easily to the lives or minds of those who survived.[48]

Of an estimated seventy tenants on the manor of Kirkhall, sixty-one died as plague ripped through Salle. There must have been a similar toll on the other manors and among wives, mothers, children and the landless. Between March and October the village was almost erased and some lands had to be returned to the lord because there was no one left to inherit. In other cases the web of relationships that wove families together meant heirs were found, however distant or young they might be. Thomas and James, sons of Robert Odonis, were among the first to die, although their sister survived. Robert Godyng's son and heir, John, was just 2 years old and the heirs of Henry atte Brigg were his sister's sons.[49] While some communities suffered similar fates, others were inexplicably spared. At Hakeford Hall in Coltishall, 23 miles southeast of Salle, the death rate over the first and subsequent outbreaks was around 70 per cent and at Aston in Worcestershire as much as 80, but at Hartlebury and Hanbury in the same county only 19 per cent of tenants succumbed.[50] To those left behind in empty homes that should have rung to the sound of familiar voices, walking deserted streets where animals strayed at will and where closed doors hid abandoned meals and bloodied, sweat soaked sheets, it probably mattered little what was happening elsewhere. Rebuilding would take time. The trauma was a permanent scar. In Norwich, where plague took at least 40 per cent of the inhabitants, unclaimed 'vagrant' pigs were still causing havoc in 1354. Buildings and gardens had been damaged, 'children killed and eaten and others buried exhumed'.[51] The Great Pestilence cast a long and grisly shadow.

In the first event of what would prove to be a 150-year run of good luck for the Boleyn family, John survived while his neighbours died, but it is unlikely his whole family were as fortunate. As the landholder only his name is recorded but he would have lived amongst many more Boleyns whose names are unknown. Perhaps a wife and young children, sisters and cousins, even landless or younger brothers. John may have been alive but he was almost certainly grieving. In June 1351 the presence of a William Boleyn is only revealed by the record of his death and the return to the lord of all the tenements he held freely.[52] There is no mention of heirs, his relationship to John or any description that might help identify what happened to his property but he was presumably a relative. Whether a later victim of underlying plague infection or a man at the end of a long life, it was another wound amongst many for his family and another mound of earth in the graveyard.

As the immediate shock wore off, England's remaining population faced a world transformed and a period of chronic uncertainty. For good or ill everything was in flux, from the rules that governed daily life to the wages in the labourers' purses and the price of the bread on their tables. Plague may have receded but further waves would regularly sweep away more lives and even the weather had become untrustworthy. Europe's climate was readjusting to a period of cooling temperatures that would be known as the Little Ice Age and erratic weather brought repeated harvest failures, particularly in the 1450s. A lack of tenants for all available land hampered production and prices rose, but it was not just food. The massive reduction in the labour force exerted upward pressure on wages and consequently the price of everything from ploughs to fuel.[53] Why would a labourer choose the backbreaking work of cutting wood when there were suddenly so many other options?

For the landlords who made up England's governing class, this looked like a threefold threat. As their villein tenants sensed new opportunity, some lords increased enforcement of the customary labour services that had enabled them to farm some of their lands directly, but it became progressively harder and there were far fewer potential workers anyway. Where such services had long been negligible or where there was now no other option, lords leased out the lands they had formerly worked with villein labour or found wages for hired hands, but this growing expense made the whole enterprise uneconomic.[54] Their response was an attempt to turn back the clock and pretend the whole awful nightmare had never happened. Between 1349 and 1351 the Ordinance then Statute of Labourers restricted wages to 1346–47 levels, compelled workers to take any employment that was offered and encouraged longer contracts, with punishments for breach of conditions. At the same time the statute sought to control the price of goods and the size of profits, with enforcement entrusted to new local justices drawn from the ranks of the gentry. It was not exactly a raging success. Inconsistent application of the vague rules meant the type of goods subject to price controls seemed entirely arbitrary and prosecutions for excessive wages targeted the employees who received them but rarely the employers who paid them. Until the 1370s, wages struggled in the face of rising food prices but thereafter the situation changed. Despite legal restraints, wages began to rise faster than prices, placing more disposable income in the purses of labourers although, to many, the compulsory service clause remained nothing more than a new and intolerable form of servility.[55]

One man's curse, however, was another man's, or woman's, blessing. There were new opportunities for women in the workplace and in London girls entered formal apprenticeship to learn trades of their own.[56] In the countryside, land, the precious commodity that had been out of reach for many, was suddenly available and at lower rents. The formerly landless could farm for themselves, produce their own food and sell any surplus and were consequently enjoying a new-found independence. But the smallholder who became a larger-holder, with more land than he could manage by family labour, might welcome curbs on wages just as much as his landlord. On the other hand, a peasant farmer might also be a labourer in quieter months or a cottage-industry cloth weaver. Experience was not uniform from county to county or from year to year.[57] Despite the problems and variations, however, it is inconceivable that life was not in some way improved for most people. It is there in the food provided for harvest workers, where a low-protein cereal-based diet gave way to better quality bread made with wheat flour rather than barley or rye and more meat and ale. It is also there in the sumptuary laws of 1363, which attempted to restrict more luxurious cloth, furs and foodstuffs to those with the appropriate social and economic standing. It was instantly unenforceable but it would have had no purpose if substantial numbers of people had not found that their purse allowed them to cut a better kind of cloth. Exports of worsted may have declined but demand from the home market continued to grow, fuelling the domestic textile industry, to the lasting benefit of places like Salle.[58]

For John Boleyn the new opportunities were more than just economic theory. Making the most of the sudden availability of land, he began to enlarge the family smallholding, picking up 2 acres here, a close and a cottage there. The difficulties landlords faced in finding and keeping tenants after the pestilence are clear from the stipulation in one of John's leases that he not depart or vacate the property during the term.[59] In 1354, together with John Solle, he took out a five-year lease on a tract of land described as 'all the pasture of Frothker and Shotker' for an annual rent of 10s. The acreage is not recorded but given the rent this was clearly a

substantial property. It would form the heart of the Boleyns' landhold-
ing, traceable through succeeding generations. In 1359, when the lease was
renewed to John Boleyn alone, and in 1369, when his son Thomas took
up the property, it had been combined with 2 acres near Reepham and in
total comprised at least 2½ acres, plus an unknown and probably substantial quantity of pasture. It is not until 1412, when John's grandson Geoffrey
became the lessee, that the total holding is described as a close plus 15 acres.
The boundaries may have changed over the years, with perhaps some land
added and a cottage given up in 1392, but the 15 acres commanded a rent
of 14s. 6d. so the land was probably broadly similar in size to the holding
taken by John in 1354.[60]

The Boleyns were evidently prospering, as were many others, but even
when plague seemed blissfully far away, tragedy might be close at hand. In
1365 John Boleyn was one of the jurors at a coroner's inquest into the tragic
death of a neighbour, 2-year-old Alice Damoisele, who had fallen into a
well at her parents' house and 'was immediately drowned'.[61] Four years
later, 1369 was a year of both famine and plague, and Thomas Boleyn's
lease of the Frothker land in that year probably points to his father's death,
as John Boleyn is not recorded again. Having been active for over thirty-
five years, John was probably in his fifties and nearing the end of his natural
life but Emma Boleyn, a customary tenant in 1377, may have been his
widow.[62] If so, she had at least eight years to see what her son would make
of the Boleyn family enterprise.

What Thomas did immediately was something the family is not
recorded as doing previously. He invested capital and purchased freehold
land rather than leasing from one of Salle's several lords. In October 1369
he paid Thomas and Margaret de Bekham 10 marks or £6 13s. 4d. for
4 acres plus half a messuage in Salle. A skilled carpenter earning the going
rate of 4d. per day would have to work for over fifteen months to earn
such a sum, but Thomas had presumably inherited it from his father.[63] This
was followed in 1382 by further land purchased for 10 marks from William
Parmenter, although in this case Thomas shared the costs with William
Derham and Geoffrey Meleman.[64] Thomas and at least some of his neighbours clearly had coin to spend, although that was certainly not true for
everyone everywhere.

For the unfree on manors where lords were vigorously enforcing their
rights, the personal dignity of freedom was a prize stubbornly out of

reach. For those at the sharp end of labour laws, interference in an area of life that had been largely unregulated was an equally grievous loss of liberty, particularly when its enforcement by gentry justices disrupted the local balance of power. Some things, however, were universally hated, and top of that list was taxation. The first Poll Tax, of 1377, was a huge shock. Never before had taxation been universal for every man and woman over the age of 14, but at 4*d*. per head it was swallowed resentfully but quietly. Version two, in 1379, graduated the payments according to wealth, but more was being squeezed from a depleted population and the tax burden per head was growing. The third-generation Poll Tax of 1380 was a monstrous creation: one flat rate but three times that of 1377.[65] Both the poorest and the newly prospering were to have their purses emptied to fund a failing war headlined by the wildly unpopular John of Gaunt. The arrival of the tax collectors ripped the lid from a cauldron of injury, resentment and frustrated aspiration that had been simmering over a low fire for three decades. Blood would flow.

Revolt erupted in June 1381 and soon Kent and Essex were in uproar. By 10 June, Canterbury had been ransacked and three of the townsfolk beheaded, and the Kentish men were kicking up dust on the road to London, having chosen as their leaders the capable and charismatic Wat Tyler and the revolutionary priest John Ball. By 12 June tens of thousands were camped on Blackheath, while across the Thames at Mile End the Essex contingent were lighting their own camp fires. As they gazed at the city's distant walls, the rebels knew they had friends inside.

Faced with a rising tide of popular sympathy and a force that vastly outnumbered the city's militia, the attempt by London's mayor to defend London Bridge barely got started. On 13 June the rebels streamed into the city, where John of Gaunt's palace of the Savoy bore the brunt of anger directed at its absent owner. In an effort to talk his subjects down, on 14 June the 15-year-old Richard II faced a large gathering of rebels at Mile End, where he magnanimously bought them off by acquiescing to their principal demands of an end to serfdom and rents capped at 4*d*. per acre. Scribes sat down to draw up charters of manumission, or freedom from serfdom, but away in the city Tyler and his Kentish men had broken into the Tower and beheaded the chancellor, Archbishop Sudbury, and the treasurer, Sir Robert Hales. The fragile façade of order crumbled and Londoners were plunged into a nightmare as violent mobs roamed the streets hunting 'traitors', dragging men from their homes and brutally beheading them. As a second day of anarchy drew to a close, Richard attempted to repeat the Blackheath strategy of appeasement. He came face to face with Tyler and his rag-tag crew at Smithfield but when Tyler began waving his dagger around, London's mayor William Walworth seized the opportunity and ran his own blade into the rebel leader's neck.[66] Further blows rained down upon the fallen Tyler and Walworth was rapidly reinforced by an armed contingent from the city, who surrounded and dispersed the commons. That would be the end of revolt in London but in Norfolk trouble was just getting started.

Disparate attacks on individuals or property crept like an infection north and east from the Suffolk border until, on 17 June, the rebels came together on Mousehold Heath just outside Norwich, under the command of one Geoffrey Lyster. In the course of that meeting Sir Robert de Salle (whose name probably betrays his family's origin) was murdered before the multitude surged into Norwich, seizing the city, killing the Justice of the Peace (JP), Reginald de Eccles, and looting houses of the elite. Amongst the victims was Henry Lomynour, whose single-minded pursuit of the perpetrators over the ensuing years resulted in the indictment of over 600 alleged looters, including at least six of Thomas Boleyn's neighbours from Salle.[67] The rebels also captured Sir John Brews, the lord of Salle's Stinton Manor, but he and several other prisoners were dispatched to the king to request the same charters of manumission and pardon that had been offered at Blackheath. Over the following days the rebels dispersed to widespread acts of destruction. Sir John Fastolf's house at Caister was attacked and there was extensive burning of manorial records, including on the Brews' manor of Stinton, although Salle's principal manor of Kirkhall remained untouched.[68]

Thus far the rebels had enjoyed a free pass, with no effective response from the forces of law and order, but that would all change with the return to the county of the fighting bishop of Norwich, Henry Despenser. On his way he intercepted the unfortunate John Brews and released him from his rebel escort, and by 24 June Despenser was in Norwich and spoiling for a fight. In a last ditch attempt to rally support, John Gyldyng of Heydon spent the following day riding around Salle, Dalling, Corpusty and nearby villages attempting to inflame the inhabitants by suggesting the bishop should be arrested.[69] Few, however, armed with little more than pitchforks and a sense of indignation, can have been in a hurry to face Despenser. Gyldyng and his fellow desperate recruiters did manage to cobble together some sort of army, which gathered to face their fate at North Walsham on 26 June. There would be little contest. The insurgents were easily overwhelmed and Lyster hanged, drawn and quartered. Barring a few isolated incidents, the Norfolk revolt was over.[70]

In the Boleyns' small world, violence had come close, with the burning of Stinton's manor court rolls, but Salle had not proved to be a hotbed of rebellion. The six villagers from Salle known to have joined the looting in Norwich were insignificant compared to the thirty-five from Ludham, thirty-one from Felmingham or even the sixteen from nearby Aylsham, and unsurprisingly none of them had the surname Boleyn.[71] Having never been servile by birth, and leasing most of his land for money rents rather than by service, Thomas probably had little reason to feel oppressed by lord or custom, and Kirkhall Manor, held by the Mautby family, seems not to have been a target for the ire of rebels. As he gathered more land, Thomas would have been moving into the role of employer rather than employee, so he was less likely to see labour laws as a burden, and he probably had other commercial interests in the worsted industry. The money he was spending on buying land must have come from the textile trade as there is no evidence he held sufficient land to produce a cash surplus on that scale.

In the end the blood-soaked summer of 1381 did not change the world but the world was changing anyway, even if it took landlords and government a while to catch up. The age in which lords controlled an unfree peasantry was dead and attempts to reanimate the corpse by statute were never going to enjoy long-term success. Villein or free, it soon would not matter. The Boleyns' neighbours the Briggs, constantly prevented from holding freehold land in the 1340s, would by the mid-fifteenth century own one of Salle's manors.[72] As the century turned and the uncertainty and turmoil settled down, the Boleyns too were riding a wave of opportunity.

Thomas Boleyn's activities soon began to expand beyond the routine business of the manorial court. He was witness to a land transaction between Kirkhall's lord John Mautby and the parson of Reepham, as well as an executor for his neighbour Richard Anabille, but it was probably worsted production or Salle's cap-making industry that facilitated contacts much further afield.[73] By 1391 he was indebted to the estate of the London grocer William de Stratton, a transaction probably related to either wool, cloth or both, and such enterprise was clearly succeeding as Thomas had cash to invest in the trappings of prosperity.[74] The family's home, clothing and diet must have been improving but Thomas also bought into the growing consumer demand for indulgences. In 1398 he received, in return for the appropriate donation, a papal indulgence granting him and his wife Agnes full remission of their sins at the hour of their death from the confessor of their choice. Conceived not as a cancelling of sin but rather a reduction of time served in purgatory, indulgences were just one way that those with increased purchasing power bought comfort for both body and soul.[75] It was also one part of Thomas's preparation for his own death or that of Agnes. The other involved careful planning for the generation to come, just as his grandson Geoffrey would do over sixty years later, 130 miles away and with vastly increased wealth.

2

'Fair Living for a Yeoman'

London, 16 June 1463

Geoffrey Boleyn drifted, twenty-four hours from death. His labours with the scribe were long over and his will borne away by Anne with its bull's head seal sunk into fresh red wax. The slight weight of the signet ring in his hand had felt so familiar. An image that had stared back at him over so many years, from property deeds and loan agreements, goods being sold, others being bought and all the countless business transactions that had made his fortune. It was the mark by which he was known. The proud beast looking confidently out of the wax impression had come to stand for the expertise and reputation that paid for everything around him.

Under his head lay soft pillows covered in the fine linens that were the root of that fortune and a relic of his youth. So many years ago, amid the crowds of Antwerp and the music of unfamiliar tongues, he had packed hats, laces and ells of linen into bale or basket destined for London. Now it was a gentle softness against his skin, a base layer of luxury in a bedchamber that defined the boundaries of his world and spoke of his worldly success. The heavily carved bedposts, the richly coloured or embroidered curtains and the splendid coverlet that weighed down his legs in the city heat were all a far cry from the house in which Geoffrey and his brother Thomas had spent their childhood. There rushes and packed earth floors, swept hard by their mother Alice, stood in stark contrast to the patterned glazed floor tiles so familiar to his feet in London. What had once been novel or luxurious had become normal and indispensable. The idea of life at Hever Castle, without the chimneys and fireplaces he enjoyed at Milk Street, had been so unthinkable he immediately summoned masons to make changes. Ten-year-old Geoffrey would have found nothing unusual in the open hearth with a smoke hole in the roof although he would have been astonished by the £300 worth of silver plate that now lay under secure lock and key in his coffers or chests.[76] But his father's well-built, timber-framed yeoman's house had been one of the best in the village and Salle's church, which he helped to build, his other great achievement. It was years since Geoffrey had seen the apostles painted on the rood screen or sat gazing up at the angels on the roof, so far above his head they seemed closer to God. Once it had all been as familiar as breathing.

Salle, Norfolk, 1399

The last year of the century had been one of new beginnings for Geoffrey's father. The dwelling house, or messuage, transferred to him by his own father, Thomas, was probably intended to be a home for him and his wife and a place to raise another generation of Boleyns, although it was not the most auspicious start.[77] Failure to observe the strictures of manorial administration by passing the transaction through the court was a fault that had to be retrospectively corrected. This was also Thomas's last recorded act as he passed the reins to younger hands. His son's name appears on later family business, although Geoffrey did not take up the lease of the Boleyn land known as 'Frothker Wood' and a further 15 acres until 1412, so Thomas's date of death, reported centuries later as 30 April 1411, may well be accurate.[78] Whether it was the messuage transferred in 1399 or another home inherited after Thomas's death, more than half a century later the younger Geoffrey would have been right to remember his childhood home as one of the better houses in Salle as his father's affluence grew.

By the 1430s the elder Geoffrey Boleyn would hold 10 acres of land in Stinton, 15 acres plus Frothker Wood in Kirkhall and presumably the 4 acres and more of freehold land in Salle purchased by his father. If to that total is added the unknown acreage that went with various messuages and possible holdings in Salle's other manors, he probably passed the 40 acre threshold that by this period earned proprietors the right to call themselves 'yeomen'. He had joined the ranks of a new but numerically small peasant aristocracy comprising, perhaps, less than 2 per cent of England's population. Despite this new prosperity, he and his young family would have lived a life still bound to the soil and the cycle of the year. His enduring connection to the land is evident from his sale of six loads of barley and oat straw for thatching in 1434 but his commercial interests in worsted or Salle's cap-making industry would have been just as, if not more, important.[79] Details of this part of his life are elusive but the £14 owed to Geoffrey by ex-Salle resident John King, a mercer or cloth merchant living in Bristol, must have been related to the textile trade.[80] It is doubtful that Geoffrey spent many hours walking behind the plough. He had become someone who could hire others to do that, a leading member of his community and a church builder.

In the opening decades of the new century, Salle's great project, emerging from scaffolding to tower over the cluster of cottages, was the parish church of St Peter and St Paul. Always larger than the depleted population required, it was built to a scale that matched the village's pride and funded by the economic might of the worsted industry. From soaring angel roof to vibrant new-painted chancel screen, it proclaimed a strength in cloth and coin that belied the half-empty Sunday nave. Construction must have taken many years, with transepts and porch added later, but there is no record of a single great donor. This was a community artistic endeavour funded by affluent villagers and manorial landlords working together. The arms of Brews, Mautby and Kerdiston record the families who had long held Salle's manors but the south porch and transept would be built by the Briggs and the north by the Roos, former tenant families with newfound prosperity sinking solid foundations. In the south aisle a window, now lost, proclaimed that it was made by Thomas Boleyn, and his son may also have made a financial contribution although no record of it survives.[81] He did, however, give his time and his effort to Salle's great project.

In 1408, John and William Meleman, Thomas Roos, Geoffrey Boleyn and Giles Bishop found themselves in hot water, having allegedly trespassed on a close belonging to Kirkhall's lord, Robert Mautby, with 'the timber of the church of Salle', entered the lord's house and damaged a small building and other possessions. The matter was taken very seriously and referred to the lord but what is made to sound like rampant vandalism was probably, at least in part, accidental damage caused in the process of storing or moving the vast timbers required for construction of the church. These men were from Salle's leading families and, it seems, were part of the team responsible for turning architectural dreams into physical reality. In the same year Geoffrey and the parson, William Schefeld, similarly trespassed over the boundaries of Mautby territory with a large ash tree that must also have been intended for the fabric of the church.[82] Once construction was complete and parishioners were ready to furnish their new church, Geoffrey gave what was probably a locally made 'tapet' or figured cloth used as a hanging or table cover and a matching set of two cushions.[83]

Not everything in Salle, however, was operating with the same degree of mutual interest and co-operation as the new church. In 1408 on Marshgate Green in Nugoun's manor, Geoffrey Boleyn was found to have dug a well without licence but no fine could be extracted from the culprit. To this was added, in 1422, the illicit digging of clay, and both offences were duly entered on record year after year, apparently without change. Not until 1439 did Geoffrey finally pay up for the well but he was far from the only resident who no longer had much regard for such petty regulation.[84] Many of his neighbours were charged with the same offences, including John Briggs and Geoffrey Meleman, men from families whose growing self-assurance and independence made them less and less reliant on a good relationship with their lord and whose actions were of increasing interest to those above them.

In 1434 Geoffrey was included on a list of men who were considered sufficiently prominent and influential that their actions might help or hinder the maintenance of law and order. All were required to swear an oath not to harbour offenders or seek to sway the judicial process in favour of their allies.[85] It was not a particularly exclusive list, with 395 names from Norfolk alone, but for Geoffrey and his other newly affluent neighbours John Meleman, Thomas Briggs and Thomas Roos it meant something to be recognised at all. With chins held high, these aspirational yeomen could look to the future with confidence, but few emerging families would prove able to go the distance. Around 50 per cent of men would die without male heirs while the fragmentation of land between those who had several posed its own problems. By the end of the fifteenth century, the march of the yeomanry had been halted by the 'new men' of the Tudor court – the lawyers, financiers and administrators who had always been there but who were gaining newfound prominence.[86] The Boleyns, however, would avoid such pitfalls. Rather than being replaced by such new men, they would become them.

Like his father before him, Geoffrey could afford the finer things in life, including a papal indulgence.[87] This meant full remission of sin for himself and his wife Alice, whose parentage would become a matter of Boleyn family legend. According to the error-strewn late sixteenth-century visitations of Norfolk, Alice was the daughter of Sir John Bracton, but there is no evidence that such a man ever existed. Within twenty years of Geoffrey's death, his son had effected such a transformation in the family's fortunes that a little creative genealogy would have been perfectly excusable. By the time the younger Geoffrey Boleyn drew his last breath on 17 June 1463, he had acquired arms of his own but having no quarterings to add to newly acquired arms made nascent families look even more nouveau riche. It was a fact of which co-operative heralds were well aware and that, being paid per grant of arms, they were happy to rectify. Geoffrey undoubtedly knew exactly who his maternal grandfather was but reality needed a little improvement. So Geoffrey's mother Alice became the daughter of a fictitious Sir John Bracton who was, conveniently, possessed of arms. The Bracton arms are unknown before their use with Boleyn, probably because they did not exist before their quartering with Boleyn, but that just meant nobody would challenge their use.[88] Such imaginative heraldry was by no means uncommon. Another Norfolk self-made man, John Heydon, not only manufactured his arms and an entire family pedigree but even his name. His father was really William Baxter, meaning baker, which had an unsavoury whiff of manual labour. Garter herald Thomas Writhe decided his name was too short to convey the necessary gravitas so changed it to the unpronounceable Wriothesley, knighting his deceased father into the bargain. Henry VII's agents Reginald Bray and Sir Henry Wyatt both borrowed the arms of better established families of the same name.[89]

All the best legends, however, have a grain of truth, and if the Bracton name was anything close to Alice's real maiden name, she may have been the daughter of a John Bacton, whose existence is not in doubt. He had married Martha Paston, sister of Clement Paston, another Norfolk yeoman whose family were on the rise. Any daughter of John Bacton and Martha Paston would be a far more likely marriage partner for Geoffrey Boleyn than the daughter of a knight, and both would have been in the same generation.[90] But a definitive contemporary connection between the Pastons and the Boleyns remains elusive. Margaret Mautby, daughter of the family who had been the Boleyns' lords on Salle's Kirkhall Manor for generations, would marry into the Paston family, but not until 1440, the year of Geoffrey's death. Clement Paston's son William, the nephew of John Bacton, had been both a feoffee or trustee for Margaret Mautby's grandfather Robert, and co-feoffee with Geoffrey Boleyn in a land transaction of 1424, so they were certainly known to each other, but acquaintance is a long way from cousins by marriage.[91]

Whoever her father was, Alice's marriage to Geoffrey certainly ensured that the Boleyns would not immediately fail for lack of male heirs. To judge from a now lost part of Geoffrey's memorial brass, the couple had at least five sons and four daughters, and although not all survived, three made it through the vulnerable years of childhood.[92] As they planned for their family's future, Geoffrey and Alice had a choice. One or both of their sons, Geoffrey and Thomas, might inherit their land, continue their careful husbandry and with luck expand the family enterprise, gradually saving shillings and pence until, like the Briggs, they could acquire a small manor or two. That, however, was the slow route and it was not the only option. Many of their neighbours had sent sons to London, using connections in the textile trades to launch new careers, but the Church was still crying out for talented men to replenish the massed ranks of clergy lost to the plague and the law had made fortunes for others. There was opportunity out there for those brave enough to leave behind everything familiar and seize it.

Lawyer, merchant or cleric, Thomas and Geoffrey could not get started without a foundation education. There were schools in Norwich that could teach reading, writing and Latin grammar but it is also possible the Boleyns had resources closer to home. Salle's mammoth church was furnished with seven guilds manned by a cast of up to seven chaplains, whose daily hours were probably not entirely filled by their regular duties.[93] Such men sometimes found other roles, particularly in the education of local children, and this may have been the case with Salle's chaplain, Thomas Drew, who formed a particularly strong relationship with Geoffrey's other surviving child, Cecily.

When he died in 1443, Drew bequeathed to Cecily a pair of coral beads with gilt paternosters, calling her his 'spiritual daughter', but he also left a book to a fellow chaplain and returned another book of devotions to Lady Ela Brews. This beautifully illustrated manuscript, which survives in the Bodleian Library, was commissioned by Ela's father but copied in 1430 for Salle's rector William Wode.[94] The presence of this text, the possible active engagement of Ela and Cecily and the numerous other personal bequests in Drew's will, particularly to women, tentatively suggest some form of scholarly spiritual community that may have had a profound effect on Cecily's future. Unlike her brothers, she would choose a far from conventional life.

Many years later, at her death on 26 June 1458, Cecily was laid to rest on her brother's new estate at Blickling under a very personal brass. Her hands clasped in prayer, she is depicted wearing a high-waisted belted gown with full sleeves and a high neckline, but without the latest fashion in headdress. Instead her long hair flows loose about her shoulders and down her back, a sure sign of a very young or unmarried woman. Should the significance of this be overlooked, the inscription is explicit: 'Cecily Boleyn, sister to Geoffrey Boleyn ... deceased in her maidenhood of the age of fifty years'. Cecily's virginal status was no accident of life, the unfortunate result of a failure to marry. It was a conscious and much-treasured choice, and her brass was probably paid for by the man whose name is engraved beside her own, her brother Geoffrey. It was crafted in London, where he had made his home, and the unusual design probably reflects his influence. Cecily had taken a little-used path and her brother wished to ensure her choice was both remembered and respected. She may, however, have met some fellow travellers along the way.

In continental Europe, particularly in the Low Countries, women who chose, as Cecily did, a life of informal piety and chastity outside male oversight but not in a nunnery were a well-established group. Living together in communities known as beguinages, many were also dedicated to apostolic poverty, but in England such institutions were rare. They are known to have existed in only one place, a city that experienced a late medieval flowering of lay and particularly female spirituality, just 15 miles from Salle. Norwich. After her childhood home was broken up by the death of her father in 1440 and her mother some years later, it was perhaps to one of these communities that Cecily turned. These Norwich beguinages have left barely a trace to tell us of their existence and there are no names recorded of the women who lived there, but one in particular fits the timeline of Cecily's life perfectly. Established in the former house of a Bruges merchant and mayor of Norwich named John Asger, it is first recorded in 1442, was reduced from three residents to two by 1457 and is no longer heard of after 1472. Even if she never moved in, Cecily may have found kindred spirits among women usually described as sisters or poor women, dedicated to God and to chastity.[95] But these enigmatic groups of lay women are so little known that this can be no more than speculation and Cecily may have made her life elsewhere. Her brother, Geoffrey, placed great trust in her, twice employing her as a feoffee and she may have turned to him for support.[96] Wherever she put down roots and however she chose to spend her days, she was blessed with at least one affectionate brother who apparently had great respect for the way she chose to live her life.

As the elder Geoffrey neared the end of his life, an adult daughter at home was perhaps of great comfort as his surviving sons built lives of their own far away.[97] Following a period at Cambridge, Thomas was well on the way to a successful career in the Church that would see him holding multiple benefices and numerous other offices, including that of a canon at St Paul's and sub-dean and precentor at Wells Cathedral, where, in 1472, he would be laid to rest in an elaborate tomb.[98] His father must have been proud, but as a cleric, Thomas would never marry, so the future of the family lay in the hands of his brother. It was probably his contacts in the textile trade that prompted Geoffrey's father to choose a mercantile rather than a legal career for his son. Following in the footsteps of many other boys from the worsted villages of Norfolk, he was packed off to a London apprenticeship, carrying hope, expectation and, as it turned out, not inconsiderable talent with him. By the time the elder Geoffrey died in 1440, he would already have known that his family's future looked golden.

PART II

Geoffrey Boleyn II: Mercer, Merchant, Mayor

1420–63

The Golden Ticket of a London Apprenticeship

London, 21 February 1421

Scattered like fireflies, carefully sheltered candles lit the labours of carpenter and joiner, painter and stainer in the cramped confines of London Bridge. With fingers stiffened by the icy grip of a February night, they plied their trade while, behind the flimsy walls of a hundred chambers, the bridge inhabitants shifted sleeplessly, on featherbed or straw-filled pallet, to the broken rhythm of hammers on nails. It was the final push in a month or more of careful preparations that had seen nimble-fingered women creating feathered wings for a cast of linen-clad virgins while a host of towering pageant figures were readied for the stage.

As the watery morning sun rose over the towers of the bridge, the bleary-eyed inhabitants looked out to find a lion and antelope, bearing heraldic shields, and two huge giants sheltering in a forest of banners. A forty-eight-hour party lay ahead as the nation's hero, Henry V, brought his beautiful new queen, Katherine de Valois, to claim her crown in the abbey church at Westminster, and London laid out the welcome mat in her usual spectacular style. Passing over London Bridge, where the lion rolled its eyes and the giants turned their heads to gaze upon their new queen, she would, by tradition, sleep one night in the Tower before following in the footsteps of Isabellas and Eleanors, Edwards and Henrys, along the spine of the city and into the shadow of the spire of St Paul's.[99]

Shoulder to fur-clad shoulder or hanging perilously from windows and rooftops, thousands of Londoners sought a glimpse of royalty. Somewhere amongst them was an apprentice boy from Norfolk, just a few years younger than the queen herself. Not for a moment can it have crossed the mind of Geoffrey Boleyn, as he slipped unnoticed through the throng or sampled the wine-filled conduits, that one day his own great-granddaughter would follow in the footsteps of that royal lady to become the queen of her great-grandson, Henry VIII.

The journey that, in 1420 or early 1421, took Geoffrey, aged around 14, from rural Norfolk to England's greatest city would not have been long.[100] Three days were enough to see the Icknield Way and Roman Ermine Street pass beneath his horse's hooves and the great spire of St Paul's break the horizon, but the distance, culturally, socially, politically and economically, was vast.[101] Seen from the much-mended Ware to Bishopsgate Road, the 3 miles of high stone walls that rose out of the northern marshy fields surrounded a world unlike anything Geoffrey had known. The territory inside the bars may only have measured a square mile but that made London vast by most contemporary standards, and certainly vast by the standards of the boy from Salle.

With over a hundred parish churches and 30–40,000 inhabitants, London was by far the largest city in England. An ocean liner in a flotilla of sailboats. She had always been England's treasure house and as more of the nation's trade flowed through her port in the course of the fifteenth century, her economic might would only grow. As custodian of the money bags, she wielded political power, and no king in Westminster could afford to disregard his influential neighbour downstream, but London was more than just money and power. She was the nation's theatre, where ceremonial spectacle lent legitimacy and prestige or where history was played out at the point of a sword. She was Charterhouse, St Paul's and a hospital for unmarried mothers. She was Geoffrey Chaucer and William Caxton, merchants from Genoa to Hamburg, the 'gong farmer' up to his knees in a cesspit and the butcher up to his elbows in offal and now she was Geoffrey Boleyn's new home.

Crossing 80ft of watery and too often stinking city ditch and slipping through the cool, shadowy archway of Bishopsgate, Geoffrey's first experience of the city in which he would rewrite his family's future was the tranquil north-east quarter, where hidden gardens still lay behind street fronts. It was a gentle introduction, an ephemeral bubble of calm that quickly burst as jetties loomed, competing tavern signs crowded in and the newcomer headed towards Cheapside and London's beating heart. The newly built Stocks market, wearing her joints and carcasses like fine goldsmith's work around a noble neck, marked the way to this shopfront of the world where linen, silks and precious jewels from beyond the sea rubbed along with carrots, cabbages and the daily loaf, and silk-clad merchants strolled elbow to elbow with labourers in much-patched woollens.[102] Between the canny housewife with a hand on her purse and the gentlewoman with silver to spare, children scurried here and there, intent on errands, and carters' horses with tired eyes pulled two-wheeled carts from wharf to warehouse. Somewhere in all this newness, among the foreign accents and the narrow lanes, Geoffrey already had a place and it lay behind a front door just off Cheapside, in the drapers' parish of St Mary le Bow.

As he stood on the doorstep of his new home with his heart pounding out of his chest, Geoffrey knew that the next seven years of his life would depend upon the nature of the man who, perhaps, had just made the journey from Salle at his side or who lay on the other side of the door. Most masters were careful of their sworn duty to teach, nurture and govern their young charges and most apprentices were appreciative of the efforts made by family and friends to secure their contract, but some boys and girls lost their way or had it lost for them. Malice or selfishness could wreak havoc in a relationship built on trust, as the apprentice fletcher Oliver Randy found to his cost. His master, he complained, taught him little and, exceeding 'reasonable chastisement', came at all hours of the night 'with dagger drawn' and beat him, as he did his own wife and servants. Other masters fared almost as badly at the hands of apprentices like Walter Andrew who betrayed those who had trusted them with their homes, families and businesses. The tailor's apprentice conspired with his fellow servants to steal goods from his master worth an astonishing £200 and gave cloth to euphemistically titled 'naughty women ... to make them kirtles'.[103]

Fortunately for Geoffrey, his father had more care of his son than to place him in danger like poor Oliver Randy. He had indentured his son to a man he probably knew personally through Salle's hat-manufacturing trade. So, on the other side of that door in St Mary le Bow, Geoffrey found a man who would not only treat him well but who would become a friend and surrogate father he would never forget. Like the 'Poor Child of Bristowe' in the fifteenth-century poem, Geoffrey 'took full well to lore' and his new master, *in loco parentis*, loved him as a son, but that probably did little to make the task of settling into a house full of strangers any easier.[104] Amongst the family, servants and other apprentices in his new home there were friends to be made but also new rules and boundaries to understand, and it all had to be done while living on top of each other like mice in an upturned bucket. For most people, privacy was still a novel concept in the fifteenth century so, as night fell on Geoffrey's first day as a Londoner, he probably found himself sleeping cheek-by-jowl with strangers, hoping they would become allies, not enemies.

Although never specifically named as his master, it is likely that Geoffrey's future was now in the hands of the hatter Adam Book, whose family were probably themselves immigrants to the city.[105] Those named Book or Buk often originated in the Low Countries (modern-day Belgium and the Netherlands) and at least twelve men with this surname settled in London and the south-east during the fifteenth century.[106] Adam was a former warden of the guild of hatters. It was a small guild, politically and economically outgunned by the Great Twelve guilds but with correspondingly small entrance fees and therefore affordable for a father of more modest means. But Adam had more to teach his new apprentice than the art of shopkeeping. He was also a successful international merchant who regularly travelled to the Low Countries, importing not only hats but everything from linen and painted cloths to laces, thimbles and spurs.[107] His not inconsiderable fortune would posthumously supply most of the windows in his parish church of St Mary le Bow and he probably could have transferred to one of the greater mercantile guilds, had he felt the need, but Adam was content to live and die a hatter.[108] He was the perfect teacher for a boy with ambition who had to start at the bottom and Geoffrey was careful to repay his debts. When Adam died, Geoffrey completed the training of his last apprentice, another boy from Salle named Geoffrey Meleman, and later made careful provision for the soul of his former master, just as if he were in truth his own father. He paid for Adam and his wife Joan to be remembered among the benefactors of Queens' College, Cambridge, and included him, alongside his birth parents, in his personal family chantry.[109]

Over the next seven years, Geoffrey would be taught the warp and weft of the hatter's trade and the florins and guilders of international commerce.

By observation and example, he would learn how to run a business and a merchant's household. If seven years seems a long time to master such specialised knowledge, that's because it was. For the bother and time spent turning naïve youths into useful citizens, London's masters were rewarded with several years of free labour. By the end of his apprenticeship and with all the requisite skills and learning under his belt, Geoffrey would have been a valuable if unpaid employee. His reward was admission to the fundamentally superior rank of a London citizen. Of an adult male population of 12–14,000, only around 3–4,000 were members of this elite club but these men held all the aces.[110] Only citizens could open a shop or engage in retail trade. Only citizens could seal wholesale deals with foreign merchants and only citizens could hold political office in London's fledgling democracy or vote in elections.

Citizenship went hand in hand with a trade or craft, as by the mid-fifteenth century most freemen, like Geoffrey, gained their wings through apprenticeship, but this locked opportunity out of the reach of those who had not passed through the door to citizenship. Almost every potential occupation, from butchers and fruit-sellers to wealthy goldsmiths and merchant tailors, was governed by a guild. Only those who entered their ranks, by apprenticeship or more rarely by purchase, could legally ply that trade or open a business. Everyone else was restricted to a life of paid labour working for their more privileged neighbours or to the few unregulated manual roles that remained, such as carters or porters. Geoffrey had come because London had the power to change lives and futures. For generations, boys like him from Kent to Lincolnshire had flocked to the city, dreaming that the ever-spinning wheels of trade and social mobility could provide a better life. Many found it. Numerous merchant fortunes (although few as large as the Boleyns') were accumulated by men who were not born to wealth, but all of them were citizens.

On 23 June 1428, Geoffrey stood in the squeaky cleanness of London's brand new Guildhall on the cusp of this new adult life. He had been there before, for the recording of his apprenticeship but then he had descended into makeshift officialdom in the western end of the crypt while an army of craftsmen wove their magic in oak and stone above his head. Now he passed under the watchful gaze of Law, Learning, Discipline, Justice, Fortitude and Temperance, who monitored comings and goings through the ornate southern porch, and entered the Guildhall itself. Over 46m long by 14.5m wide, paved in Purbeck marble and spanned by the second largest unsupported roof in England, the space in which Geoffrey and Adam stood was unlike any other in London. Constructed in emulation of Westminster Hall and continental cloth halls like that in Bruges, it was the city's pride and ambition made tangible and beautiful. Stretching upwards from north and south, seven vast stone arches bore the weight of the roof and soared gracefully over the heads of the two men below, making them puny by comparison. Along the walls, a harmonious rhythm was created by tall Gothic windows and matching blank tracery, while to east and west brightly painted glass in two huge windows threw broken rainbows carelessly onto the pristine floor.[111]

Their words echoing in the vast space, they stood before the city's chamberlain, John Bederenden, as Adam confirmed that his young protégé had faithfully completed his term of apprenticeship and Geoffrey spoke the transformative words.[112] Swearing from this moment on to 'be faithful and loyal unto our lord the king … obedient to the mayor and ministers that keep the city', to maintain the city's 'franchises and customs' and to keep the city harmless, he (not for the last time) assumed a new rank and status.[113] A fee of 5s. 10d. went into the city coffers, a clerk wrote 'Geoffrey Boleyn' into the now lost record of freedoms and Geoffrey walked back into the sunshine a citizen of London.[114] Outside, the streets were rapidly filling with bonfires, lanterns and precautionary buckets of water as everyone prepared for the coming nocturnal revels of the Midsummer Watch. For a newly minted citizen, it was just the time to celebrate. For a night or two the future could wait.

4

Commerce and Commodities

God had listened to him speak the words of the freeman's oath. With sword and helm, the mounted Midsummer Watch had clattered through London's narrow streets and the ashes of forgotten bonfires had been swept away by passing breeze or fastidious housewife. Regretful revellers nursing delicate heads sought to ease their problems with cabbage juice and sugar as they faced a new day and Geoffrey faced the rest of his life.[115] Now he was a man, with a man's responsibilities, a man's ambition and a man's fears. Every guild included journeymen or post-apprenticeship wage labourers who would never know the satisfaction of leaning on their own shop counter, never mind join the premier league of merchant wholesalers. There was no guarantee of success but to get started Geoffrey had to find his first foothold with some starting capital.

In most merchant trades, an aspiring ex-apprentice needed a stock of goods worth around £40, and the grocers tried to set this figure as a minimum requirement in 1480.[116] Today it would be nearly £25,000, a significant sum, but young men like Geoffrey had various resources at their disposal. Some apprentices were younger sons of gentry stock who could have appealed to family for their seed capital but Geoffrey would probably have asked in vain. His father may have been able to supply something but as he could only afford an apprenticeship with one of the minor guilds for his son, it is unlikely he could have found such a quantity of silver. Many young men worked for years for a former master or other merchant, carefully saving their wages until they could branch out on their own. Others were fortunate to receive generous bequests from former masters. Adam was still alive and it is possible that Geoffrey's beloved mentor made a loan to his favoured apprentice. There was, however, another time-honoured way of making money quickly, and all it took was a short walk up the aisle.

While there is no direct evidence that wedding vows secured Geoffrey's foothold on life or that his first marriage even took place in the years when he was yet a newly minted citizen, it remains one possible explanation for his early and rapid ascent. The lady in question was named Dionisia but that is almost everything that is known about her. Geoffrey remembered her in his will, ensuring that prayers and masses would speed her soul to heaven, but further knowledge of her identity, wealth or family remain elusive.[117] She certainly died at least twenty years before Geoffrey and, despite suggestions to the contrary, their marriage produced no children, so it is possible she was substantially older, perhaps a widow with a modest fortune of her own.[118] If so, this would certainly explain how, within three years of completing his apprenticeship, Geoffrey had his £40 and was ready to make his mark on the world.

How to begin? He could have acquired premises and set up a little shop but Geoffrey's ambitions were greater than the life of a jovial shopkeeper with a long-suffering wife and a brood of offspring in two sparse rooms above the shop. Probably guided by Adam, he gathered up his precious coin and set out to see whether a fortune could be made beyond the breakers of the North Sea. To succeed he would need to master numerous different currencies, coins, exchange rates and languages as well as the constantly shifting sands of European politics.

It was summer 1431, three years after completing his apprenticeship, when Geoffrey first boarded a ship on London's crowded quayside and rode the outgoing tide, into the Thames estuary and onwards to the Low Countries. Beneath the salt-soaked planks of the deck lay a cargo of prized English woollen cloth, but the less well-protected passengers had to find shelter where they could. On some ships, travelling merchants could at least make use of sleeping facilities and shelter under the stern-castle but carpenters were often summoned to build or improve cabins for royal or noble passengers, suggesting these spaces were a far cry from the comforts of home. Sailors or less exalted travellers had to make do with large hooded sacks or hammocks to sleep in and the leeward side of the gunwale. Confined to a few square metres of deck for the next two days, any wind-swept merchants who were not losing their lunch over the side had to be fed. Some ships had a cook's room with a permanent hearth, while others employed a sand- and clay-filled wooden box on deck as a fireplace, but this was far from the captain's table. For a voyage to Zeeland in 1487, the *Margaret Cely* was provisioned with the nauseating combination of salt-fish, salted ox meat and ship's biscuits.[119] Geoffrey and his fellow seafaring merchants must have prayed vigorously and often for favourable winds, a swift, placid crossing and deliverance from ship lice.

Finally the horizon offered up relief but rather than the congested wharves of Antwerp, the young hatter's first glimpse of a foreign shore would have been a more spacious port on the Scheldt delta, called Middelburg. Here the streets echoed to the familiar accents of home, for this was the commercial base favoured by English merchants. The docks were lined with plentiful warehouses for the woollens and worsteds unloaded from wind-battered ships or for purchases stored in anticipation of the voyage home. Local ship's captains awaited a commission to head back out to the North Sea while hundreds of smaller, more nimble craft plied the waterways of the delta up to Bergen op Zoom and Antwerp. On this occasion, Geoffrey was probably heading straight to Antwerp for Bamis Mart, one of the four great fairs that formed a framework to the lives of 'adventurers', or Englishmen who traded with the continent. This commercial festival opened in late August and continued to early October but was quickly followed by Cold Mart, in Bergen, from late October to late November.[120] Geoffrey would have travelled from one fair to the other, pausing only briefly in Middelburg to deliver his first consignment into the hands of the skipper Heyn Bulscamp and speed it back to London. After Cold Mart, he and his latest purchases were homeward bound, but for other merchants, the fair cycle began again at Bergen's Easter Mart, which ran for a month from Maundy Thursday, followed by Whitsun Mart, from about 25 April to 13 June, back in Antwerp.[121]

A short journey through the branching delta waterways from Middelburg brought Geoffrey to the booming town of Antwerp, where as soon as he set foot on the bustling wharf, by the waters of the Scheldt, he would have known he was far from home. The sailors, dockworkers, merchants and travellers around him no longer spoke the familiar words of his native land but a dozen different tongues. As the Spanish nobleman Pedro Tafur found in 1435, 'whoever wants to see the whole world or a large part of it, concentrated on one place, he can do so' in Antwerp.[122] Weeks of travel, by land and sea, brought European merchants from Baltic ports and Mediterranean city-states to stroll elbow to elbow through the crowded stalls of the Grote Markt, at the heart of the old town. Although Geoffrey was without the companionship and advice of his old friend and mentor on this first trip abroad, Adam would have packed him off with sage advice, so the green young hatter would have known to avoid crowded inns, where thieves were rife, and find safer lodgings with a local host.[123] In a tall mercantile town house on one of the main commercial streets, goods could be stored more securely and all that the city had to offer lay just around the corner.[124]

In Antwerp's market square, overshadowed by the impressive façade of the new town hall, all 'the most beautiful things in the world are to be seen'.[125] It was a dazzling choice for a young man whose horizons were growing by the day. Should he select the resin, wax and furs of sable that evoked a frozen Baltic winter or the sun-soaked dates, citrus and olive oil from the far-flung warmth of the Mediterranean? Perhaps cloth was the thing. Something more exotic than the woollens of England. There was fine, soft linen from the looms of Flanders or heavy fluid silks from Italy or Paris, but from every side the carefully honed skills of a thousand artisans sought to distract the merchant's eye. Precious gold and silver, highly polished armour and leatherwork and saddles, redolent with bees-wax, may have been beyond the reach of Geoffrey's purse. He had to set his sights on the retailers of less glamorous wares. Between Antwerp and Bergen he parted with £44 10s. in return for 100lbs of white thread, 384 hats, 2,100 ells of linen cloth, 16 packets of laces and an astounding 5,600 wooden combs.[126] Not the exotic luxuries that made the fairs so exciting but the everyday necessities that would be sure to find buyers back in England. These mundane commodities, carefully packed and distrib-uted between three separate ships to guard against catastrophe in autumn's storms, were the unremarkable foundations of a family fortune that would take the Boleyns all the way to a crown.

For the next few years this was Geoffrey's life. In spring winds or autumn storms he was to be found heading out into the North Sea bound for the next great fair. Straw hats replaced felt in the summer months while hemp, decorative painted hangings, thimbles, girdles, spurs and paper all made their way into Geoffrey's baskets and bales when the merchant's astute eye saw the price was right.[127] Although records are scant, Geoffrey probably funded these purchases with the sale of cloth in Antwerp, where England's woollens and worsteds undercut the prices of Flemish producers. It was an established pattern of trade that made many merchant adventurers rich and Geoffrey could have carried on for the rest of his career. As his resources grew, he might have expanded into manuscripts, tapestries or other luxury wares, while hired factors or former apprentices shouldered the burdens of overseas travel, but he did not. First, European politics got in the way and then, by compulsion or design, Geoffrey set out on a different path.

The collapse of cordial relations between England and her accustomed Burgundian ally was the first point of failure that rerouted the Boleyn train. Duke Philip of Burgundy ruled over a diverse, composite territory that included the commercial jewels of Antwerp, Bergen op Zoom and Bruges, so a friendly ear and a welcoming arm were essential to English trade with the Low Countries. However, the introduction of English restrictions on the Calais wool trade had pushed up the price of raw materials and that, in turn, hindered the looms of the duke's Flemish weavers. In 1434, he retaliated by switching allegiance to France and banning all imports of English cloth. It was not universally enforced but it was, nevertheless, devastating for trade. The number of cloths exported by Englishmen collapsed from 26,708 in 1433–34 to only 10,830 in 1435–36.[128] Alien (foreign) exporters picked up some of the slack but many London merchants, like Geoffrey, were forced to abandon travel to the great fairs.[129]

These were equally tough times for English weavers as their formerly prized cloth languished in warehouses but it was not, as it may appear, a total catastrophe for Geoffrey. Although the simplistic commercial model of exporting cloth and using the proceeds to fund imports had been stopped at a stroke, the insatiable desire of English men and women for Low Countries linen, leather or laces had not disappeared. Geoffrey's import business might yet thrive if he could just get money or credit to Antwerp or Bergen to fund the necessary purchases. Fortunately, the financial institutions of medieval Europe stood ready to help. In 1436, on narrow St Nicholas Lane, in the heart of London, the Milanese Borromei family opened the doors of a new bank. With typical Italian commercial opportunism, they would run it until 1441, specifically to take advantage of England's sudden difficulties, and their enterprise was a great success. While the bankers made a nice profit from fees, interest or exchange, merchants such as Geoffrey were able to keep the shelves of Cheapside stocked with linen.

What the Borromei offered seems at first glance incredibly modern. A short stroll along the Italian stronghold of Lumbard Street would have brought Geoffrey to the bank clerks of St Nicholas Lane. Here he could make his sterling deposits and just as it does today, the bank's financial wizardry enabled that money to be transferred and withdrawn in Bruges. Without the benefit of computers or telephone lines, however, a transaction that today takes hours was far more laborious. Two copies of a bill purchased in London had to be physically delivered to Bruges or elsewhere, one sent by the merchant in London and one delivered by the bank's long-suffering couriers. Constantly on the road between Europe's great cities, this army of dusty messengers kept trade alive and taxes flowing into insatiable royal coffers. They would have helped Geoffrey maintain his business while European politics were getting in the way but even without such hurdles the Borromei were always useful as they facilitated credit. In 1438, Geoffrey passed just over £422 through the Borromei ledgers, the equivalent of over £260,000 today and one of the largest annual turnovers in London. His transactions involved the transfer of funds from London to Bruges (for which the bank extended credit by paying out the money before it had been fully deposited) plus bills or loans taken up in Bruges and Antwerp for repayment in London. Such access to credit would have allowed Geoffrey to expand his activities but the profits of the Borromei lay in the variable exchange rates they offered, so he would have had to pay for his money, possibly as much as 10 per cent.[130]

If Geoffrey was in London, however, who was receiving the money in Bruges and taking up those bills? The answer was his factor, Thomas Hethe, a newly qualified ex-apprentice of the mercer John Edmund. When small amounts of cloth again began to filter into Middelburg, in 1437, Hethe sailed from London on a ship laden with bales of cloth that were listed under his name but may have come from Geoffrey's stockpile, and more would be sent out under his master's name in June the following year.[131] In May 1438, he was in Bruges to withdraw Geoffrey's funds from the Borromei and in June, Geoffrey's familiar mixed cargo of linen, laces and thread, augmented with grey furs and 36lbs of jet, was hauled onto Southampton's docks.[132] Hethe would still be riding the continental fairs cycle a year later.[133] Despite the hiccup with exports, Geoffrey's business was evidently thriving and he began to feel a little pot-bound in the minor guild of the hatters. He 'had long used, and was now using, the art of mercery and not the art of hatter' so he sought to spread his roots, alongside similar specimens, in the great mercantile guild of the mercers.[134]

On 1 February 1436, Geoffrey again made his way through the imposing Gothic arches of the Guildhall to stand before the assembled aldermen and the mayor, Henry Frowyk, himself a mercer, and sought permission to transfer from the guild of the hatters to that of the mercers. Although technically a change of trade, this was not practically a change of career. The 'art of mercery' was a trade that specialised in luxury imported textiles, laces and accessories, something akin to the fabric department at Liberty, and as Geoffrey said himself, very much the wares that were already hitting London docks bearing his name.[135] Mercers were not strangers but an assembly of familiar faces, men who sent goods or even travelled on the same ships to the same great fairs, and several of them supported his application.[136] There was more to this switch, however, than the semantics of the trade he wrote after his name.

The mercers' company formed the most influential group among English adventurers in the Low Countries and membership would have given Geoffrey powerful allies to protect his overseas interests, but they were also one of the dominant forces in London. Controlled by hugely wealthy international merchants, the mercers and the eleven other guilds of the Great Twelve effectively ran the city. In the fifteenth century, none of London's mayors or aldermen was chosen from outside their ranks but Geoffrey was accepted with ease. He paid a 2*s.* administrative fee for admission and £5 13*s.* 4*d.*, equivalent to £3,500 today, to skip straight over the rank-and-file and join the 'livery' or upper ranks of the guild.[137] This would be both a secure resting place and a safety net as he climbed ever higher.

The way ahead even began to look a little less hostile when, in September 1438, a new commercial treaty with the duke of Burgundy meant London's merchants were finally able to empty warehouses of cloth that had been gathering dust for years. Geoffrey, however, had already moved on. In 1443, twelve years after he first explored Antwerp's Grote Markt, his last recorded cargo of linen, hemp and paper was hauled onto a London dock.[138] Woollen cloth may have been flowing back to the markets of Flanders and Brabant but as the middle of the century drew near, English overseas trade slid inexorably into depression. Further international discord did not help and neither did prohibitions on the use of credit or Lancastrian trade policies that seemed to favour foreign merchants. As far as Geoffrey was concerned, others could deal with the risks and the ship's biscuits. He had found another way to prosper while keeping his feet and his fortunes firmly on English soil.

Now approaching 40 and with a new marriage on the cards, Geoffrey was in a phase of life when many merchants stepped away from overseas travel, if not from overseas trade, but he seems to have largely stepped away from both. There were avenues of opportunity closer to home where an enterprising middleman could turn a profit connecting the weaver with the wharf and the wayfaring pedlar. These were the paths where Geoffrey chose to roam for most of his remaining career. Cloth did not have to be sold in Antwerp. It could be sold in London to others on their way to Antwerp or to Italians on their way home. Silk or spices did not have to be purchased abroad. They were already en route in Venetian holds to be sold by foreign merchants who were, by law, a captive audience for the London wholesaler. From his comfortable city base, Geoffrey set himself up as a collector of goods destined for abroad and a distributor of imports to English consumers. Piggybacking on the overseas trade of others, he carved out a niche where the risks belonged to someone else and the coins could pile high.

Key to this wholesale enterprise were the cosmopolitan Italian merchants who regularly sailed into London. Out of their heavily laden galleys, floating low in the Thames, London's lightermen hauled just the goods that Geoffrey wanted to buy: silk brocade and cloth-of-gold, pepper and ginger for spiced wine and sauces, or the woad and madder that dyers transformed to blue and red.[139] Into their empty holds went what he had to sell, such as the £981 (£630,000) worth of West Country broadcloth and other woollens shipped home by the Venetian merchants Federico Corner and Carlo Contarini in 1440.[140] Any woollens and worsteds not snapped up by adventurous Italians probably went abroad with merchant adventurers, but the silks and spices were destined for English backs and English bellies. Some could have passed through the hands of London shopkeepers, whose well-stocked shelves attracted an army of well-to-do shoppers, but thousands of men and women, with disposable income burning a hole in their purse, were unable to make the long and costly journey to London. Geoffrey would make his fortune supplying their needs. Like many other mercers, he worked closely with rural chapmen, who filled their packs with London's imports and plied the highways and byways of the realm. From Robert Green in Bridgwater, Somerset, who owed him £60, to John Hunt of Leicestershire, who owed £40, these men would carry Geoffrey's wares the length and breadth of England.[141]

Geoffrey's withdrawal from overseas trade was, however, distinctly unconventional. Most London merchants made their fortune shipping English wool to Calais or cloth to Antwerp and bringing linen, wine or other wares back home, yet Geoffrey was not unique. His near contemporary, the draper Simon Eyre, amassed a fortune of around £7,000 from a very similar trade and a near identical career path. Arriving in London from Brandon, Suffolk, Simon was apprenticed to an upholder or dealer in second-hand clothes, but like Geoffrey he soon swapped this trade for something better. It took him six years (in comparison to Geoffrey's eight) to join the ranks of a mercantile guild, in his case the guild of the drapers, but there the difference ended. Just like Geoffrey, Simon shunned overseas trade and operated as a middleman. Just like Geoffrey, he specialised in the supply of cloth for others to export and the distribution of Italian dyes and spices throughout England. In the first half of the 1440s, when Geoffrey was withdrawing from the North Sea trade, Eyre was at the height of his powers, and his face and fortune would have been familiar to all. During Eyre's mayoralty of 1445–46, Geoffrey was a common councilman and over the ensuing years, Simon would have been hard to miss, as his great vision for a new market, granary, chapel and three schools took shape at Leadenhall. Although there is no direct evidence of any friendship between the two men, it is hard to believe that Geoffrey was not swayed by this object lesson in how to succeed.[142]

Whether selling cloth or buying spices, the commercial world of Geoffrey, Simon and every other merchant was held together by the warp and weft of bonds and bills. Only small-time traders or fools paid for anything with ready coin when deals could be done on credit. Merchants such as the ironmonger Gilbert Maghfeld conducted as much as 75 per cent of their business this way. Geoffrey was, doubtless, no

different but there was another form of credit that could make rich merchants even richer.[143] By the early 1440s, Geoffrey had collected enough
personal capital to join in partnership with other citizens and begin
advancing loans. Like a small merchant bank, he and a variety of associates made numerous loans to London merchants, some of whom can
be traced using it to import linen or paper from the same fairs Geoffrey
frequented in his youth. Lady Luck might smile on their ventures but if
she turned her face away, losses could be recouped from the goods and
chattels the borrowers had already gifted as security.[144] As Geoffrey's
career advanced, the loans became greater and his partners fewer until he
was able to lend £200 to his brother Thomas and £100 to his uncle-in-
law Thomas Hoo.[145] At the same time, a Europe-wide shortage of coin
was pushing up interest rates and encouraging many merchants and their
capital away from the recession-blighted world of trade and towards the
easier gains of financial services. When Geoffrey lent money to London's
Genoese community in 1456, the 14 per cent interest rate he was able to
impose was nothing out of the ordinary.[146]

This comfortable and familiar world of domestic trade and commercial
finance saw Geoffrey grow from a naïve youth to an experienced merchant.
His success built a secure safety net for him and his family, so by the 1450s
he was prepared to be a little more adventurous and try something new.
Other merchants, such as his fellow mercer William Cantelowe, based
their fortune on wool export and royal finance, but Geoffrey had hitherto
found little to recommend either enterprise. As with cloth, any interest
he had in wool was that of the middleman dealer.[147] Credit restrictions
combined with an unpaid, mutinous garrison in Calais and the infiltration
of Italians wielding preferential export licences made the life of a wool
exporter less than appealing. In the later 1450s, access to his own export
licence and its corresponding discounted subsidy rate briefly tempted him
to dip a toe into the swirling currents of the Calais trade but it was not a
habit that would stick.[148] This was not a sea where he particularly wanted
to swim and neither were the unpredictable waters of Lancastrian finance.

Some men, such as the mercer William Estfield (d.1446), seemed to
maintain a natural buoyancy, successfully supplementing the profits of
trade with the rather more uncertain rewards that came from bankrolling
the Crown, but Geoffrey only tried this once and evidently decided
never to do so again. It was not an avenue open to a merchant until he

had amassed substantial capital but by 1451, Geoffrey was ready to take a chance. Together with a number of leading citizens, he lent a total of £1,246 13*s*. 4*d*. to the Crown to fund an expedition to rescue Gascony.[149] Such advances had their attractions, with interest rates that may have reached 30 per cent, but a chill wind often whipped through the barren coffers of the Lancastrian Exchequer and straight into the hearts of royal creditors.[150] While Estfield seems to have fared well, John Fastolf died in 1455 with all of his loans to the Crown, totalling over £2,400, unpaid.[151] Geoffrey was assigned repayment of his loan from the clerical subsidy but the Boleyn coffers were slammed firmly shut against any more grasping hands from the House of Lancaster.[152]

For twenty years, Geoffrey and a rotating cast of his own apprentices and servants gathered in the goods and shepherded the silver. By the end of it all, that newly minted citizen with the salt spray in his hair and his dreams in his pocket must have seemed a very long way away. Geoffrey could look down upon almost everyone around him. With estates worth over £150 (£96,000) a year and moveable goods or debts worth at least £5,500 (£3.5 million), he had entered the ranks of the super-rich. In 1436, when the city was assessed, only eleven citizens had a landed income that came anywhere near.[153] Behind him he had left men who had once been his peers, such as his fellow parishioner and hatter Thomas Frary, who never made it beyond the ranks of his minor guild and died leaving cash bequests of only £19.[154] Geoffrey was exceptional and yet also unexceptional. There is no evidence that in business he did anything that was not being done by countless other merchants. If anything he did less, with apparently little taste for royal finance, wool or much in the way of overseas trade, but he was not averse to pushing the boundaries of correctness. Having suffered the accusing fingers of popular disapproval for allegedly breaking the rules that governed the credit terms available to foreign merchants, he obtained a royal pardon in 1445, but in 1459, along with many of his friends or peers, he was formally prosecuted for extending credit to alien merchants beyond the legally permitted six months. Such technically dubious trading was, however, routine practice, targeted by a financially desperate Lancastrian regime as a way of prising money out of merchants. Geoffrey had to be distrained before he deigned to respond but he eventually sent his attorney wielding yet another pardon to escape sanction.[155] What then can explain his staggering success? Could it be that the Boleyns exploited the less fortunate or less skilful on their way to the top?

Around 1457, Geoffrey's honour was dragged through the courts by a struggling haberdasher who vociferously alleged that this was the case. Slinging mud left, right and centre, he made accusations of overcharging, covetousness, 'usury and untruth' and 'malice and evil' which, he claimed, Geoffrey sought to hide by the falsification of legal documents. This was defamation that could hardly be allowed to stand and it elicited a much more energetic defence than the Crown prosecution for illegal credit. All of it, Geoffrey replied, was entirely untrue and he directed the court to 'every other place of worship within this realm and without where his conversation [way of life] is or at any time hath been understood or known'. Woodward's accusations were 'but feigned, coloured … and imagined to … defame the said Geoffrey' and delay his suit of debt against the haberdasher.[156] There is no surviving judgement in this case, and there probably never was. Such Chancery disputes were usually settled out of court but Woodward's own history throws his credibility into doubt. This would not be the last time he initiated dubious or even criminal proceedings to hinder a creditor. Despite being a second-generation haberdasher who married the daughter of a small landowner, Woodward was sinking, not swimming. Geoffrey was not the only creditor who would pursue him for debts accrued in the late 1450s and neither was he the only merchant damaged by the haberdasher's struggles to stay afloat.

Around ten years later, having amassed such debts that he was forced to flee London, Woodward allegedly resorted to violence and fraud. The vintner Thomas Hyltofte, one of Woodward's many creditors, recounted his assault at the hands of the desperate haberdasher who, together with 'diverse persons in riotous wise' took him at his lodgings in Huntingdon, 'menaced him of his life and would not suffer him in any wise to depart' until he had sealed an obligation for £7. Woodward then started legal proceedings to obtain the sum exacted with menaces and back home in London, Hyltofte found himself under arrest.[157] The matter was ultimately settled by agreement between the parties but Woodward emerges as a less than reliable witness. His vexatious prosecution is most useful in revealing not how Geoffrey exploited others, but the commodities he traded in (fustian, woad and madder) and how he ran his business. Amongst the factual or fictitious accounts of their business dealings put forward by Woodward and confirmed or disputed by Geoffrey, one thing is clear. Geoffrey commissioned Woodward to buy wool on his behalf in the Cotswolds with the intention of selling it to another London merchant, in this case the mercer John Tate, rather than exporting it himself. Such middleman dealing must have been at the heart of his business and his success.

Beyond Woodward's dubious accusations there is nothing to suggest that Geoffrey's wealth was less ethical or less lawful than any other merchant's honestly earned fortune. His neighbours would have understood that his star rose while others fell, according to the wishes and whims of God, and society happily absorbed such meteors of fate.[158] Even in London's meritocracy, where the most able bricks shuffled to the top of the wall, the psychology of a pre-destined order was still the mortar that kept the house standing. For Geoffrey, with his feet firmly planted on coffers of silver, or at least on piles of credit notes, it was universally accepted that all the coveted prizes of London's civic or political life would fall, naturally, into his hands. London, however, was not the world. Realities that had little bearing on a merchant's status, such as lineage or landed wealth, assumed greater weight beyond the city's walls. It was not impossible to progress without them but if the Boleyns were to enjoy the same rank and regard outside London as they did in mercantile circles, it would help if they had something that money could not buy, or at least not directly: noble blood.

Enter the First Anne Boleyn

London, May 1445

As spring slipped into the summer of 1445, London's carpenters, stainers and artisans were once again hard at work. Carefully stored angel wings were sorted into mouse-munched or magnificent while Noah emerged, complete with ark, as the city, once again, prepared her finery. The child-king Henry VI was of an age to be married and 15-year-old Margaret of Anjou was on the road from her old home to her new. The lengthy journey from France, however, precipitated a week of rest at Eltham, so while the queen recuperated, the city's craftsmen laboured and anxious civic dignitaries awaited their moment in the sun. On 28 May it finally came. London's mayor and aldermen, resplendent in the civic colours of scarlet and white, joined liverymen in blue gowns and red hoods for the short ride to Blackheath. There they 'abode and hoved on horseback' as they waited to escort their tardy teenage queen back to the Tower. It was the same well-rehearsed ceremony and pageantry that London had staged many times before but for Geoffrey Boleyn the difference between Queen Katherine's entry in 1421 and that of her successor twenty-four years later could not have been more stark. No longer was he an anonymous apprentice boy concealed in the crowd. Now he had the right to be an active participant, a livery man of the Great Twelve. Inside his heavy robes, in the early summer heat, he basked in the warm glow of success.

After a further night of rest in the Tower, Margaret emerged, clad in virginal white, with her long hair loose about her shoulders. She was still feeling unwell so rather than horseback, opted for a litter, drawn by two white horses, for her procession through the city, and behind her went the mayor, aldermen and liverymen. They passed 'sumptuous and costly pageants and resemblance of diverse old histories' which celebrated Margaret as a virtuous bringer of peace and future mother of heirs. Their progress halted in the churchyard of St Paul's, where the lightning-blasted remains of the spire loomed ominously over the start of a queenship that would turn out to be far from peaceful.[159]

Margaret, however, was not the only young wife in London. Geoffrey too was embarking upon a new relationship that would shape the rest of his life and transform the future of his children. His first wife, Dionisia, had died, as silently as she lived, leaving Geoffrey, now a wealthy man, to contemplate the alliance those riches might win for him. It has been suggested that her demise left him a widower with a young son, named Dionisius, but the evidence for such a boy is flimsy at best.[160] His entire existence is founded upon a bede roll compiled for Queens' College, Cambridge, around 1484, listing the souls to be remembered in the prayers of members. Sometime between this date and the foundation of the college in 1448, donations had been recorded on behalf of Geoffrey Boleyn and his second wife, Anne, his brother Thomas, Adam Book and his wife Joan and a name written by the scribe as 'Dionisi' Boleyne' but transcribed when later published as 'Dionisi[us] Boleyn'. The unnamed Cambridge scribe, lacking detailed knowledge of the family and compiling his list from a collection of older records, simply used a general abbreviation mark and inadvertently created a son from a name that evidently should read 'Dionisi[a]'.[161] Neither Dionisia nor Adam Book could themselves have made donations to Queens' as both died years before the college was established.[162] It was Geoffrey who provided this money and named the souls for whom he was buying remembrance, the same people he would later recall in his own family chantry. By the early 1440s, therefore, Geoffrey was rich, single and unencumbered with offspring. An excellent catch for any of London's mercantile daughters.

Geoffrey's sights, however, were set on a far more aristocratic match, as he sought to win the hand of a young noblewoman named Anne Hoo.

She came from a family far removed from the warehouses, wharves and company halls of London and from a world that did not naturally collide with Geoffrey's own. The matchmaker in this case may have been his brother Thomas, whose high-flying clerical connections had carried him into the realms of the titled and entitled. While Geoffrey left home bound for London and commerce, his brother Thomas took a more studious path, becoming a fellow of Trinity Hall, Cambridge, by 1420. He was ordained a priest, at Norwich Cathedral, the following year and the fledgling cleric quickly found his first benefice via a local Norfolk family who would draw him into the orbit of some powerful noblemen and women.[163] The Kerdeston family owned the manor of Reepham, adjacent to Thomas's home in Salle, as well as the advowson (right to nominate the priest) of the parish church, and it was here that Thomas Boleyn was installed by Thomas Kerdeston in 1422.[164] The Kerdestons, however, were in the process of forging even grander connections. In this same year, Thomas Kerdeston married Elizabeth de la Pole, the sister of William de la Pole, Earl (later Duke) of Suffolk. Suffolk, who spent his youth fighting in France, was a rising star at the court of Henry VI, and Thomas Boleyn perhaps had early aspirations to move in such circles. In 1434 he attended the church council at Basle in the retinue of Edmund Beaufort, then Count of Mortain, later Duke of Somerset, and he may have encountered Anne's father, Sir Thomas Hoo, amongst the many satellites of the earl of Suffolk.[165] By the 1440s Hoo was a veteran campaigner who had served under Suffolk in the Pays de Caux and who acted as feoffee or trustee for the earl's large estates.[166] But he was also a father with an unmarried daughter urgently in need of a husband.

The combination of social network and faction that brought Geoffrey and the Hoos into the same orbit was the bread and butter of medieval high society as families sought advantage and formed affinities, loyalties and, crucially, marriages. When the possibility of an alliance between Geoffrey and Anne was first raised, it would have appealed to both parties, but perhaps particularly to the prospective bridegroom. Wealth, that indispensable pre-requisite to acquired gentility, he already had in abundance, and more would follow, but riches alone did not a gentleman make. If Geoffrey's children were to enjoy a different style of life, the profits of trade had to be combined with other attributes. He might buy landed estates and with them a place in the feudal hierarchy or secure advancement through royal service but the most important gift he could bestow upon future sons and daughters was a blood relationship with an established noble line. For Geoffrey the Hoos were the perfect 'Goldilocks' family. Although well connected at court, they were not too exalted. Dukes and earls would never have entertained a son-in-law so recently descended from the yeomanry, no matter how many Borromei bank accounts he had, and yet Anne was far more aristocratic than the ordinary mercantile bride. Around a third of the city's fifteenth-century aldermen married the daughters of country landowners but most came from far humbler gentry stock. Sir Thomas Hoo was already a knight at their marriage and would soon be welcomed into the Order of the Garter and ennobled with a peerage as Lord Hoo and Hastings.[167] Two of Anne's three half-sisters would also go on to marry London mercers but only a handful of merchants, such as the famous Richard Whittington, who married the daughter of Sir Ivo Fitzwaryn, came close to such aristocratic matches.[168]

Of course Anne also had more mercenary attractions. With her hand in marriage came a dowry, which, if similar to that bequeathed to her younger half-sisters, would have been worth around £225, around £145,000 today, but any further inheritance was uncertain. In the summer of 1445, Thomas Hoo, who spent much of his career in France, returned to England, where it seems he set about reordering his family. Now a widower, he arranged a second marriage for himself, revoking the settlement that would have given the manor of Mulbarton in Norfolk to Anne and adding it, instead, to the property entailed upon the male offspring of his new marriage to Eleanor Wells, or upon his brother thereafter.[169] It seems likely that it was around this time that he also disposed of his older daughter, clearing the way for a new household and, hopefully, new children. At her marriage Anne had a claim to the unentailed portion of her father's estate, which was not settled on the male line, but a new brother would trump that entitlement. Ultimately sons would elude the Hoo family and Lord Hoo's brother would follow him to the grave without a male heir, but as Anne and Geoffrey exchanged vows, their union meant pocket money and a gamble for the groom, not a lottery win.[170] Anne's prestigious relations were her real treasure.

But what of Anne and her family? Why did she agree to become the wife of Geoffrey Boleyn? As a well-born young lady she would lower her own status by marriage to a merchant in a way that noble sons, hunting mercantile heiresses, did not. There must have been a compelling reason. After the death of Anne's father, in 1455, the attraction of the fabulously wealthy Geoffrey Boleyn suddenly becomes clear. It was not that Lord Hoo was impoverished. He still owned extensive landed estates but he probably suffered a financial hit as a result of English military defeats in France and ran up considerable expenses in the process. In 1441 the Crown granted him an annual pension of £40 in compensation, but by his death, he was in such debt that the value of all his moveable goods and chattels and the sale of his lordship of the 'rape of Hastings' for 1,000 marks could not pay his creditors.[171] The executors named in his will, his half-brother Thomas and widow Eleanor, 'expressly refused to act' and the difficult task of administering his estate was entrusted to his step-brother Richard Lewknor.[172]

The bare facts laid at the feet of the prospective couple made for a practical match but their true feelings remain a mystery. As a young gentlewoman, Anne would have been raised to understand that love or affection in marriage was something desirable to be cultivated in time, not an essential pre-requisite. That type of romance was for chivalric literature, not real life. A marriage in the summer of 1445 would fit neatly with Lord Hoo's time in England and with the birth of the couple's first child in late 1446. This means on her wedding day Anne would have been around 20, while Geoffrey was twice her age, but such a match would have been commonplace at all levels of society and not, generally, a reason for objection.[173] Anne was a slightly mature bride in an age when the daughters of nobility regularly married in their teens but it is possible that she had for some time simply lacked close relatives, particularly female relatives, to seek and negotiate a marriage on her behalf. The date of her mother's death is unknown but it certainly occurred before 1445 and her father spent much of his time overseas. The deaths of parents and subsequent remarriages are known to have contributed to the fate of a small number of aristocratic women who, with no one to focus on their future, never married at all. When Sir Roger Darcy died in 1508 he left two daughters, Margaret and Eleanor. Their widowed mother, who had been Elizabeth Wentworth before her marriage, would bury two further husbands while Margaret and Eleanor Darcy both remained unmarried, despite dowries of £200 apiece, seemingly for no other reason than a lack of attention in the crucial years of their late teens and early twenties.[174]

It would seem that Anne's father belatedly caught up with his family responsibilities in the summer of 1445 and disposed of his unwed daughter to a convenient wealthy merchant. Like many girls born to wealthy or noble families, Anne probably made herself content with the husband chosen for her, although a clue to her true feelings may lie in how she went about marrying her own daughters. Anne seems to have been particularly solicitous of their feelings but it is impossible to know whether this was because she was denied such self-determination herself or because she wanted them to enjoy the same marital happiness she had freely chosen.

Whatever the affections or otherwise of the bride and groom, one morning, probably in the summer of 1445, as the sun climbed towards the noonday cut-off for wedding ceremonies, Geoffrey met Anne at the door of a church. Perhaps they stood before the rough flint walls of All Saints on the river in Chelsea, where Geoffrey's brother Thomas served as rector from 1442, or perhaps in the shadow of the great Bow Bell, at the groom's parish church in the city.[175] Garbed in the softest English woollens or brightest imported silks, the mercer and his soon-to-be wife displayed family fortune and mercantile art as they came together to exchange the familiar words barely changed over 600 years. Anne's father or another relative placed her right hand into Geoffrey's own as the family of her birth literally and symbolically handed her over to the care of her new husband. For the confident, worldly merchant, it was not the first time he had stood before a woman who would soon be his wife and taken her by the hand, but for Anne, it was the one and only time she would speak the words that gave herself away. First she listened, as Geoffrey vowed to 'take thee Anne, to my wedded wife, to have and to hold from this day forward, for better, for worse, for richer, for poorer, in sickness and in health, till death us do part, if holy church will it ordain and thereto I plight thee my troth'.[176]

Then it was her turn to repeat those familiar words, but unlike brides today, Anne would also have promised to 'be bonour and buxom (good/ obliging) in bed and at board'. A welcoming bed-fellow and a well-provisioned table were not all that was expected of medieval wives (who can equally be found running businesses or estates) but it was part of the model of an ideal, happy domestic life. Church and society similarly expected Anne to obey Geoffrey, although this she would not have sworn. Not until the Protestant Book of Common Prayer replaced bonour and buxomness with obedience, in 1549, were wives required to be obedient by a vow before God.[177] With the gold ring on her finger, the formalities were complete. Anne Hoo became the first Anne Boleyn and a joyous crowd of friends and family trooped into the church. There the newlyweds knelt at the altar for a nuptial mass and all offered prayers for their future happiness, peace and fruitfulness.[178]

Not all wedding ceremonies were this elaborate or adhered to the full form of liturgy known as the Sarum Rite, but as a wealthy couple and a daughter of nobility, Anne and Geoffrey would have expected the full ceremonial extravaganza, not kitchen table promises. A public event blessed by the Church, witnessed by their friends, family and community and followed by an expensive wedding feast, a post-wedding knees-up being as old as marriage itself. With tables groaning under the weight of roast meats, pastries and wine, some wedding celebrations cost the father of the bride as much as his daughter's dowry, which can have done little to help Sir Thomas Hoo's finances.

Whether on her wedding night or shortly thereafter, Geoffrey would have brought his young wife to a new house far removed from her childhood home. Gone were the flat Norfolk expanses of Mulbarton, to be replaced by crowded little tenements and bustling streets.[179] Down a cramped alleyway beside the church of St Mary le Bow, Anne's new husband led her past the narrow shopfronts of tailors and shoemakers and through a large gateway into the front courtyard of one of the great merchant houses that lay hidden behind London's retail streets. Every night from now on, the dolorous tolling of the great bell at St Mary le Bow, ringing the 9 p.m. curfew, would remind her how much life had changed.

Geoffrey certainly lived at this address between 1445 and 1448, and perhaps for some years both before and after these dates, paying a substantial annual rent of £6 13s. 4d to the hospital of St Mary within Cripplegate.[180] Excavation of the site, carried out in 1979, suggests that Anne stood in the shadow of a large, imposing building stretching as much as 45ft across the full width of the property. Crossing the courtyard and entering her new domain, she would have found herself in the open expanse of a great hall. Below lay a vaulted stone undercroft, packed with silk and linen or fragrant with Geoffrey's bales of spices, while above lay smaller, private family chambers. To the rear, another courtyard, with its own well, was the daily workplace of the household's numerous domestic staff.

Sadly, no contemporary description of the interior remains but a much later inventory, from 1599, describes some of the rooms that made up the house Anne would call home. Beyond the great hall there was a parlour and buttery; a room described as the 'great chamber', probably above the parlour; a 'matted chamber', with a window looking towards the gate on Bow Lane; and a kitchen. A 'frame of glass' provided light for the stairway that led up from the hall to the chambers, while outside, the yard housed the practical realities of a lead cistern, pump and two stills.[181] Elsewhere there were probably servants' chambers or other unfurnished rooms, which were excluded from this short inventory because they had no contents to record. As Anne explored she may have found small rooms, such as the parlour, fitted with expensive painted wood panelling, known as wainscoting. Other rooms would have been simply plastered and whitewashed to better display the colourful painted cloths or tapestries imported from the Low Countries by men like her husband.

In the bright afternoon sun, such a luxurious house would have been well lit by plentiful windows, although glazing was only installed in large public buildings or the occasional private home and shutters would have been commonplace elsewhere. The hall of a great merchant house would be furnished with at least one large fireplace, while in more private moments, the newlyweds could have warmed themselves by smaller fireplaces in the principal chambers or with braziers on wheels used to move heat around.[182] When snow lay thick in the lane outside, Anne would also have found warmth in the rich, sumptuous textiles of her husband's trade, in furnishings like the red worsted hangings with matching cushions that graced the hall of the draper Thomas Salle, whose name probably derived from the same home village as Geoffrey.[183] Numerous testamentary bequests suggest that the Boleyns would have retired at night to a bed cocooned with feather mattresses, coverlets, bolsters and elaborate hangings. These domestic textiles were often the most valuable household items, after jewellery and silver vessels, but inexpensive wooden furniture, produced by skilled English wood carvers, put the art and artistry into relatively simply furnished rooms.[184]

This new, spacious and comfortable home, squeezed cheek-by-jowl between the markets, merchants and tradesmen of Cheapside, was now Anne's domain. Here she had to build a life, both within her new household realm and in the community beyond. Her easiest entry into London's largely invisible and unrecorded female society would have been via the wives of her husband's friends and her new neighbours. Geoffrey's closest companions were his fellow mercer Ralph Verney and the lawyer Thomas Burgoyne. Both men were regular business associates and it was to them that he later assigned the important task of executing his will. Verney was the younger man, completing his apprenticeship the same year Geoffrey joined the mercers' company, but the two were often engaged in the same enterprises, regularly served as feoffee for each other and both founded wealthy family dynasties. Verney was not an immediate neighbour, however, as he lived in the parish of St Martin Pomary, in Ironmonger Lane, on the opposite side of Cheapside, and he was probably still a single man when Anne came to London. He would go on to marry Emma, widow of the mercer John Pykyng, and their children would have been around four years younger than Anne and Geoffrey's brood.[185] Serving as London's undersheriff from 1434 until his death in 1470, Thomas Burgoyne was one of the city's legal advisors, and Geoffrey made use of his friendship and his expertise throughout his career. He and his wife lived even further away, outside the city walls, in a large house within the precinct of St Bartholomew's Hospital, but the physical distance would have been easily erased by affection, for Burgoyne was probably still married to his first wife, Isabel, the daughter of Geoffrey's old master and friend Adam Book. Along with the Verneys, the couple must have been regular visitors to the Boleyns' home, bringing companionship, local gossip and commercial or political news to the parlour at Bow Lane.[186]

Closer to home, just a few steps down the lane, lived John Lok and his wife Elizabeth, a native-born Londoner and daughter of a salter (salt importer and merchant). Lok was not only a fellow mercer but also a fellow Norfolk man who owned lands in Salle, and the couple would have a total of six children growing up around the same time as the Boleyn boys and girls.[187] Living in such close proximity and with young families of a similar age, Anne and Elizabeth must have been naturally thrown together. Elizabeth's knowledge, born of a life spent in the city, would have helped to point Anne in the right direction but she may also have found friendship and hard-won maternal expertise at the hearth of Alice Nedeham. As the widow of the tailor John Kinge, Alice already had five young children when she married Geoffrey's friend and executor Richard Nedeham in 1444.[188] Like the Boleyns, the union of Alice and Richard spanned the void between the aristocracy of blood and the aristocracy of trade. While Alice brought years of experience in London's mercantile society, Richard's life as a mercer was secondary to his service with Humphrey, Duke of Gloucester.[189]

Even without her new friends and neighbours, under the tiled roof of the house on Bow Lane, Anne would have rarely been alone. By 1444, Geoffrey had six young apprentices and many more would follow, adding to a large household that by his death included two former servants and one maid servant, remembered by name, as well as a much wider body of anonymous staff.[190] Like all married women, Anne would have been the helmswoman of this unwieldy vessel: managing and hiring servants, balancing the books and overseeing apprentices or other business matters while Geoffrey was out of town. It was an extensive establishment for a relatively inexperienced young woman but her education and upbringing would have prepared her to be a useful domestic partner, albeit a junior one. Crucial to her success or failure were the friendships and alliances, enmities and rivalries of all the young men and women who called the house on Bow Lane home. As she sought to find her footing, she would quickly need to learn who she could lean upon and trust and who might be better off in someone else's household.

These many helping hands would have freed her from personal involvement in the laborious tasks of cooking or cleaning but like her wealthy friends and neighbours, she would have needed to supervise her staff and maintain an awareness of market prices in order to keep and check accounts. The mistress who remained aloof from such mundane matters risked embezzlement and loss at the hands of unscrupulous household staff, so when it came to putting food on the table, Anne had to learn her trade. From produce and poultry on Cheapside to the fishmongers down by the bridge, she had to know who sold quality goods honestly and who used false weights to sell rancid meat or watered wine. In the streets and markets of London it was normal to see women, both rich and poor, everywhere but this was something remarkable to foreign visitors. Alessandro Magno, a young Italian merchant, wrote that 'Englishwomen have great freedom to go out of the house without menfolk ... the women themselves carry the goods if they are poor or make their maids do so if they have them and they are free to buy whatever is needed'. In 1575, a Dutch traveller to England similarly remarked that English women were not kept strictly at home as they were in Spain. Instead they had 'the free management of the house or housekeeping', they went 'to market to buy what they like best' and they 'sit before their doors, decked out in fine clothes, in order to see and be seen'. They were free to attend banquets, visit their neighbours or 'gossips' and 'make merry' with them at childbirths, christenings and churchings.[191] For Anne, the retail delights of Cheapside and the neighbourly conclaves were already hers to explore and before long, she too would be in the deep waters of her own childbirth and churchings.

6

'A Multitude of Riff Raff'

London, September 1446

Assuming that her pregnancy was full term, Anne would have become aware of the impending arrival of a baby around the Christmas and New Year festivities of 1445. The news must have added a special joy to the Boleyns' yuletide celebrations, but for Anne and every other medieval woman, such happiness would have been tinged with fear. Poor nutrition, a large number of pregnancies in quick succession and either particularly young or particularly old conception made childbirth perilous even before a lack of effective midwifery care is considered. It has been estimated that 6 per cent, or around one in seventeen, medieval women died during or because of childbirth, meaning most women would have known someone for whom pregnancy meant death, not life.[192] Geoffrey and Anne would have been showered with congratulations by their friends and relatives but such well-wishing was often accompanied by prayers that Anne have 'a good time and good deliverance'.[193]

By the time late summer's heat had descended on the city, Anne would already have loosened the laces of her gown several times, apprehension growing with her waistline. To keep her mind occupied, there was much to prepare as she collected around her the precious paraphernalia of a mother-to-be: not only the tiny linens and wrappings to keep the precious life safe but probably a selection of supernatural aids that were an expectant mother's only talismans against the coming ordeal. A chamber must be chosen and prepared, both for the birth and the ensuing period of seclusion, but as the wife of a wealthy mercer, Anne's bedroom was probably already well furnished with luxurious hangings. The special linens she may have added were those endowed with properties helpful in childbirth, such as the sheets and pillowcases included in the bankruptcy inventory of an unnamed widow from the late fifteenth or early sixteenth century. This unfortunate lady had evidently fallen from a state of some affluence as her possessions included:

A sheet for a woman when she lies in childbed with bone lace of white in the same, 8s.[194]

3 pillowcases with the same bone lace, 9s.

A face cloth of cambric for a child, 4s.

3 pillowcases with pearls, 6s.

A plain sheet for a woman's bed, 5s.

Some mysterious quality of the first sheet clearly made it apt for use by a pregnant woman, while to the pearls on the three pillowcases was attributed the ability to stem post-partum haemorrhage.[195] If not linens and pearls, then a host of other items may have been borrowed or gifted to Anne as an aid in her labours. Amber and coral beads were believed to be helpful in childbirth and at least one mid-fifteenth century midwife in London was employing the supernatural assistance of water that had lain in contact with jet for three days. This unknown goodwife's discarded jet bowl has been recovered from the city's waterfront, where it had lain undisturbed for over 500 years.[196] However, the most powerful and important aid that could be offered to an expectant mother, other than the hands of an experienced midwife, came in the form of the ancient, pre-Christian tradition of the birthing girdle. Westminster Abbey housed the supposed girdle of the Virgin Mary, which was loaned to expectant royal ladies, but Anne would never have had access to such a sacred relic. Like other less exalted women, she perhaps turned to parchment or paper scrolls, inscribed with prayers or charms, which were placed across the stomach of the mother-to-be.[197] All such items, imbued with a special resonance for women, were commonly passed from mothers to daughters and lent between relatives and friendship groups. Their repeated use invoked ties of family, ancestry and community as each new generation entered the world and new bonds were forged between the women in the birthing chamber. Anne could not call upon her own mother but the sharing of objects, memories and prayers to St Margaret, the patron saint of childbirth, would have helped to deepen her new friendships.

Fortunately all was well and the arrival of a healthy son, Thomas, on 7 September 1446 would have been welcomed with great joy and celebration.[198] The vulnerable infant would have been quickly hustled to the family's parish church of St Mary le Bow for baptism, in case God called him back before he could be washed clean of original sin. When Geoffrey brought his baby son into church for the first time, the fragments of light that fell upon him shone in through windows paid for at the bequest of his own beloved mentor and father figure, Adam Book.[199] His old friend could not be there but his legacy sprinkled multi-coloured sunbeams upon the child he never lived to see. Undoubtedly, the newborn Thomas cried heartily for his mother as the priest immersed him three times in the font, once on each side and once face downwards, but Anne was probably not present at the baptism.[200] Like all newly delivered women, she was still secluded in the chamber where she gave birth, attended only by other women. This period, known as lying-in, continued for a month, although after the first two weeks or so she would have been permitted controlled exercise within the confines of her home. So it was to the chill of an autumn day in early October that Anne emerged for a choreographed re-entry into society known as 'churching'. This important ceremony never completely escapes overtones of clerical misogyny, given that it was built around the ritual cleansing of post-partum women, but in practice, it seems to have been welcomed as an opportunity for celebration and thanksgiving. Anne had safely traversed a perilous twilight realm between life and death and was to be welcomed back into church and society as a mother. One by one, her female friends would have gathered at the house on Bow Lane, ready to play their part in the ritual. Over her head Anne draped a special veil, known as a 'care cloth', perhaps the one St Mary le Bow had available for new mothers to borrow, and took a lit candle in her hands. With her jubilant friends clustered around her, she processed a few short yards, out through the gate and up the lane to the churchyard. Before the entrance, Anne would have knelt on the stone steps to be sprinkled with holy water by the priest as they spoke together the words 'thou shalt purge me, O Lord, with hyssop'. It was a small but significant rite that brought her back into the world. Rising to her feet, she and her companions filed into the church for a mass, to offer prayers of thanksgiving and to present the candle and a penny at the altar.[201] It was a time to reconnect with friends and neighbours, share the gossip of the day and indulge in feasting and rejoicing at the family's great good fortune.

Over the coming years, Anne would repeat the whole process at least four more times, for another son, William, and three daughters, Anne, Isabel and Alice, who survived to adulthood, and probably several other children who did not. Perhaps to accommodate their growing brood but probably also to acquire a higher status address, around 1448 the family packed chests, baskets and valuable coffers into the moving carts and decamped to a new home among the mercantile oligarchs of Milk Street.[202] Not even this refined enclave could, however, provide shelter from the dark clouds gathering on the horizon. The approaching storm would be unlike anything the city had seen since the rebels of 1381 flooded over London Bridge, and at the eye of the tempest was a man closely linked to Anne's father, the de facto leader of Henry's government, William de la Pole, Duke of Suffolk.

The first clouds began to gather with the opening of parliament in November 1449 in an atmosphere infected with an anxious distrust of royal government. Demands for change at the top were only reinforced by a campaign in France that brought humiliation followed by gradual retreat. French armies had marched into Normandy, causing London's wool merchants to fear for the continuing security of the wool staple port at Calais. Cloth exports had again collapsed in the face of another Burgundian cloth ban and the French campaign in Gascony threatened a similar fate for wine imports. The Royal Exchequer was almost empty of funds and London's mercantile community fretted about growing royal demands for loans with insecure prospects of repayment. But medieval political correctness dictated that the king himself was not to be censured. Instead, opponents argued, corrections must be made to his team of incompetent or malevolent advisors, and top of the list was his chief minister, the duke of Suffolk. After an abortive attempt at impeachment or prosecution by parliament, Henry agreed to impose a milder and temporary punishment of banishment for five years. Under cover of darkness, on 17 March 1450, Suffolk was spirited from his confinement in the Jewel Tower of the Palace of Westminster. The intention was a discreet departure for his manor at East Thorp but the mob got wind of his intended flit and he was pursued part of the way by a crowd of 2,000 angry Londoners. The duke set sail from Ipswich on the last day of April, bound for the duke of Burgundy's lands in the Low Countries, and a small reconnaissance craft went ahead to verify his welcome at Calais, but the crew betrayed his whereabouts and Suffolk was intercepted outside Dover by a ship from London called *Nicholas of the Tower*. Forced or persuaded aboard by a hostile crew, he was subjected to a show trial and summarily condemned. On 2 May he was put into a smaller boat, with a chaplain to shrive him, and there a sailor from Bosham, later named as Richard Lenard, smote off his head with a rusty sword. Two days later his body was found dumped on Dover beach, his head impaled on a pole next to the bloody corpse.[203]

In London and elsewhere the atmosphere remained fraught. The head of the beast may have been removed but popular fury and thirst for blood continued, seeking out a wider cancer in the body politic among Suffolk's cronies and associates. Not least amongst the crowd of men blamed for England's problems was Anne's father Thomas, who by this time had been rewarded with the barony of Hoo and Hastings under Suffolk's patronage. As chancellor of France, he was damningly connected, both politically and militarily, with the recent defeats and territorial losses. He had taken a leading role in negotiations for the surrenders of Rouen, Caudebec and Harfleur and would later be accused of financial impropriety.[204] As rumour and report swirled into the city, Geoffrey and Anne must have listened in horror to news that the perpetually rebellious commons of Kent had once again risen in revolt. Thousands of armed men marched for London, demanding reform and hunting down Suffolk's cronies wherever they could find them. On the lips of rebels and Londoners alike, that summer, were popular verses and ballads that ridiculed Suffolk and his circle, including one that cruelly indicted fifty councillors, household and government servants, including Thomas Hoo.[205] Singing about Anne's father, the rebels were coming.

The trouble began in April 1450, when the threat of a French invasion saw the Kentish coast thrown into a state of alarm. In preparation, the government issued a commission of array (the order to raise the county militia) and men gathered in each hundred, or administrative division, to be provided with clothing, equipment and armour. However, on finding themselves organised into a fighting force, the men of Kent saw enemies not only over the seas but closer to home in the form of those dangerous and untrustworthy advisors still clustered around the king. The Kentish men elected as their leader a local man named Jack Cade and marched towards London, gathering reinforcements along the way. By 11 June they were encamped on the field at Blackheath last occupied by their forebears in 1381 and were busy digging entrenchments. In the city, guards were stationed day and night along the Thames, while ordinance was prepared and the bridge masters were issued with the rudimentary and unpredictable hand guns of the time, which must have offered little comfort.[206]

The king had returned to London but, unlike the teenage Richard II in 1381, he refused to meet with the rebels in person. Instead there followed several days of fruitless discussion with government negotiators, followed by the withdrawal of the rebels back into Kent, pursued by a royal army. When the two sides met near Tonbridge, the king's forces were ambushed and slaughtered. Both royal commanders, Humphrey Stafford, Duke of Buckingham, and his kinsman William Stafford, were killed, while large numbers of fighting men who should have been loyal to the Crown lost heart and threatened to defect to the rebels. This catalogue of disaster persuaded Henry to flee London for the relative safety of Kenilworth Castle, leaving the city exposed to the rebels. By 2 July, Jack Cade and his forces had returned to occupy Southwark at the southern foot of London Bridge, while the city walls around Aldgate were surrounded by men from a separate uprising in Essex. London was besieged.

The following day, the rebels fought their way past the city militia, who had been hastily assembled to defend the bridge, and slashed the ropes of the drawbridge to ensure London's defences remained open as they surged into the city. Many of London's inhabitants sympathised with the rebels' demands and even the ruling patriciate had some degree of understanding, but minds were quickly changed as Londoners endured a short but brutal occupation by what one chronicler scathingly described as 'a multitude of riff raff'.[207] The Boleyns watched anxiously as other city families with links to Suffolk's poisonous reign were ruthlessly targeted by the rebels. The alderman Philip Malpas had his house ransacked and much of his property stolen, while Robert Horne, with whom Geoffrey had recently served as sheriff, found himself thrown into Newgate prison. With the rebels in complete control of the city, they proceeded to eliminate their perceived enemies wherever they could find them. The despised royal treasurer, James Fiennes, Lord Saye and Sele, was beheaded in the middle of Cheapside, while his son-in-law William Crowmer, sheriff of Kent, was dragged outside the city to Mile End and viciously hacked to pieces. Both had their heads impaled on spears and paraded around the streets, to the horror and dismay of the resident population.

Fearing that his father-in-law's connection to Suffolk and to military disaster in France would endanger his family when the 'riff raff' ran out of more direct targets, Geoffrey must have worried about how to keep his children and possibly pregnant wife safe.[208] The safest course of action would have been to send Anne and young Thomas, who, by this date, had probably been joined by at least one sister, out of the city. However, Geoffrey had not yet acquired his country estates in Norfolk and Kent, so could not send his wife and young family to the safety and tranquillity of their own rural retreat. It would have been unwise for Anne to go to her own family home when her father was himself a potential target, and travelling the countryside was perilous, so the family were probably compelled to remain where they were and watch the drama unfold around them.

With the prospect of imminent threat to his home, property or family, Geoffrey would have been eager to expel the rebels, and he was certainly not alone. By 5 July, Londoners had had enough and, with their militia reinforced by the garrison from the Tower and under the command of two veterans from the French wars, Thomas, Lord Scales, and Mathew Gough, they were ready to attempt a counter-attack. All of London's citizens had a duty to contribute to the defence of the city in moments of crisis and as Geoffrey was still a relatively young, healthy man and a prominent member of his community, he may well have joined the fighting force raised from his ward of Cripplegate and led by their alderman and Geoffrey's fellow mercer, William Cantelowe. As twilight approached, the Londoners turned out in harness, and battle was waged on London Bridge. It would continue through the hours of darkness and long past sunrise. In the narrow confines of the carriageway the conflict was bloody hand-to-hand fighting by torchlight and both sides were soon tripping over the bodies of their dead and injured comrades. In desperation, Cade set fire to the wooden drawbridge, choking the air with smoke and sending men to a cold death in the river below. Finally, the frantic Londoners managed to close the gates at the northern end, leaving the rebels outside. Floating in the river or strewn on the bridge lay the bodies of around forty Londoners, including Mathew Gough, the alderman, John Sutton, Roger Heysant, a draper, and around 200 Kentishmen.[209] The following day the rebels, on the advice of Queen Margaret, were offered a pardon, which many accepted, and they gradually dispersed back into Kent. Jack Cade, however, refused, preferring to fight until the end. On 12 July, he was declared a traitor and a few days later was captured 'in a garden' in Sussex. On the road back to London he died of injuries sustained during his capture and justice had to content herself with the posthumous beheading of his body. As was traditional, his head was placed on London Bridge, which would bear the scorched scars of battle for some time to come.[210]

The crisis may have passed but London and the south-east remained volatile throughout the late summer and autumn. Demobbed soldiers from Normandy continued to swell London's population. In August the armoury at the Tower was broken into and emptied of weaponry, while riots accompanied the mayoral election in October.[211] Suffolk's fall had left a vacuum at the heart of government which the 28-year-old ineffectual monarch was unwilling or unable to fill. It was by no means clear who, in the immediate future, would be holding the reins of power, which left many wondering where to turn. When Richard, Duke of York, returned from Ireland in September, it seemed the vacancy would be filled and a number of Suffolk's former allies rushed to switch sides, including Anne's father, Thomas. It was a risky move and he was not exactly welcomed with open arms when he caught up with the duke at St Albans. The 'western men' accompanying Richard greeted him with such animosity that he had to be protected by the duke's chancellor, Sir William Oldhall.[212] York brought his army through London on 27 September 1450 and after two weeks in residence, departed on 9 October for his own estates, leaving behind him a restless city unconvinced by the Hoo family's realignment of loyalties.

Cade's rebels had been appeased with a royal inquiry into the failings and abuses of various officials and proceedings opened at Rochester in late summer. A number of men, including Thomas Hoo, were indicted but punishments were light or non-existent and few were satisfied. As Christmas approached, parliament launched its own concerted attack, demanding the removal from the king's presence of Lord Hoo and twenty-eight other named individuals, about whom 'universal noise and clamour of … misbehaving reign'.[213] It came to nothing. The king refused but sympathy for the attempt prompted the London mob, on 3 December, to ransack the lodgings of Anne's unfortunate father along with 'many divers lords' and 'they bore away all the goods that were in them'.[214] Whether Thomas Hoo's lodgings were an inn, his own residence or even his daughter's home, we may never know, but this dangerous brush with national politics was not the last one for the Boleyns. Geoffrey's standing in his company and community had been growing and for such men the duties of public service and civic government were inescapable. As the nation stumbled towards civil war, he would be sucked into the maelstrom, seeking to reconcile the safety of neutrality with a growing personal loyalty to Richard, Duke of York.

7

Common Council to House of Commons

London, 24 June 1442

It was a truth universally acknowledged that any role in civic or company government was usually time consuming, rarely paid and often extremely personally expensive. So, as the temperature rose in the crowded hall and venison-filled stomachs strained against gilded belts, something unwelcome was about to happen to Geoffrey Boleyn. Wine cups were emptied, the relics of the great feast cleared from the boards and the mercers sat back to watch the formal selection of a new set of wardens. Crowned with garlands of flowers and preceded by cup-bearers, the four wardens processed into the hall. Each held his garland over the heads of the assembled candidates before laying it in front of the man he intended to succeed him in office.[215] The choice of the widely respected John Olney as master for the third time would have been no surprise to anyone but it seems that the garland of office that fell into Geoffrey's own lap was in no way welcome.[216] That fateful circle of roses and gillyflowers was just the kind of distraction that the commercially driven mercer had spent the early part of that year desperately trying to avoid.

By early 1442 Geoffrey must have realised that his card would soon be marked for civic office. He had reached the level of personal prominence and professional success at which London respectfully required her foremost citizens to repay the opportunity and riches she had provided by taking up the reins of civic government. Some positions were appointments, others were elections, but unlike today, when only those who agree to stand can be chosen by voters, in the medieval city men could be, and frequently were, elected in their absence or against their will. Some went to great lengths to try and escape this costly and burdensome noose. When John Stokton was substituted for an incumbent sheriff who had died in harness, in 1467, he paid the substantial sum of £100 to ensure he would not be subjected to the office a second time, and when John Gedney was elected an alderman, in 1415, it took a spell in prison to persuade him to take up his position.[217] For Thomas Walsingham, vintner, the burdens of an aldermanry were such that he preferred to pay the considerable cost of glazing the new great east window of the Guildhall as the price of his release.[218] It must have been with a similar sense of impending doom that in March 1442, Geoffrey secured a royal exemption from being forced into various official roles against his will.[219] He was safe from the burdensome duties of mayor, sheriff, juryman or tax collector but this did nothing to protect him from company appointments, a loophole that had just become painfully apparent.

At least it was not the worst job going. Every year the mercers were governed by four wardens. The most senior, usually an alderman, was known as the master but the greatest drudgery of office was shouldered by the fourth or 'renter' warden. With responsibility for gathering rents, maintaining properties and, crucially, balancing the books, this was the position where up and coming men shed their training wheels. Here they would either prove their mettle or founder under the pressure but Geoffrey was at least allowed to skip this year of hard labour. Instead the burden fell to John Burton, with whom he would maintain a friendly relationship for many years to come.[220] As third or 'house' warden, Geoffrey's rather less onerous responsibilities encompassed the oversight of the company's goods and chattels, the safe keeping of official records, such as property deeds, and the care and updating of the mercers' books. The latter included the volumes used in the chapel, the working and fair copies of both the company and rental accounts and the rolls of members' names and seniority.[221] Something of Geoffrey's tidy mind and systematic approach to business can perhaps be read in the fact that, by the end of his year in office, the company's filing system had been improved by the purchase of one box for the deeds, another for the leases and a large wooden chest with four locks, costing 6*s*. 8*d*., that would ensure all such documents were safe and secure.[222] Fortunately Geoffrey's year in office was not too onerous or expensive but civic duty was inescapable and the net was closing in.

By early 1445 Geoffrey had been elected to membership of London's common council, a body inferior to the court of aldermen but formed to represent the wider community of London's citizens. It was the first rung of civic office and it seems to have prompted frantic efforts to escape. His royal letters of immunity from public office specified the office of mayor but not that of alderman, common councilman or numerous other positions specific to London and it seems to have prompted some debate. Through the summer of that year, Geoffrey vigorously pursued a petition for a parallel and comprehensive exemption from duties within the city. But London's rulers could not easily let men like Geoffrey escape or everyone would be doing it and who would be left to govern? Neither could they allow significant legal precedents that touched upon the jurisdiction and scope of such royal pronouncements to slide by unchallenged. By September, the aldermen and common council had decided that they would not grant Geoffrey's petition unless he was willing to abide by the judgement of three doctors of theology, although what they were judging remains unclear. The freedom from jury service that was part of Geoffrey's Crown exemption was officially recognised by the city and that seems to have put an end to the matter.[223] Until everything changed.

In September 1446 Geoffrey took his first-born son into his arms and the money, the commerce, the warehouse full of cloth and spices, which had hitherto been all about his own personal wealth and success, became about something else. Now he had a family and a future that stretched beyond his own demise. He could look ahead and dream of a son recognised by all as a gentleman by birth, with a noble wife on his arm. Such a dream, however, would require more than just gold and silver. Landed merchants who lacked the ambition to take aldermanic office were half as likely to marry gentry wives and a similar tendency might rub off on his children.[224] Suddenly prestigious government offices looked far more appealing. An alderman and his family were held in higher regard than a mere merchant, and a mayor or ex-mayor even higher still. London's rulers were not yet routinely knighted but with a place in the civic hierarchy of London, he and his family could borrow some of the honour and dignity of the city itself. Suddenly he was willing to start climbing the ladder he had previously been so vigorously avoiding.

Just two weeks after the birth of Thomas, Geoffrey appeared at the Guildhall, before the mayor, aldermen and 'very many commoners', and was elected one of the two sheriffs of London and Middlesex.[225] Although the city held the right of election, this was still technically a Crown position, from which he was already specifically exempted, but tellingly he now chose to abandon that exemption. Only twelve months after the fervent petitions and the desperate writhing to escape, Geoffrey Boleyn buckled down to one of the most onerous offices in London.

Before he faced an in-tray of writs and wrongdoers, however, there were formalities of appointment to go through, both in the city and before the barons of the Exchequer. On the morning of the eve of the feast of St Michael the Archangel, before the clock at St Paul's struck ten, Geoffrey and his fellow sheriff for the year, Robert Horne, entered the Guildhall to take their oath of office.[226] There, before the assembled mayor and aldermen, they swore to guard the counties of London and Middlesex, to keep the assizes of bread and ale (which regulated quality and price), only to execute royal writs or instructions after first showing them to the mayor and council (which probably meant the recorder, the city's legal officer), to carry out the reasonable wishes of the mayor and not to 'farm' or lease out the county of Middlesex or the gaol of Newgate. They were also responsible for the annual sum of £300 that the city owed to the Crown. If the revenue raised did not meet the required amount, Geoffrey and Robert would be held personally accountable for the difference. Just the sort of personal financial liability that probably helped to deter Geoffrey from civic office in the first place.

At noon, power officially transferred from the old to the new sheriffs and the assembly headed off to refresh themselves with dinner after a hard morning of oath-taking. All that remained was the legal handover of the prisoners of Newgate from the outgoing to the incoming sheriffs. Geoffrey and Robert made their way to this perpetually fetid establishment built into the city gate to meet the now ex-sheriffs, John Derby, a draper, and the mercer Geoffrey Fielding, whom Geoffrey knew well as one of his fellow wardens. The day's events had placed city-wide authority and responsibility into his hands for the first time. The coming year would reveal how he dealt with it but first the glory and the grandeur.[227]

The sheriffs' 'riding' to Westminster was much overshadowed by the razzmatazz of the mayor's procession a month later but it was, nevertheless, a significant event. In a city that loved a parade, the populace would have been sure to turn out for a display of civic finery, music and celebration. Although the term 'riding' persisted, from 1389 the ceremonial journey of the sheriffs to Westminster was made by river barge. Spiralling expenses had been restrained by banning the issue of new liveries for the occasion but the costs that remained were borne either by the incumbents themselves or more often by their company. From mercers to drapers, fishmongers to grocers, all were keen to celebrate the elevation of one of their own by swelling the ranks of the procession. Through the noise of the crowd and the clamour of musicians and trumpets, Geoffrey, Robert and the assembled dignitaries made their way down to the Thames. Along with eight musicians adorned with new hoods, the mercers had provided two barges at a total cost of nearly £4, or £2,500 today, to carry Geoffrey and his party to the formal presentation before the barons of the Exchequer in Westminster Hall.[228] It was the final act in the merrymaking. Now the work began.

Geoffrey's new list of duties was enough to make any man thankful they only had to serve once. As well as actioning around 200 royal writs a year, the sheriffs were principally responsible for law and order, a not inconsiderable task in a city of 30–40,000 people. Geoffrey's role would have included arresting criminals; ensuring witnesses or suspects appeared in court and fining or seizing the goods of those who failed to do so; arranging executions; overseeing the operation of the city's prisons; and presiding over his own twice-weekly law court. It was essentially a full-time job for men who already had full-time jobs running their own businesses but Geoffrey and Robert would have had a household of experienced staff on hand to provide assistance. There were three undersheriffs, or legal advisors to the sheriffs, as well as a large body of clerical staff and valets or sergeants to do the unpopular work of arresting people or seizing their goods.[229] One of Geoffrey's undersheriffs, Thomas Burgoyne, was an experienced hand who had been in office since 1434, and with his friend at his side, Geoffrey's year in office was busy but free from major problems.

Over the next two years, he was able to give his full attention to merchandise, trade and investments, but the city's aldermen and commonalty had not forgotten the potential usefulness of Geoffrey Boleyn. At the end of January 1449 he was elected to be one of London's four MPs for the upcoming parliament.[230] The House of Commons would sit for over sixteen weeks between February and July, another considerable distraction from business, but in return Geoffrey would have received some recompense beyond the warm glow of being chosen to represent the nation's greatest city. As one of the city's 'commoner' or non-aldermanic MPs, he would have been paid a wage of 2s. per day and would have been entitled to a clothing allowance of five yards of cloth, at 15s. the yard, and 33s. 4d. for fur. To ensure that both he and those around him were turned out to the credit of the city, he could also have claimed four yards of cloth, at 28d. the yard, to clothe one servant.[231] For a labourer it was a fortune but for a man whose life was founded on cloth, it was probably scant compensation for the time away from his commercial concerns. Perhaps his experience on the periphery of government was reward enough. It was certainly a useful and often obligatory step up the ladder.

On Friday 12 February, Geoffrey and his fellow London MPs, the aldermen John Catteworth and John Norman and the Common Sergeant, Thomas Bylling, set out on the journey of a little over 2 miles to the Palace of Westminster. A further 272 members had been returned in answer to royal writs and some would have been on the road for weeks. Men newly arrived from Cornwall and Carlisle, Norwich and Newcastle made their way into the vast, echoing confines of Westminster Hall. Here, in a hum of conversation muffled only by the layers of wool and fur that cloaked the members' shoulders, old hands could offer wisdom to parliamentary virgins or voice shared concerns as they awaited the call to join the Lords. When the moment came, it was only a short procession, past St Stephen's Chapel and into the long, narrow, ornate hall known as the Painted Chamber. This spectacular space was, from floor to ceiling, an ostentatious display of royal wealth and power. From the lower part of the walls, scenes from the life of that most saintly of kings, Edward the Confessor, gazed down upon the throng, while around the windows, Largesse defeated Covetousness and Gentleness overcame Wrath. Tales from the Old Testament marched around the top of the walls, including the righteous revolt of Judas Maccabeus against the tyrannical rule of Antiochus. The assembled members, meeting for the first time in almost two years and amid growing tension and disillusionment with Henry's government, must have wondered whether to be inspired or cowed.[232]

The chancellor, John Stafford, Archbishop of Canterbury, got proceedings underway with the opening sermon and while the lords settled down to their deliberations, Geoffrey and his fellow MPs made their way over to the refectory of Westminster Abbey, where the Commons would sit. The most pressing item on the agenda, and the reason these men had been summoned to that place, was the Crown's desperate need for money. Geoffrey's father-in-law, Thomas Hoo, sitting in the lords for the first time as Lord Hoo and Hastings, had crossed the Channel with letters of credence from Edmund Beaufort, Duke of Somerset, to aid this cause. Hoo, as chancellor of France, and Reginald Boulers, Abbot of Gloucester, were specially commissioned to speak to the Lords on the dire situation in Normandy and the urgent need for financial assistance. It fell to Boulers to make the speech but possession of a relative at the heart of diplomatic and political affairs probably played a part in Geoffrey's election to this particular parliament. Of equal importance, however, was his own expertise, as mercantile concerns were the inescapable cry of the Commons. Geoffrey had been elected alongside members of London's other great import-export trades, a grocer and a draper, and although there is no record of his contributions to the debate, the voice of the merchants is loud and clear.

One son-in-law in the refectory, however, would do little to aid Lord Hoo's mission. In the first session limited funding was begrudgingly granted but much of it was earmarked for the defence and supply of that mercantile priority, the wool staple at Calais, which did little to service a royal debt of £372,000, or nearly £240 million today. On 4 April, members were released for a month until the second session opened on 7 May but the breather did little to soften the hearts of the tight-fisted merchant faction, who were ill-inclined to throw good money after bad. Over the course of the parliament, their words can be heard in petition after petition. The Calais staple was not only underfunded but undermined by royal licences to sell elsewhere. The duke of Burgundy had again banned English cloth imports and alien merchants were not spending their profits in England but instead were carrying silver out of the realm, contrary to longstanding statute. After only three weeks, members were again dismissed.

Discussions over taxation had probably reached deadlock and it seems the Crown hoped that a cooling-off period, combined with a move far away from the mercantile might of London, would dilute resistance.

Geoffrey and his fellow MPs were compelled to trail 70 miles to the cathedral town of Winchester, where the substantial priory was large enough to accommodate the assembly of Lords and Commons. There they sat for a month and by the end of this final session the government had successfully extracted more taxation, albeit less than was needed. Lord Hoo's efforts to secure support for Normandy had, however, proved fruitless.[233]

The widening gap between the government and the governed, revealed by this parliament, would only get worse in the next, with the attempted impeachment and subsequent downfall of the duke of Suffolk. Geoffrey and his family would live through the invasion of London by Cade's rebels before we find him again with aldermanic robes almost within his grasp.

The office of a London alderman was no easy sinecure. With the court of aldermen meeting at least once a week in normal times, and as often as three times a week during the troubled years of the 1450s, those who had to labour for their living could never have found time to fulfil the many demands of the job. Election was, therefore, confined to those well established in mercantile trades, who were sufficiently wealthy to withstand the financial burden of public service. From 1469, it was laid down that a personal fortune of £1,000, equivalent to around £650,000 today, was essential to ensure aldermen were not impoverished by their office. Despite these challenges, London's twenty-five aldermen found value in their position and ways around the problems. Generally, only the mayor attended all the court meetings in any given year. His fellow rulers routinely skipped sessions to attend to more pressing affairs and if they had a particular need, were allowed to appoint deputies to handle some of their duties. Many men must have taken comfort, however, from their quasi-noble status and their prestigious robes of office, which marked them out from their peers and from fellow citizens.[234] Here were rank and privilege not determined by birth but derived from a lifetime of hard work and achievement, and Geoffrey Boleyn had his eyes on that prize.

On 10 July, only five days after Londoners had defeated Cade's rebel intruders in the battle of London Bridge, Geoffrey was nominated for his first aldermanic seat. It is tempting to imagine that some heroic part he played in the defence of the city prompted his selection by the electors of Lime Street ward, but it was probably just his turn. Since Geoffrey's year as sheriff had proved his personal capabilities, there had only been two aldermanic elections. One of those took place while he was sitting as an MP and for the other, the election of Philip Malpas had been forced through by royal decree. Whatever the reasoning, the citizens of Lime Street felt he was ready to serve. As was customary, four names were put forward by the ward and the aldermen made the final decision about whom they would welcome to their ranks. Usually they achieved consensus but when this proved impossible they resorted to voting, and on this occasion Geoffrey faced stiff competition. Two of his rivals were grocers, Richard Lee and John Walderne, but neither of them had yet served as sheriff. His real competition came from the fishmonger William Hulyn, the hero of the recent battle on the bridge, who had managed to close the gates against Cade and his rebels.[235] It was really no competition at all. Hulyn was installed for the ward of Lime Street and Geoffrey had to bide his time.[236]

Meanwhile, he was given another, less illustrious appointment. At the end of the month, along with his fellow mercer John Olney and the salter John Beaumond, he was given the thankless task of collecting from the wards a loan of 2,000 marks for the defence of Calais.[237] He would have to wait another year for his next aldermanic opportunity and then two came along at once. The transfer of Simon Eyre to Langbourn and Thomas Scott to Walbrook left their former wards of Cornhill and Dowgate vacant and on 16 July 1451, Geoffrey was nominated for both simultaneously. In Cornhill the election of Nicholas Wyfold, grocer, was a formality as he was the sitting mayor, exercising his right to transfer to any vacant ward during his year of office. In Dowgate, however, the competition was fierce. John Feelde and John Yonge were the outsiders, having not yet proven themselves as sheriff, but William Dere was a worthy adversary. Not only was he by far the senior candidate, he had been unsuccessfully nominated for office eight times over the previous seven years. Nevertheless, the aldermen could not agree and had to resort to voting, with Dere taking ten votes and Geoffrey only four. Having finally progressed from his role as the perpetual runner-up, Dere would not be given long to enjoy his success as he was released from office only five years later on the grounds of age and infirmity.[238]

For the time being Geoffrey had to turn his attention back to his own affairs and, intermittently, to the business of the common council until the next opportunity arose. In August, the ward of Farringdon Without fell vacant but he was not nominated, probably much to his relief, as this large extra-mural ward was the most burdensome aldermanic seat in the city. In November, he was entrusted with custody of one of the keys to the chest that held the city's common seal but it was not until summer came around again that he was able to take another shot at aldermanic office.[239] William Combes, who had done fourteen years carrying the weight of Farringdon Without, was only able to enjoy his transfer to the relative retirement of Castle Baynard for a little over a year before he died in 1452, leaving his new seat vacant. Again Geoffrey's name was put forward by the citizens of the ward, along with John Feelde, Thomas Oulegrave and Thomas Davy, none of whom had shrieval experience. It should have been a shoo-in but Feelde had support and again the aldermen could not agree and had to resort to voting. Five aldermen who had voted against Geoffrey a year earlier now lent him their support, including his fellow mercer John Olney. Two further mercers, Geoffrey Fielding and William Cantelowe, who had previously been absent, were now also on his side. Feelde was defeated by eleven votes to five and on 19 July 1452 Geoffrey was installed as alderman for the ward of Castle Baynard.[240]

His new territory lay in the far south-west of the intra-mural city on the banks of the Thames but the northern arm wrapped around the west end of St Paul's and reached almost as far as Newgate. It included the bishop of London's palace and the king's wardrobe as well as three parish churches but the most significant structure in Geoffrey's new ward was undoubtedly Baynard's Castle itself, soon to become the London residence of Richard, Duke of York. In the years that were to come, Geoffrey would display a subtle but growing affinity and sympathy for Richard's cause. An affinity that perhaps put out its first green shoots at a time when the duke and the merchant walked the same streets.

8

'The Rising and Wanton Rule'

London, Summer 1452

Geoffrey's first few weeks in office involved multiple meetings about the financial irregularities of William Melbourne, much discussion of the city's case regarding parish clergy and the excessive fees they charged for services such as baptisms or marriages and the appropriate reprimanding of William Welles for his 'obstinate and scandalous words' about the usefulness of the common council.[241] It was hardly the most thrilling fare for the new alderman for Castle Baynard but there would be more than enough excitement and fateful decisions to be made in the years ahead. While the elevation in rank may have been welcome, Geoffrey took to his new duties with all the foot-dragging enthusiasm of a schoolboy on the first day of term. During his first three weeks in office, he attended only three out of a total of eleven meetings, one being his own election, but this gentle routine of meetings, committees and deputations soon became a normal part of his life.[242] Of the 122 meetings of the court of aldermen that were held in his first year in office, he attended fifty-three, a level of commitment only slightly below average but one that allowed time for yet another unavoidable duty.[243]

Geoffrey's commitment to the routine business of his company was just as sporadic. He had been fined seven times between 1437 and 1446 for failing to attend meetings of the mercers' court but from the summer of 1453, he had to toe the line as his fellow mercers demanded his service as master for the next twelve months.[244] Fortunately, this was largely a prestigious rather than an onerous position. Geoffrey would have had the help of his long-term friend and associate Ralph Verney as second warden, and most of the routine work of running the company, collecting rents, repairing properties, fulfilling obligations to benefactors and dispensing alms was carried out by the lower wardens, John Littleton and Ralph Marche, just as Geoffrey had done eleven years earlier. He and his fellow wardens were required to inspect the company's numerous properties at least once a year but were treated to a free dinner in return for their trouble.[245] In October, however, Master Boleyn's routine calendar of ceremonial outings was subject to a welcome interruption as the nation paused to celebrate.[246] The mercers splashed out 4s. 4d. on barge hire and Geoffrey and his fellow liverymen took to the river, along with the city's other great companies, to provide a ceremonial escort for Queen Margaret as she arrived in Westminster for the birth of, hopefully, a heaven-sent heir. Prince Edward put in a timely appearance on 13 October, auspiciously the feast of St Edward the Confessor, and his arrival was celebrated throughout the city by the pealing of church bells. The messenger Giles Senclowe, who brought Londoners news of the birth, was generously rewarded with a purse of 10 marks, the equivalent of nearly £4,000 today.[247]

Behind this façade of royal joy, however, a secret was lurking. As winter's grip tightened on the city, the comforting blanket of order and routine, which had briefly settled over the nation, was cruelly and suddenly ripped away. At the manor of Clarendon, near Salisbury, in August 1453, while on a royal tour of the west country, the king had been suddenly and catastrophically overwhelmed by illness: a mental and physical malady that would afflict him for the next seventeen months, leaving him unable to speak, move his own limbs or feed himself.[248] When his realm needed him most, the king became a vacant, catatonic absence. For several months Henry's condition remained shrouded in silence. Those around him desperately hoped for an equally sudden recovery and prayed that the queen would provide the country with an heir but both at home and abroad, pressing demands for governance could not be ignored for long. Henry's realm teetered on the brink of chaos and Richard, Duke of York, seized his opportunity.

In November Richard returned to London, summoned along with twenty-four other lords, for a great council meeting at Westminster, but in the well-cushioned comfort of their council chamber, the city's aldermen were sitting very uncomfortably. That the king's incapacity would inevitably result in a power struggle between the queen's faction and the Yorkist contingent was apparent to all. Now with the arrival of all the main players in London's backyard, they were forced to attempt a juggling act between loyalty and neutrality that demanded they face in opposite directions at the same time. Would it be prudent to pay an official, cordial visit to the duke in his residence at Baynard's Castle? To do so risked inciting the hostility of Queen Margaret, whose star might prove to be in the ascendant. But to snub the great magnate could be equally damaging if he ultimately became the de facto ruler. On 20 November, Geoffrey and eleven of his fellow aldermen met to formulate a course of action. His voice in the discussions is unrecorded but he formed part of a cautious assembly so paralysed by indecision that they were too afraid to do anything until more news arrived from the royal council.[249]

England's government lay in a state of suspended animation and London held her breath. In the New Year, Margaret formally proposed herself as regent, a concept of astounding novelty for England, but the final decision lay in the hands of the parliamentary lords who were due to meet at Westminster. As the summoned magnates and their well-armed retinues again descended on London, the city became a political tinderbox. Adherents of York's great rival, Edmund, Duke of Somerset, who had been committed to the Tower in November, were rumoured to have taken lodgings in the city in preparation for a rescue attempt, while York and his own followers were expected at any moment. The queen was also in attendance as the moment of long-delayed decision neared. For London's rulers the stakes were now even higher. There was a risk that York would attempt an armed coup while the crown lay in the feeble grip of an invalid and yet the city still had to maintain a Janus-like composure between these two bitter enemies. On 22 February, with York and Margaret then both in residence, Geoffrey and his colleagues again gathered to consider their options. This time they could not dodge the bullet. The queen would be favoured with a formal delegation of the mayor and aldermen in their scarlet robes and the duke of York would be extended the same courtesy, but on the following Friday. Prudence and impartiality were yet the order of the day and formal precedence had been maintained by establishing a clear order, but as Geoffrey and his fellow aldermen bade farewell to Richard at Baynard's Castle, they must have been crossing their fingers and praying that neither party had taken offence.[250]

Ultimately, the realm was not ready for a female regent, which left the lords with no alternative. On 3 April 1454, York was formally appointed protector until the king regained his faculties or Prince Edward attained his majority, whichever occurred first.[251] While hardly ushering in an era of peace and contentment, it at least brought an end to the relentless, corrosive uncertainty.

Let the crown fall where it may, however, the cycle of London's year continued unabated. The end of Geoffrey's rule over his own small realm of mercers was fast approaching, along with an irresistible opportunity to impress his peers with sparkling surroundings and an abundance of food. In years past, the mercers' annual feast had been held in the hall of St Thomas of Acre but some of his illustrious predecessors, including John Olney, Henry Frowyk, William Melreth and William Estfield, had hosted the gathering in their own large mansions and now that Geoffrey was living in Melreth's old house on Milk Street, he chose to do the same.[252] In their new great hall the Boleyns would probably have played host to around a hundred hungry and expectant guests. All the liverymen were invited and usually each made a small contribution of around 5s. but most of the tradesmen's bills would have been paid by Geoffrey and his fellow wardens and were probably met principally by Geoffrey himself.[253]

On 17 June, the kitchen of the Boleyns' house would have swarmed with many extra hands as, sweating in the heat, they produced the most impressive fare that human skill and an appropriate budget could produce, while in the hall, long tables would have filled a space glittering with candles, silver plate and money. Only a gentleman could offer such largesse. Once the livery-clad merchants had filled their bellies and made inroads into the family cellars, Geoffrey chose John Olney for yet another term as master and Ralph Verney chose Robert Baron, who had been the fourth warden in 1446.[254] Such a conspicuous display of wealth and success was a form of civic involvement Geoffrey could embrace.

Playing the gracious hostess, however, can hardly have been Anne's natural inclination in the summer of 1454 as her father's health was failing fast. The family would have been aware that the old soldier and courtier was likely entering his final weeks or months of life. In May, the records of the Privy Council record his plea that he was too sick and feeble to attend the imminent session of parliament and he was again absent from his place in the House of Lords in July. He survived over Christmas, when most of the nation, if not the duke of York, rejoiced at news that the king's break from sanity had ended as suddenly as it had begun, but he saw only a few weeks of the New Year before his death on 13 February. His mortal remains would be laid to rest at Battle Abbey, where he was later joined by his half-brother Thomas, in an elaborate tomb topped with Caen stone funeral effigies.[255] Fortunately, the loyal Lancastrian retainer did not live to witness the humiliating defeat of his royal master in the opening act of a war that would tear England apart for the next thirty years.

Within weeks of the king's recovery, York's old enemy, Somerset, had been restored to his former position of power at the side of the throne. For safely piloting the country in the absence of a monarch, York was deprived of position, authority and dignity, with a single-mindedness that amounted to persecution. It was a turn of affairs that could not go unchallenged. The duke and his allies rode north to gather troops and the royal court followed suit. York had previously raised an army in 1452 but this time swords would not remain in their scabbards. A psychological boundary was about to be breached as subjects met their anointed monarch with violence.

On 22 May 1455, the two forces came together in a brutal skirmish through the narrow streets and lanes of the unwalled and defenceless town of St Albans. York was triumphant. The duke of Somerset, Henry, Earl of Northumberland, and John, Lord Clifford, lay dead. James Butler, Earl of Wiltshire, managed to flee dressed as a monk and the pathetic figure of the king was found abandoned and alone, bleeding from a wound to his neck, in the reeking confines of a tanner's shop, where he had found a place to hide.[256] Richard was, as yet, however, no usurper. It was Somerset he sought to supplant, not the king, and so in the peace of St Albans Abbey, York and his allies, the earls of Salisbury and Warwick, knelt before Henry, pledged their loyalty and were received back into the king's grace.

With the dawn, they prepared to convey Henry to London 'as king and not as a prisoner' but 25 miles away, in the city, news had travelled faster than the combatants themselves.[257] The shocked populace, probably with the Boleyn family among them, thronged onto the streets to view the aftermath of events, the like of which only the most aged had witnessed in their lifetimes. Henry rode, surrounded by his new ministers and advisors, who had so recently been the enemy forces. The duke of York flanked his right hand side and the earl of Salisbury his left, while the earl of Warwick carried the king's sword, which he had borne from the battlefield. On Sunday 25 May, in a solemn ceremony staged at St Paul's Cathedral, the king sat in state and was handed his crown from York's own hands. The significance of the gesture would not have been lost on the London crowd or the nation. If Henry had been weak and ineffectual before, after his ill-ness and St Albans, the king was little more than a cipher.[258] The future would be a strange and volatile country.

While the new regime set about the difficult task of establishing legiti-mate authority and reconciling warring magnates, the annual cycle of London government continued. On 13 October the city had to select a new mayor to see them through these increasingly difficult times. Eighteen of the twenty-five aldermen and 'an immense commonalty' assembled at the Guildhall to carry out the traditional ceremony of election. The alder-men and outgoing mayor, Stephen Forster, clad in their robes of office, gathered at the west end of the chamber, where the mayor was accustomed to hold his court. Facing them, at the east end, were assembled a number of 'the more sufficient and more discreet' citizens, which, in practice, meant the members of the common council, the masters or wardens of the livery companies and other 'good men' who had been especially summoned.[259] The nomination of suitable candidates was a matter for them, but a pro-spective mayor had to be an alderman and had to have served as sheriff, so that he might already have practised his 'governance and bountee' before taking office.[260] The assembled citizens put their heads together and came up with two men to whom they were willing to entrust the rule of their city in a year that could bring even more unheralded and dangerous events. Their decision was conveyed to the sergeant-at-arms, who strode to the other end of the hall and announced the names of the grocer William Marowe and Geoffrey Boleyn. Neither man was in the room.[261]

It had, in the past, been common for aldermen to stay away from the election in order to avoid being chosen, but fines had been imposed for absenteeism and by the early fifteenth century officialdom was harder to avoid. If the elected mayor was not in the chamber, the current mayor, aldermen and sheriffs would simply proceed to his house to inform the lucky candidate of the happy news.[262] Nevertheless, aldermanic truancy remained a reality and Geoffrey attended fewer than half of the mayoral elections held between 1452 and 1462. Whatever was distracting him, it seems it was not official city business. On 22 September, he had been dispatched to negotiate with the Archbishop of Canterbury, in an ongoing dispute between the city and St Martin le Grand over sanctuary, but this would not explain his absence from the mayoral election three weeks later.[263] When the aldermen re-entered the hall with a decision, their journey took them not to Milk Street but east and north from the Guildhall to the parish of St Botolph Bishopsgate and the home of William Marowe.[264] In the year following St Albans, the collective mood was one of uncertainty and disquiet and the new mayor would have a rough ride.

In the second half of the 1450s, London, which had long been turbulent, erupted in a series of riots and disturbances that were the beginning of the end for healthy relations between King Henry and his capital. Popular sympathy for York and mercantile exasperation with Lancastrian commercial and foreign policy, together with general antipathy towards Italians all went into a crucible of violence, with the mercers at its heart. Geoffrey, as one of the city's rulers, would have been responsible for settling the city and restoring order to his ward, but civic duty did not preclude a personal sympathy with the troublemakers or their proxy attack on Henry's failing government.

This turbulent half-decade began with a minor altercation and a familiar name. On 28 April 1456, John Edwards, the servant of Geoffrey's neighbour, associate and fellow mercer John Lok, accosted a well-known merchant from Lucca, in full view of the Cheapside crowds. Edwards and two other mercer apprentices seized the dagger of Alessandro Palastrelli, broke it over the unfortunate Italian's head and were 'about to do evil' to him. What stopped them is unknown but early the following day, Palastrelli complained to the mayor, William Marowe, and Edwards was located and imprisoned. This did not go down well, however, with the culprit's friends. As the mayor headed home for lunch, he was stopped by a threatening gang of mercers' apprentices and London 'rent-a-ruffians' who demanded the delivery of 'their fellow out of prison'. It was probably on account of this skirmish that John Lok stood bail for his apprentice in the sum of £20 that same afternoon.

That, however, was far from the end of the matter as the mob, buoyed up by success, took the opportunity to escalate their protests. Young men from a number of crafts rampaged through the city, ransacking and robbing the houses of terrified Italian merchants. At this point the forces of law and order were compelled to intervene lest the king conclude that Londoners could not manage their own affairs. Geoffrey and his fellow aldermen, together with the sheriffs and their household, had to act to recover control of their personal domains. Some of the miscreants were rounded up and thrown into Newgate but Edwards and his cronies, who had started the riot, sought sanctuary in Westminster Abbey and the king, seeing uproar at the heart of his realm, chose to intervene in person. On 30 April, he was rowed down the river from Westminster and landed at Blackfriars' stairs, from where he made his way to the Bishop of London's palace, by St Paul's. It was a journey of only a few hundred metres, through Geoffrey's own ward, but the violence and menace that filled the streets meant the mayor, aldermen and a number of men-at-arms had to escort and protect their royal visitor. Once installed in the safety of the bishop's walled and gated residence, Henry appointed a judicial commission to investigate the disorder, but their work had barely started before a rumour of further armed uprising caused their deliberations to be adjourned.

Evidently the presence of the monarch had little effect and it would be up to the mayor, William Marowe, and his aldermen to restore tranquillity to the city. Having secured the formal co-operation of the mercers and the other companies, a force of some 260 to 300 armed men was raised and Geoffrey and his fellow aldermen rode out to retake control. In helm and harness, they patrolled the tense city streets in a show of force designed to quell any further outbursts. It worked. By 5 May the royal commissioners were able to resume their session at the Guildhall, albeit surrounded by an intimidating crowd of armed heavies, and the result was the hanging of two or possibly three men at Tyburn amidst a din of popular outrage.[265]

The icy days of winter kept troublemakers off the streets and London remained just on the right side of peaceful, but, fearful of the volatile city, Henry removed the royal court to Coventry, from where he wrote multiple letters reminding the mayor of his obligation to preserve peace. Londoners amused themselves with the capture of two whales, a large swordfish or narwhal and a walrus in the Thames but trouble was not long coming.[266]

As the weather warmed, in the summer of 1457, so did the temper of the London mob. Again the target was Italians and again the agitators were mercers' apprentices, particularly Thomas Thurston and Thomas Graunt, apprentices of Ralph Marche, who had both been key players the previous year. This time, however, their actions were more premeditated.

On 16 June, a great gathering of conspirators assembled to plot the murder of the Italian Galiot Centurione, alias Scott, and other foreign merchants. They were confident of support, for 'much people then hated deadly the said merchant strangers', believing them to be 'false extortioners, common lechers and adulterers, wherefore they thought it a good deed to slay and murder them', but they were fearful of discovery, and they were right to be. The new mayor, Thomas Canynges, and the aldermen had been alerted to the danger and swiftly agreed enhanced security measures to prevent a repeat of the previous year's violence. Each day the mayor and sheriffs vigilantly patrolled the city with men-at-arms, while at night each alderman was required to personally supervise the watch in his own ward. For Geoffrey that would have meant several anxious, sleepless nights, riding the dark streets and lanes to the south and west of St Paul's, accompanied by eight armed men of his ward, but the efforts paid off and a full-scale riot never materialised.[267] It was not, however, the last that would be heard of Thomas Graunt. The frustrated young firebrand attempted to provoke a more spontaneous uprising ten days later. Marching out of a shop on Cheapside, with his arms full of wooden staves, he threw them to the ground and declared, 'Go we hence, for there is an Englishman slain by the Lombards in Lumbard Street', whereupon he was immediately arrested by the mercer Hugh Wiche. Later, Graunt seems to have been able to flee, but his master, Ralph Marche, was imprisoned for failing to keep his apprentices in order and had to pay a hefty fine to bail himself.[268]

What really lay behind these violent and tumultuous years, and Geoffrey's own part in proceedings, are a puzzle with many parts. At first glance the mayhem appears to be an outbreak of the general xenophobic rumblings that periodically convulsed the city, but the involvement of prominent mercers or wool merchants and their apprentices, together with the timing, suggests an incident that was as much top-down as it was bottom-up. London's lower orders had long been sympathetic to York, or at least disillusioned with Henry VI, but by the middle of the century, a growing 'fifth column' of prominent merchants had been forced to conclude that their interests could no longer be protected or advanced under the prevailing Lancastrian rule.[269]

Mercers' apprentices, in particular, would have absorbed complaints about the encroachment of Italian merchants, and the government favouritism they enjoyed, along with their bread and ale before their masters' hearths. These Mediterranean speculators, it was claimed, robbed the country of bullion in return for useless and unnecessary 'nifles [and] trifles, that little have availed'.[270] For mercers in particular, the scale of Italian involvement in trade that overlapped so closely with their own, combined with their obvious commercial success, inevitably fostered hostility. How much better for London mercers if the profits from all that wool, cloth, silks and spices could be gathered into their own coffers? To make matters worse, Italians, amongst others, were regularly granted royal licences to export wool to places other than the wool staple at Calais, either free of the subsidy (export duty) or at a reduced rate, and often in return for a loan. To Londoners it appeared that these foreigners were catastrophically stealing their trade. On the docks and wharves of the city, resentment grew as the volume of alien wool exports skyrocketed by over 500 per cent, from a paltry 664 sacks to an astonishing 3,359. Much of this was pre-existing trade, transferred to the capital from the outports of Southampton and Sandwich, but in London nobody knew, or cared.[271] Meanwhile, in Calais, an urgent need to deal with the unpaid, mutinous garrison had forced the staplers into bed with the town's new captain, Richard Neville, Earl of Warwick. The vast sum advanced by these men of wool, many of whom were both Londoners and mercers, inescapably bound them to the Yorkist cause.[272] Only nine days after their deal was struck, violence against the Italian favourites of the Lancastrian regime exploded onto the streets of London. The newfound commitment of some members of the mercantile community to the House of York had let the riotous genie out of the bottle.

Geoffrey's involvement in this melting pot of mercantile resentment and popular violence is largely shrouded in silence. As the post-mortem began he was among the first of the mercers summoned to the Guildhall to account for the behaviour of his apprentices, but this position of prominence could owe as much to his status and to the fact he was also sitting as an alderman on the investigating panel as it did to any implied culpability. As far as it is possible to ascertain from the heavily damaged record of proceedings, Geoffrey simply claimed that he or his apprentices had no part to play in the uproar.[273] As a London alderman, he would undoubtedly have taken part in the efforts to restore order, taking up arms and armour in his duty to his city, but it was entirely possible for him to fulfil this role while also sympathising with the motives of the rioters, if not actively encouraging them. The master of his company, William Cantelowe, spent several weeks imprisoned in Dudley Castle for his involvement with the riots despite simultaneously being an alderman who had sworn to maintain the peace of the city.[274]

There is nothing to suggest that Geoffrey's active involvement went as far as Cantelowe's but in what was effectively a proxy attack on Lancastrian rule, and by implication an endorsement of York, his heart was probably aligned with the cause of the troublemakers, if not with their actions. The weight of circumstantial evidence points to a growing familiarity with the duke of York and his circle in the second half of the 1450s, the groundwork for which had long been in the making. Geoffrey's great friend Thomas Burgoyne had served as Richard's bailiff in Cambridgeshire and Huntingdonshire in the last years of the 1440s. It would, however, be several years before Geoffrey began to forge closer links with the House of York.[275]

During Geoffrey's time as master of the mercers, William Neville, Baron Fauconberg and brother-in-law of the duke of York, had been admitted as an honorary member of the company. This move symbolised the desperate hopes of many mercers and merchants that the Yorkist lords could offer stable government but was possibly also evidence of a growing affinity between Geoffrey and York.[276] In 1458, Geoffrey was one of three Londoners chosen to act as feoffee for William Oldhall, one of Richard's closest advisors, and Anne's uncle Edmund Wychingham was also one of York's councillors.[277] Even Geoffrey's prosecution for offering illegal credit to aliens, in 1459, may indicate that his Yorkist allegiances were well known.[278] Long-term credit was common mercantile practice but prominent Lancastrians seem to have escaped censure, while Yorkist sympathisers found themselves called before the bench as Queen Margaret launched a campaign of intimidation against those she regarded as enemies in London.[279] When York's son Edward finally triumphed in 1461, he would recognise Geoffrey's loyalty, issuing a new grant of exemption from office-holding that specifically recalled the good service (*grata obsequia*) offered by 'our beloved and faithful Geoffrey Boleyn' to the new king's late father.[280]

Neither was Geoffrey alone in his borderline treasonable sympathies. By the mid-1450s, the men with whom he dealt and the company he kept were decidedly Yorkist, or otherwise implicated in the riots. It was John Lok's apprentice, John Edwards, who triggered the violence in 1456 by his attack on Palastrelli, while Ralph Verney, an even closer friend, had marked Yorkist leanings and would later be knighted for his services to Edward IV. As early as 1454, he and four other mercers provided bail for the earl of Salisbury's (York's brother-in-law) men who had been imprisoned for riot and disorder.[281] His fellow sureties on this occasion included other decided Yorkists: John Harowe, who would lead London's forces north to fight with the duke of York at Wakefield, and Ralph Marche, whose servants had caused such trouble in 1457.

In 1456, however, Geoffrey was the only man in this clique who as yet enjoyed a seat on the aldermanic bench and as such he was probably more cautious about the merits of disturbing the dynastic status quo. London's leaders may have been divided in their sympathies but they were yet united in their determination to maintain the city's neutrality for as long as possible. In the months and years to come, this policy would stretch the city, her aldermen and Geoffrey himself to breaking point and beyond.

9

'Our Honourable and Worthy Mayor'

London, 13 October 1457

In the vast echoing expanse of London's Guildhall the crowd waited. Friends and neighbours cloaked hushed whispers behind expensively gloved hands while rivals, of the personal or professional variety, pointedly avoided a hostile gaze. The great south door was locked and barred against the thugs and heavies who, in years gone by, had marred the peaceful integrity of city elections, so there was nowhere to go and nothing to do as the minutes ticked by.

Closeted in the cushion-lined comfort of their meeting room adjacent to the mayor's court, the assembled fur-robed aldermen had their heads together. Before them was the same decision they faced every year on this October day. Two men were nominated but only one could be mayor. Would it be the draper Thomas Cook, just twelve months an alderman, or the more experienced Geoffrey Boleyn? The outgoing mayor, Thomas Canynges, was perhaps less concerned with the identity of the new incumbent and more relieved that it would not be him. Over the past tumultuous twelve months he had policed a riot, managed a prison break from Newgate and narrowly avoided mopping noble blood from the paving stones of Cheapside.[282] Finally he could offload responsibility for the unpredictable, impulsive and downright dangerous populace onto the shoulders of a more or less willing colleague.

Back in the hall, the hum of voices faltered and failed as the scuff of leather boots on flagstones signalled the aldermen were on their way.

Canynges, they knew, would be holding high the arm of the victor, and men strained to see between jostling hats and hoods as the news broke over the crowd in a wave. London's new mayor was Geoffrey Boleyn.[283] The former apprentice hatter from Norfolk finally held in his hands the rank and power to go with his silver and gold but reality galloped hard on the heels of triumph. For now the realm was at peace but it was a peace as fragile as the great glass window that filtered autumn sunlight onto the back of Geoffrey's head. A day's ride away, the helpless tanners and tailors of St Albans had not forgotten their bloodstained, body-strewn streets, and as the new mayor elect stood and smiled with his arm held aloft, he could not know if, or when, London would suffer a similar fate. Over the next twelve months, Geoffrey Boleyn would have to answer for the safety and security of the 40,000 men, women and children within the city's sheltering walls.

The transfer of power, however, was not immediate. Incoming mayors were traditionally given a little over two weeks to arrange their business affairs so that they might devote themselves fully to their new office. Geoffrey would take his oath at the Exchequer on 29 October 1457 but the preceding Friday was set aside for the city's own ceremonial installation. Early on that autumnal morning, swathed in his costly aldermanic robes, Geoffrey would have joined his fellow aldermen, commoners and officials in the great chamber of the Guildhall. Thomas Canynges took his place, probably for the last time, in the mayoral seat and the sergeant-at-arms called the assembly to silence to allow the Recorder, Thomas Urswyck, the city's legal officer, to address the crowd. As was customary, he reminded the assembly of London's ancient traditions and heaped praise upon the numerous accomplishments and triumphs of the outgoing mayor before the suitably flattered Canynges vacated his position as London's leader. For a brief moment, the mayoral seat stood empty, before Geoffrey stepped up and assumed his new high place. The 'book with the calendar with the effigy of Him crucified on the outside', probably a copy of the Gospels, was brought before him and Geoffrey placed his hand on the holy book while the common clerk read his oath of office. For all to hear, he promised to 'well and lawfully' serve the king and to exercise the powers conferred on him by royal authority, without prejudice or favour to rich or poor.[284] As the clerk's final syllables faded into the rafters, Geoffrey leaned forward and kissed the sacred book. Canynges pressed upon him the official mayoral seal engraved with images of London's arms, St Paul and St Thomas Becket, and Geoffrey Boleyn became mayor of London.

His first task would have been to address the crowded hall but sadly, the inaugural speeches of incoming mayors were not recorded. However, his theme for this opening public performance would traditionally have been the pressing issues facing the city and the help and support he would need from his audience in governing London for the next year. With the formalities of the day complete, the congregation spilled out into Guildhall Yard and arranged themselves into a procession to escort Geoffrey on his short walk back home. The two mayors led the throng, preceded by the city's ceremonial sword, borne aloft by the Swordbearer, and followed by the aldermen and populace. In Milk Street, Geoffrey was welcomed back into the arms of his proud family and the great sword was borne onwards to Canynges's house. The outgoing mayor would continue to exercise power, in case of any dire emergency, until Geoffrey took his oath at the Exchequer in the morning.[285]

The following late October day, the whole city would have been in carnival mood for the most important ceremonial and celebratory day in London's civic calendar. Geoffrey was back in Guildhall Yard early, as the participants began filtering in by 9 a.m., ready for the civic pomp and circumstance of the mayor's progress to Westminster. For most of the city's history, the mayor would have ridden this short distance on horseback but a popular innovation, introduced four years previously, meant Geoffrey would travel down the Thames by barge to take his oath. Clad, along with his aldermen, in new scarlet robes and attended by the liverymen of the mercers and other city companies, similarly arrayed in the finery of their rank, the men who gathered at the city's heart displayed wealth, power and civic pride in every fold of their gowns or sparkle of a silver belt mount. It was a matter of particular pride to each livery company when one of their number was chosen to be mayor and the mercers accordingly spared no expense in their preparations for Geoffrey's big day. They spent 29s. 2d. on 'murrey' cloth, of a purple-red hue, to make new hoods for seventeen trumpeters, including 'Thomas with the big trumpet', and 14s. 10d. on fine red cloth and yards of fringe, ribbon and laces, used to make new banners painted with the 'mercers' maiden'. With the cost of sewing the new apparel, paying the trumpeters and providing the barges and drinks along the way to Westminster and back, the mercers expended over £10 3s. 8d., equivalent to over £6,000, welcoming one of their own into office.[286]

Geoffrey and his fellow aldermen, accompanied by the sheriffs, civic officials and numerous minstrels, would have made their way to the Thames through crowd-lined streets as the populace turned out to admire the spectacle and celebrate their city. In the Exchequer Chamber adjacent to Westminster Hall, before the chancellor William Waynflete and the barons of the Exchequer, Geoffrey repeated the oath he had sworn at Guildhall. The chancellor's vehement direction to attend to his most important duty of maintaining a peaceful city was both customary and poignantly apt. Geoffrey would have been well aware that this would be his greatest challenge.

When these ceremonies were complete, Geoffrey and his array of attendants made their way back to the barges moored on the Thames and returned in state to the city. There a host of invited guests and dignitaries would have streamed into the house on Milk Street, where Anne and her household were again called upon to produce an elaborate banquet. None of the revellers, however, could afford to descend too far into their cups for there was still one ritual set-piece event to be completed. When they had consumed their fill, the crowd of aldermen, liverymen and officials assembled at the east end of Cheapside, near the church of St Thomas of Acre. From there, they rode the full length of Cheapside, London's great ceremonial street, to St Paul's Cathedral, where they offered a prayer at the tomb of St Thomas Becket's parents, before riding back along Cheapside in a torchlit procession that brought a day of carnival-like celebrations to a close. Geoffrey returned home, undoubtedly to an excited 11-year-old Thomas and his younger siblings, who had spent a thrilling day watching their father installed in temporary dominion over London's square mile.[287]

Geoffrey would soon find that the burdens of office were numerous and expensive and the privileges and perquisites limited. As well as sitting with the court of aldermen, he had general oversight of all civic officials, was required to ensure that traders complied with regulations, took a leading role in all political and religious rituals and had ultimate responsibility for the safety and security of the city. He also presided over the mayor's court, which mostly heard commercial cases regarding debt or broken contracts. For all of this he would have received no salary, although there were a few perks, including monetary perquisites to the value of at least £50 and the annual gift of four casks of premium Gascon wine and a boar's head from the butcher's.[288] The mayor also enjoyed the right to transfer to any alder-manry that fell vacant during his term of office, and less than three weeks after his oath-swearing at Westminster, he made use of this perk, becoming alderman of the small mercer-controlled ward of Bassishaw. The elderly mercer, Henry Fowyck, who had served the ward for thirty-three years and twice been mayor, stood down and Geoffrey took his place, giving up Castle Baynard to his ever-present friend Ralph Verney.[289]

To assist him in his many tasks, Geoffrey would have had a corps of sergeants, esquires and valets who made up the mayor's household. Some received a salary from the city but most had to be paid a wage and provided with a livery out of Geoffrey's own pocket. Fortunately, the mayor's staff were at least provided with accommodation by the city, so the Boleyns did not have to find them beds, but Geoffrey would have been expected to provide food and drink in the same way that a great lord would have provisioned his retainers. For the next year he would be almost constantly attended and rarely alone, as befitted the quasi-noble status of his office, as the house on Milk Street became akin to a lord's great hall. As mayor he was held to be second only to the king, when within the city's jurisdiction, and although ordinarily ranked below a baron or abbot, within the bars of the city, Mayor Boleyn now took precedence over an earl.[290]

Precedence, however, was the least of Geoffrey's problems with earls and dukes. While London had been venting her spleen on Italian residents and shaking out her finery, the simmering animosity between magnates and Crown had not gone away. Following what appears to have been a short partial relapse in the king's health in late 1455 and a second protector-ate for Richard, Duke of York, Henry was back to what, for him, passed as being in charge. Wary of the uproar and tumult in London's streets, he had withdrawn the court to Coventry in the Lancastrian heartlands, but while Geoffrey was swearing his mayoral oaths, the king was back in his capital, preparing a proactive but characteristically naïve plan to force peace on magnates and metropolis alike. The mailed fist, in the form of thousands of archers mustered around the city from St George's Field in Southwark to Longfield Park, near Haringey, probably came from Henry's council, while the theatrical velvet glove can only have come from the mind of the king himself.[291] Determined to 'eradicate the roots of rancour' that had taken hold among younger nobles whose fathers had been killed at St Albans, the king called a great council. But summoning the lords and their armed retinues to the already volatile capital was a potential recipe for disaster and one man was ultimately responsible for heading off the threat. The buck stopped with Mayor Boleyn.

In the final week of January 1458 they began to arrive. York lodged 400 men in his house at Baynard's Castle while Richard Neville, Earl of Salisbury, took a force of around 500 to his family inn, The Erber, just north of Dowgate. They were soon joined by the Lancastrian contingent. First Henry Holland, Duke of Exeter, and Henry Beaufort, Duke of Somerset, arrived with 800 men between them, followed by the Percy brothers, Henry, Earl of Northumberland, Thomas, Lord Egremont, and Ralph Percy, who together with Lord Clifford commanded a substantial force of 1,500 men. Fortunately, the Lancastrian lords remained outside the city, taking lodgings to the west, beyond Temple Bar. Finally, Richard, Earl of Warwick, was the last of the principal magnates to arrive. On St Valentine's day he brought 600 retainers clad in ostentatious red jackets with the earl's device of the ragged staff emblazoned on front and back. They headed for the north-west corner of the city and lodged in the Grey Friars.[292] The unwelcome garrisoning of London was, for better or worse, complete.

A total of around 3,800 armed men, from opposing factions, residing either within the walls or just beyond, not only created logistical problems but also seriously threatened the continued peace of Geoffrey's mayoralty. His response and that of the aldermanic bench was emphatic. On 8 February arrangements were made to impose a curfew from 6 p.m. to 6 a.m., during which time the gates were locked and guarded and the carrying of weapons was forbidden. Each ward was required to produce a levy of between 100 and 400 armed men who, when brought together, would have formed a contingent some 5,000 strong, more than enough to overawe and contain the magnates' belligerent retainers. It was not enough, however, simply to have such a force at hand. They had to be visible and several of the chronicle accounts compiled later in the century attest not only to the numerical advantage of London's militia but also to Mayor Boleyn's personal dedication to his new military role. Every day he 'kept great watch', riding his hastily recruited men from Newgate, along Holborn and Chancery Lane to Fleet Street, re-entering the city at Ludgate and proceeding via Thames Street to the Tower. It was a carefully planned route that took in the lodgings of all the main antagonists, impressing upon them, with the clatter of Geoffrey's passing column, that the might of the city stood ready to suppress any trouble.[293] It was a routine that had to continue for weeks and the threat of violence was unremitting. On 1 March rumour swirled that Somerset and Northumberland intended to take bloody retribution on Warwick as he passed their lodgings on the way to Westminster but Geoffrey's fragile peace held. Not until 24 March was it announced that an arbitration award had been agreed. Most of the concessions were made by the Yorkist lords, with York, Warwick and Salisbury reaching financial settlements with the families of those slain at St Albans. A façade of harmony had been produced but bitter enemies smiled at each other through gritted teeth.

To celebrate his hard-won illusion of peace, Henry planned a spectacle of celebration which, while fooling nobody, at least gave anxious Londoners a festive holiday. The feast of the Annunciation was on 25 March; it was generally known as Lady Day but renamed Love Day for the occasion, and an astonishing procession of lords was to be seen making their way through the militarised streets of London to St Paul's. Enemy was paired with enemy, so the new duke of Somerset linked arms with the old earl of Salisbury, followed by the duke of Exeter in harmonious animosity with the earl of Warwick. Behind them came the remarkable sight of Queen Margaret accompanied by her most detested foe, Richard, Duke of York, while Henry, as arbitrator of peace, walked alone. In majesty and splendour they entered the lofty arches of the cathedral to be greeted by 'a great multitude of people'. Amongst the crowd there must have been a much-relieved Geoffrey Boleyn, who was perhaps more sincere than many of the participants in giving thanks for the blessing of peace that had descended upon the realm.[294]

For Mayor Boleyn, as much as for England, however, it would be a fleeting peace. Throughout May the royal celebrations continued, with jousting at the Tower and the queen's house at Greenwich, but the city continued to seethe. While the court was in residence at Westminster, a fight broke out within the city boundaries between one of King Henry's men and one of Warwick's retainers, injuring the former.[295] The earl settled the matter without intervention from the mayor but for Geoffrey, October cannot have come around fast enough. It must have been with great relief that he handed responsibility for the riotous city to Thomas

Scot, a draper, and returned to the relative peace of Milk Street to count the costs, both emotional and financial, of his year as London's mayor.[296]

England too would soon be counting her losses as the fragile framework of Henry's contrived peace came crashing down. Mistrustful of the menacing military levy that accompanied the great council meeting of 1459 and suspicious that these forces heralded an imminent attainder for treason that would strip them and their heirs of lands and title, York and his allies again resorted to arms. On 23 September 1459, Salisbury's contingent of around 5,000 men crossed paths with royal forces at Blore Heath, south of Newcastle-under-Lyme, resulting in a slaughter that would earn the site the name 'Deadmen's Den', but no decisive victory. That battle still lay ahead. By the second week of October, Queen Margaret, with the king in tow, had run the Yorkists down to the fields below Richard's stronghold of Ludlow Castle. The fortress above them sheltered the duke's wife, Cecily, with his two youngest boys, George, aged 9, and Richard, aged 7, while his older teenage sons, Edward, Earl of March, and Edmund, Earl of Rutland, were at their father's side. This was now a contest on which York gambled his whole family. If he did not emerge victorious, would any of them be treated mercifully by the queen encamped on the other side of the newly built Ludford Bridge over the river Teme? The royal forces were larger, more legitimate (as the prominent royal standard proclaimed) and soon to be reinforced by the men and intelligence of the turncoat Andrew Trollope, one of Warwick's own captains. Slowly and quietly, defeatism crept through the Yorkist ranks and the magnates crept away under cover of darkness. Cloaked in dishonour but with his family intact, York made for Ireland with his second son, Rutland, while Warwick, Salisbury and his elder son, March, took ship for Calais, leaving his unsuspecting troops to surrender without him.[297]

For the time being, at least, the game was up for York and his allies. The queen was in the ascendant and she proceeded to crush her enemies ruthlessly. The Yorkist lords were all attainted at the next parliament, their lands forfeit, their power destroyed, and Duchess Cecily and her children were taken captive and closely monitored. London's rulers would have been foolish to abandon loyalty to the Lancastrian monarchy at this juncture and they were certainly not that. When Henry wrote from Nottingham, on his way to Ludlow, they resolved to hold the city for their king and prohibited the sale of arms to any adherent of York, Warwick or Salisbury.[298]

Four days after York sailed for Ireland, they hastily made the king a gift of 1,000 marks, or £666 13s. 4d., to 'relieve his great expenses after the recent perturbations'.[299] None of this, however, meant the undercurrent of resentment or individual partiality for the House of York had gone away. London's great merchants simply knew how to trim their sails to the prevailing wind. Their final destination had yet to be determined.

York may have been down but he was not yet out, as Henry's government was well aware. The duke was now backed so firmly into a corner that the only way to save his extended family from perpetual ruin was to seize control of either government or the Crown itself. Further bloodshed was inevitable so the king sent out numerous commissions of array, including, on 14 January 1460, a letter to London's mayor and aldermen requesting that they raise men and archers to resist the Yorkist rebels. It was a missive that backed the city's rulers into a corner of their own. Physically to enter the field of battle, risk life and limb and shed blood for one side or the other was a decision that it would be difficult to walk back from, but that was not the city's only concern. For over 130 years, no king had been able to compel Londoners 'to go or send to war out of the city'. A monarch might ask for military support but London had the right to refuse, and to submit now might undermine that ancient privilege.[300] In the inner chamber of the Guildhall, personal preferences were forced to confront practical policy as the aldermen chose a course of action. In the written record they appear resolute and united, as only their bare decision was committed to pen and parchment. But beneath the shroud of sterile officialdom there must have been a healthy debate, in which, it seems, Geoffrey took a leading role.

On 25 January, the aldermen took the diplomatic decision to send a deputation to Northampton to speak to the king in person about the matter. But the men they chose to send says as much about the tenor of those privy discussions in the Guildhall as it does about the individuals themselves. At the head of the delegation that rode north from the city with their breath thick in the bitter January air was Geoffrey Boleyn. He was accompanied by two of his close friends, fellow mercer Ralph Verney and the undersheriff Thomas Burgoyne, and also by the recorder Thomas Urswyck, travelling in his official role.[301] Geoffrey would later choose two of these men to be his executors, so we can safely assume that the presence of this clique was more than a happy coincidence. Burgoyne was a man trusted by the royal court, having previously served on several of Henry's commissions of array for his native Cambridgeshire, but he also had established, if outdated, links to York, so on this little jaunt he was probably, like Urswyck, the neutral voice of London's civil service.[302] Geoffrey and Ralph Verney, however, were both known Yorkist sympathisers and the only aldermanic representatives. It would appear that their arguments for defying royal instructions had carried the day but they had to tell the king to his face.

Whatever words Geoffrey or his companions spoke to their king apparently did the trick. Henry was convinced that the capital remained loyal yet concerned for their privileges and the emissaries were back in London by 5 February, with a letter reassuring the citizens that the king did not intend to infringe their liberties as long as that loyalty endured.[303] But pressure was mounting both within the city and without. Not for long could the aldermen continue to walk a tightrope between opposing armies, keeping personal politics separate from civic action. Soon they would be forced to choose a side.

Within the city's enfolding walls, the rising feelings, not only of the disenfranchised masses but also of more moderate citizens, would no longer remain quietly contained beneath a veneer of civic diplomacy. In February a lawyer named Roger Neville, probably a kinsman of the earls of Warwick and Salisbury, was arrested along with nine mercers and vintners on their way to deliver bowstrings and arrows to the Yorkist earls at Calais. Their punishment was swift and brutal. Hanged, drawn and quartered, their heads went to adorn London Bridge while their dismembered bodies were distributed around the city gates.[304] The king, increasingly dubious of the Londoners' professed loyalty, sent a commission to investigate this potential hotbed of treason. But Londoners were no strangers to such intimidation or to executions and the consequent gory decoration of the bridge. They were not cowed but as more news filtered in, they were increasingly alarmed.

Henry was heading back to Westminster and rumour flew that the Yorkists might descend on England at any moment. It was one thing to long for a change of regime and another to contemplate London succumbing to the fate of St Albans and becoming a battleground. By St Valentine's Day the aldermen were more concerned with war than romance and were desperately exhorting the masters of the companies to raise contributions towards the purchase of arms.[305] They feared not only for the future of civic governance or London's relationship with the Crown, but for their own skins. Geoffrey and his fellow aldermen knew that a wrong step might mean bloodshed and citizens could die. He could die. So, on 28 February 1460, he wrote his will.[306] The records of the court of aldermen show he was neither ill nor embarking on a long journey, both common reasons for making a will. It seems he was simply preparing for the worst.

Despite the prevailing anxiety, however, York in Ireland and the earls of March, Salisbury and Warwick in Calais did not get their ducks in a row until well into the summer. It was 26 June before the denizens of Sandwich sighted the cluster of sails on the horizon that heralded the Yorkists' return. That first night they spent in Canterbury but rumour had no need to tarry with saints and shrines and flew quickly up to London, putting the city in a spin. On 27 June, Geoffrey and his fellow aldermen met urgently with the common council. They knew that within the next forty-eight hours an army would likely be knocking on their gates. The years spent pursuing a policy of neutrality, despite personal inclination, were about to come to an end. Following the Parliament of Devils in November 1459, the Yorkist magnates were attainted traitors, and to assist them could be construed as nothing other than treason. Unless of course they proved to be victorious. Desperately London's rulers tried to avoid the looming decision.

With the Lancastrian commanders, Thomas, Lord Scales, and Robert, Lord Hungerford, closely watching their actions from the Tower, the aldermen and common council set in motion preparations to hold the city for the king but determined that they would do so without any assistance from the Tower garrison. If Londoners were not seen to be fighting along-side partisan troops from either side, perhaps they could claim to have held the city on behalf of whoever came out on top. Meanwhile they scrambled to head off the threat. A deputation was sent to the approaching earls to warn them that the city had been ordered to halt their entry and to per-suade them to make a detour around London. It was a plea that fell on deaf ears. Warwick would not be so easily distracted from the powerful prize that was the city of London.[307] By this time the earls had reached Blackheath, on the outskirts of the city, with a force swollen by enthusias-tic recruits to at least 20,000 men. The city's rulers had their backs against the wall. To defend the walls against such a force would inevitably shed Londoners' blood into London's streets and many who assembled in the now daily fevered meetings at the Guildhall must have had little will to do so. When Warwick sent a letter querying the city's disposition, the 'little division' that arose as the aldermen swallowed the bitter pill they had so long avoided was 'soon ceased'.[308] No record has been left of the sides taken in that 'little division' or the names of those men who rode out to meet their new allies but when the deputation reported back, on 1 July, Geoffrey Boleyn was among the almost full house of aldermen and common council packed into the Guildhall.[309] The following day the die was cast and the earls of Warwick, March and Salisbury entered unopposed over London Bridge. For better or worse, London had become a Yorkist city. As Geoffrey stood amongst his fellow aldermen to welcome the earls at St Paul's, his heart was probably comfortable with this sudden change of course but he must also have feared the rocks and shoals ahead. If York could not gain control of the government, a resurgent Queen Margaret could demolish city privilege and punish the rebellious Londoners where it hurt, in their purses.[310] From now on, the city and her citizens would rise or fall with the House of York.

Geoffrey and the city's rulers were under no illusion about the role they were expected to play in pursuit of Yorkist rule and in defence of their own futures. Those closely guarded purses must be opened wide. Between July 1460 and April of the following year, the city lent York or his family a total of £11,000, while further loans came from the companies, including 500 marks from the mercers, to which Geoffrey and his fellow mercer Geoffrey Fielding made the largest contributions.[311] It would be a tumultuous year before the fate of London and of England was finally determined.

The Lancastrian garrison of the Tower was less than impressed with the city's new allegiance and flung wildfire from the battlements into London's streets. Londoners joined the earl of Salisbury in a full-scale siege, taking the remarkable step of firing towards their own city from the Southwark shore. To fund what would ultimately be a successful campaign, Geoffrey and six other aldermen were appointed to persuade the wealthiest citizens to cough up.[312] By the time Richard, Duke of York, finally arrived in London in October, his heir Edward, Earl of March, together with the earl of Warwick, had gained victory at the Battle of Northampton on 10 July and, crucially, had taken Henry VI into custody. With both London and the king in his grasp, York made a play for the throne, but parliament resisted his claim for immediate possession and instead installed him as Henry's legal heir, supplanting Prince Edward. It was a compromise entirely unacceptable to both sides. The ultimate victor had yet to be determined on the battlefield and both claimants were growing increasingly desperate.

In December, when armour was usually mothballed for the winter, news reached London that, despite the hostile conditions, the Lancastrians were mustering their forces near Hull. Now the city would send troops to fight beyond her walls. York, his son Rutland, the earl of Salisbury and a contingent of Londoners under the command of the mercer, John Harowe, embarked upon a desolate trudge north through freezing mud and snow to meet a force equally pushed to the edge. It was a bloodbath. At Wakefield on the penultimate day of 1460, misjudgement by York, combined with a larger Lancastrian force, put an end to his ambitions and his life. Amongst the dead were his son Rutland, the earl of Salisbury, his son Sir Thomas Neville and London's captain John Harowe. The future looked bleak for London's gamble on the Yorkists.[313]

Hope, however, remained in the person of Edward, now Duke of York, who had inherited his late father's claim to the throne. News of his victory at Mortimer's Cross, in Herefordshire, on 3 February 1461, must have gone some way towards soothing the anxious minds of London's rulers but it would be short-lived relief. Only two weeks later Warwick was crushed in a second battle at the long-suffering town of St Albans. Henry was again abandoned, this time under a tree, and deposited back into the custody of his queen by the loyal Thomas Hoo, half-brother to Anne's father.[314] Down but not out, Warwick was able to effect a rendezvous with Edward, but the victorious Queen Margaret, back in possession of her husband, was not about to be outmanoeuvred. Both armies turned and headed for London.

This was exactly what the civic authorities had been trying for years to avoid. Now there was not just one hostile force marching for the capital, but two. Shops stood with shutters closed 'and nothing is done either by the tradespeople or by the merchants and men do not stand in the streets or go far away from home'.[315] Margaret was in the lead so the mayor and aldermen tried to play for time. Desperate to save the city from the pillage and plunder that had marred the queen's march south, they attempted to pay her off with much-needed supplies for her army. On 22 February, a delegation of aldermen and commoners set out for Barnet with cartloads of food, but at Cripplegate a mob slammed shut the gate and seized the carts. Whether this was simply an outbreak of looting, direct action against the provisioning of Margaret's unruly and much-feared troops or the act of a populace who had long been Yorkist at heart, it had the same effect. Fearful of the approaching Yorkists and believing she could not secure London, Margaret retreated north with her husband and Edward entered the city unopposed, to a rapturous reception.

On 4 March 1461, the mayor and aldermen, with Geoffrey among them, joined the lords and magnates in Westminster Hall to see Edward claim the kingdom as Edward IV.[316] His security on the throne was later assured by a bloody victory at Towton, south-west of York, on 29 March, and Geoffrey and his fellow aldermen attended his formal coronation on 28 June, clad in new liveries of light green cloth, carefully chosen to distinguish themselves from the burgesses of Coventry who, rumour had it, had also chosen to appear in green.[317]

The Boleyns had made it through on the right side of history and the next two years would provide a respite, for the family and the nation, from the mayhem and menace of recent events. London would remain a part of Geoffrey's life until its end but from late April 1462, he no longer attended meetings of the city's aldermen and was probably spending more and more time at Blickling, the family's grand new house in Norfolk. This country retreat was part of an immense property shopping spree that occupied Geoffrey's later years, all of it carefully chosen to solidify his liquid mercantile capital into the foundations of one of England's most famous noble families.

10

Blickling or Bust

Norwich, 5 November 1451

In temporary lodgings with the Talvas family in Norwich, the redoubtable Margaret Paston, of that famous Norfolk letter-writing family, sat down to dictate a letter to her husband John in London. Building works at their manor of Mautby were plodding along slowly, hampered by a familiar tale of bad weather and unreliable tradesmen, and her uncle Philip Berney was gravely ill. John was reminded of a pressing need that he return home and find a house to buy in Norwich that could accommodate his growing family, but pertinent local rumour and gossip also found their way into her latest bulletin. Margaret had been speaking with Lady Hastings, who had heard that John Heydon, the former henchman of the duke of Suffolk, had 'spoken to Geoffrey Boleyn of London and is agreed with him that he should bargain with Sir John Fastolf to buy the manor of Blickling'.[318] Then in his mid-forties, Geoffrey was still very much occupied with his burgeoning political career in London, but he had also been blessed with two sons as well as daughters, and it was time to think about translating mercantile success into that most elusive of commodities, gentility.

The manor house of Blickling was not, however, Geoffrey's first foray into the land market. He had already dipped a toe, followed rapidly by both feet, into London property, although that was a domestic and commercial affair, not the ambitious acquisition of a new identity. It had started nearly ten years earlier, in 1442, with a modest tenement uncomfortably situated near the stench of the Thames in the riverside parish of St Michael Queenhithe.[319] This house, along with part interests in several other tenements in the adjoining parish, had belonged to a man whose life could so easily have been Geoffrey's own. Thomas atte Wood was a hurer, a maker and dealer of caps. He and his wife, Joan, were the parents of just one daughter, Agnes, but like many other Londoners, both rich and poor, the hazards of childhood combined with endless outbreaks of plague or, in the 1420s, a deadly form of influenza, extinguished any hopes they may have harboured for the future of their small family. Within the space of two years, Joan would bury first her husband, then their daughter, before remarrying the fishmonger John Wyverton, but he too preceded her to the grave, in 1441.[320] Wyverton described Geoffrey as a close friend, someone to be trusted not only with the execution of his will but also with the money he left for the support of his elderly mother, so when his widow came to sell the Thameside property, Geoffrey was a natural purchaser.

For the atte Woods there was no transfer to a greater guild or ascent to the mercantile elite, just an all too frequent walk to the silent parish graveyard. But it was also the ubiquity of such personal tragedy that helped to make fifteenth-century England such fertile ground for ambitious men like Geoffrey Boleyn. When the Paston family inherited the lands of the Mautbys, the Boleyns' former landlords in Salle, it was through John Paston's marriage to the Mautby heiress, Margaret. The Pastons' gain would never have been possible without the decline and male line failure of the Mautbys.[321] If all families had been blessed with prosperity and hearty sons to inherit their father's lands or pick up his tools, the upward pressure exerted by rising merchants or lawyers on the lower margins of the gentry would have found no release valve. There would have been fewer landed estates to buy or acquire by marriage and successive generations of rich merchant families or successful lawyers would have been stymied, frustrated or confined to the urban realm.

For Geoffrey, the atte Woods' house by the Thames was just a modest investment, a buy-to-let, not a new home. His family were already installed in the comforts of the house on Bow Lane and would remain there for at least the next six years, with no desire to exchange the environs of Cheapside for the humble residence of a hurer and a relentless cacophony from the hooves and iron-shod cartwheels that served the port of Queenhithe. But owning, rather than renting, the keys to his castle was just as compelling to a fifteenth-century Englishman or woman as it is to their twenty-first-century successors. It was just a matter of waiting for the right house.

The Boleyns' new front door lay on the other side of Cheapside at the north end of Milk Street, just 350m or so from where they had previously hung their cloaks, and it was the former home of another wealthy London mercer, William Melreth. Like Geoffrey, a self-made man who had served as sheriff, MP and alderman, Melreth died in 1445, leaving numerous properties in the heart of the city to his two married daughters, Margaret and Emma.[322] What he did not leave, however, was enough hard cash to bankroll his debts, his other bequests, the elaborate tomb he required for his body and the commemoration he desired for his soul. Under the terms of his will, the shortfall would come out of his daughters' inheritance. All his London properties were to be sold to fund his will and the surplus, be it large or small, divided between Margaret and Emma. It was all too much bother for most of his executors. Three of the four refused to act, including Melreth's fellow mercer and neighbour on Milk Street, John Olney, and Robert Rooke, vicar of the church of St Lawrence Jewry, which was set to benefit from Melreth's memorial provision.[323] This left Melreth's former apprentice, William Pickering, to deal with the estate alone, but he did not have to look far for a purchaser with liquidity and an eye for a bargain. Within the livery of the mercers there must have been no shortage of interested parties but it was Geoffrey Boleyn who was attracted, not only by the useful investment but by the prospect of a suitable home.

The range of property put up for sale was considerable. As well as Melreth's own great house on Milk Street, Pickering was selling six other smaller tenements in that street and Lad Lane, a house and shop in the adjoining parish of St Michael Woodstreet, five houses in the parish of St Mary Aldermary church, a shop in West Cheap next to the Broadseld (covered market) and 7s. of rent from a shop in the Broadseld.[324] At the time of the sale, in July 1448, Melreth's widow, Beatrice, still had a life interest in the houses on Milk Street and Lad Lane, and Margery, widow of the former owner, Adam Norbury, had a life interest in the rest, so it could have been some time before Geoffrey and Anne were able to move in, but Beatrice would die later the same year, vacating the home she had shared with her husband and making way for a new mercer and his wife. The Boleyns would have packed the latten and brass, linens and silver that furnished their home into hired carts and made a short journey to their new life on Milk Street.

It was not only the wainscoting on the walls and tiles on the roof that were new and unfamiliar. It also meant a new parish church on Sundays and, crucially, new neighbours. Milk Street had long forgotten its origins as a dairy market and was lined with large merchant houses, home to some of the most wealthy and powerful men in the city. As the moving carts rolled up to the front door, Geoffrey was not just changing his address but making a statement about where he was heading, even though, in 1448, he had only recently finished his stint as sheriff and was yet to become either an MP or an alderman. As they walked down to Cheapside or to their new parish church of St Lawrence, Geoffrey and Anne would have come across familiar faces, such as the wealthy mercers Richard Lovelace, John Olney or Henry Frowyk, as well as those whose names carried handles such as 'gentleman' or 'esquire', like John Padyngton, whose house lay north of the church of St Mary Magdalen.[325] Here, amongst the rich and influential and just yards from London's heart at the Guildhall, Geoffrey would don aldermanic robes and lift the mayor's sword of office, but a more distant home was also calling to the heart of a son who had travelled far since his boots last stood on Norfolk soil.

The extent of Geoffrey's involvement in his native county since he rode south as a young, aspiring apprentice would appear to have been very limited. He does not seem to have been involved in any property transactions in the county before the 1450s and it is entirely possible that he was a stranger to Norfolk, beyond a possible visit to Salle for his father's funeral in 1440. The family's freehold land on Salle's Stinton Manor had been sold to Alan Roos, from another newly prosperous family, and their other holdings probably suffered a similar fate.[326] Margaret Paston certainly regarded him as Geoffrey Boleyn 'of London', not Salle, although she would have been fully versed in the family's origins. When it came to acquiring a rural estate, however, like many Londoners before him, Geoffrey favoured the county of his birth.

It was not a bad time to buy, but for any merchant, choosing the moment to turn silver into manors was never an easy decision. With instinct and experience, Geoffrey knew that liquid capital was more profitable. The returns from trade would always outstrip those from land but they would never carry the same social cachet or open the same doors. Only income from land could determine the right to vote or enter parliament as a 'knight of the shire' and those who drew most of their income from land (without lifting a hand or breaking a sweat) were a class apart. Land ownership under the Crown was the rich ground that nourished the tree of nobility.

Without crowds of lordly ancestors, Geoffrey and his family would have to rely on the security and prestige of landed income and the culture and lifestyle afforded by a great country house to establish their gentle credentials. When Anne gave birth to a second son, William, in late 1450 or 1451, building this future assumed even greater importance. Two potential male heirs made Geoffrey's legacy far more secure. The idea of future Boleyns leading Norfolk society was no longer a precarious dream that could disappear with one childhood illness, outbreak of plague or equine accident. It was something solid and dependable. Geoffrey was spurred into action. If Thomas and William were to grow up inhabiting this new future, he needed to do some serious shopping and put down some roots, deep into the land he knew best.

Exactly how Geoffrey opened negotiations for Blickling is unclear. News that Fastolf wished to sell may have reached Geoffrey via the perpetual rumour mill that, in fifteenth-century society, did the job of estate agent, matchmaker, news outlet and social media, but the timing, just as Geoffrey was celebrating the arrival of the spare to his heir, seems improbably convenient. Margaret Paston's gossip, Lady Hastings, conveyed the impression that the impetus came from Geoffrey, in discussion with the lawyer John Heydon, and she was probably right. Heydon certainly acted as Geoffrey's legal counsel in the matter but he would have been a peculiar choice of go-between to bargain with Fastolf, given that the old knight was in the process of prosecuting Heydon for alleged wrongdoing while serving as agent and henchman for the lately murdered duke of Suffolk. A deal negotiated by sworn enemies was unlikely to be a good one for the man whose purse would be lighter as a result. Geoffrey later wrote to John Paston about his purchase of Blickling, indicating that discussions with Fastolf occurred at Fastolf Place in Southwark, opposite the Tower.[327] So Geoffrey would have strolled over London Bridge or hailed one of the countless small boats that beetled back and forth, to cross the Thames and conclude one of the most important deals of his career.

There is no mystery, however, in Fastolf's willingness to sell. By 1451, he was a widower in his seventies, keen to shed some of his estates to raise annuities for his old age, and Blickling had been much damaged and depleted in the 1440s during disputes with both John Heydon and Phillip Wentworth. The bailiff and tenants at Blickling had suffered harassment and various parcels of land had been seized, on dubious legal justification, by the lackeys of Heydon or his master the duke of Suffolk. The legal costs, alone, that Fastolf had incurred fighting these numerous disputes were considerable. Geographically, Blickling did not lie within the concentration of Fastolf's other properties and was closer to Heydon's family seat at Baconsthorpe than to the Fastolf stronghold at Caister Castle, so it could readily be dispensed with.[328]

For Geoffrey, however, Blickling was not only indispensable; it was irreplaceable. Not because it was an architectural gem with all the mod-cons of the late Middle Ages, but because of where it was. Nestling in the valley of the river Bure with an extensive estate and pasture for hundreds of money-making woolly tenants, Blickling was only 7 miles from Salle. The house offered room for improvement but the location trumped everything else. Where better for Geoffrey to make a triumphant return to the county of his birth than a neighbourhood where everyone would appreciate his transformation of the family's fortunes? This had to be where he put down roots. It was where his heart lay and, despite all the other estates that would come into Boleyn hands, over Geoffrey's lifetime and in the generations that would follow him, it was always the place that mattered most. The house on Milk Street was bought from executors who had to sell. Blickling was bought by a purchaser who just had to buy and he paid a high price to get his heart's desire, but the Boleyns had Blickling. Everything else was just the cream on the apple pie.

The manor and house on which Geoffrey set his sights had originally been owned in its entirety by the bishops of Norwich but in the twelfth century, the large manor was divided. The bishops retained their country residence in the north of the parish and the southern portion was conveyed into secular hands. The Blickling estate subsequently passed through several families before coming into the hands of Sir Nicholas Dagworth in 1378.[329] Dagworth, a soldier and royal servant, was not a man of vast wealth. He owned only a handful of manors beyond Blickling but it was he who built the modest manor house that was at the top of Geoffrey's shopping list. After his death, the manor passed briefly through the hands of Sir Thomas Erpingham, whose executors sold it, in 1431, to his old comrade in arms Sir John Fastolf, for the princely sum of £1,647, or over £1 million today.[330] Geoffrey, with his characteristic sense of ambition, coveted the most expensive property in Fastolf's extensive portfolio.

With or without the assistance of John Heydon, it was ultimately Geoffrey who had to approve the purchase details for Blickling and it was a typical merchant's gamble, which, for once in Geoffrey's life, failed to pay off. He agreed to pay 2,000 marks (£1,333) up front and an annuity of 90 marks (£60) for the rest of Fastolf's life, however long that might be. If Fastolf lived for a further five years, Geoffrey's total purchase cost of £1,633 would be only slightly less than Fastolf had paid. If the old knight hastened to his grave, Geoffrey would get a bargain. If he soldiered on, Geoffrey would have to keep paying and paying. Fastolf had the last laugh, collecting that annuity for another seven years, and the thought that someone had got the better of him in business was evidently a thorn in the side of Geoffrey Boleyn. When he wrote to John Paston nine years later, with hopes of buying the manor of Guton, the wound was still raw and he could not help opening his letter by lamenting 'the great payment that I paid … and the yearly annuity during his life … [that] was to me great charge'.[331]

Before Geoffrey knew whether he was a winner or a loser, however, his purchase of Blickling had already degenerated into conflict, as both he and Fastolf found themselves in court. In 1452 Fastolf hauled Geoffrey into the court of the Chancellor at Fulham to explain why he had only paid 1,000 marks, was continuing to withhold two obligations for the remaining sum and had also failed to set up the required annuity. Geoffrey countered that the purchase agreement should have included 559 sheep and other unidentified belongings that had not been relinquished. From the start he was clearly determined that he would get every ewe and ewer he was entitled to. The court determined that Geoffrey should hand over one of the obligations for 500 marks and seal a deed of annuity but that the remaining 500 marks could be withheld until the missing sheep appeared and the other 'stuff' mentioned in the sale agreement had been valued by John Heydon (acting for Geoffrey) and Sir William Jenny (Fastolf's lawyer).[332] Despite the painful cost of Blickling, however, Geoffrey was soon lavishing more of his precious coin on the enlargement and improvement of Dagworth's old manor house and the wider estate. In 1452 he purchased all the houses and lands in Blickling owned by Edmund Love and united the property into what was later referred to as 'the new manor of Blickling', but multiple small cottages were far less important than a great family mansion.[333] Notes collected by the Tudor antiquarian John Leland, between 1538 and 1543, record that Geoffrey 'built a fair house of brick at [Blickling] in Norfolk' and although Leland is not always reliable and elsewhere got Geoffrey's place of birth wrong, evidence for a substantial brick house built by the Boleyns is indisputable.[334]

The Jacobean mansion that now stands at Blickling was built in 1619 by the lawyer Sir Henry Hobart but it occupies the same footprint as the house built by the Boleyns. Hobart rebuilt walls and floors, replaced roofs, moved internal walls and added turrets but much of the double courtyard house, in which four generations of Boleyns lived, loved and lost, remained, while the retention of the medieval moat constrained both the site and the costs. The house that Geoffrey was at such pains to acquire was probably a fairly standard, square plan, single court-yard fourteenth-century manor house. Crossing the moat and entering through the gatehouse range, to the south, the Boleyns would likely have found themselves in an enclosed open space with the great hall in front of them and family accommodation or the servants' domain to left or right. But this was far too mean and mundane for the future lifestyle of Geoffrey's family. The 'fair house of brick' that Leland recorded was probably an enormous extension that more than doubled the size of the house by adding a second courtyard and surrounding ranges to the north. A partial skeleton of this house, as it existed before Hobart's rebuild, can be glimpsed in the lease of the west range to a William Cardynal of Norwich in 1617. For £100 a year, Cardynal acquired the right to reside in what had been the service wing of the Boleyns' home. There he would have found a kitchen, two larders, pantry, washing house and two fur-ther chambers on the ground floor, as well as the porter's lodge at the south. Upstairs there were eleven further rooms, including one known as 'the corner chamber', meaning this range alone contained more rooms than the Boleyns' old home on Bow Lane.[335]

Hobart's grand plan involved extensive reconstruction of the ranges to the south and east and less substantial changes to those on the west and north, but the arrangement of bridge and gatehouse leading to the Little

Court, with the hall opposite, and beyond that the larger Long Court, would have been as familiar to the Boleyns as it was to the Hobarts.

What is harder to disentangle is which generation of the Boleyns at Blickling was responsible for these improvements and enlargements, and whether Leland can be trusted in his assertion that this was all the work of Geoffrey Boleyn. If Geoffrey's grandsons Thomas or James were responsible, this large project would have been taking place during Leland's own lifetime, making it far less likely that he would make an error in naming the man behind the plan. Geoffrey was certainly not shy of calling in the builders as he certainly set about the immediate modernisation of Hever Castle, when it later came into his hands, and was engaged in the aggrandisement of other parts of the Blickling estate. His will records that Norfolk's masons and carpenters had been hard at work on the church of St Andrew at Blickling, building a new chapel adjacent to the north aisle. Dedicated to St Thomas, it was intended to be the last resting place of himself and future generations of his family. But if money was lavished on a place to rest the heads of deceased Boleyns, it seems likely those builders were also employed at least to start work on a home fit to shelter those who yet lived. Geoffrey may not have survived to see the end of this project, given that Hobart's remodel of the Boleyn framework took over eight years to complete, but there is no reason to doubt Leland's assertion that he was the impetus behind the new house at Blickling. It was big, it was showy and in its innovative use of the new building material, brick, it was just the thing for a self-made man keen to exhibit both his wealth and his sense of style. Geoffrey's son William, who spent most of his life in Norfolk, would have both the leisure and the cash to complete or improve what his father had begun.

Despite the 'great charge' of Blickling and its continued improvement, Geoffrey would plough on collecting landed estates to support his two sons, but future purchases were made with a clearer head and his more usual eye for advantage.[336] Geoffrey's father-in-law, Thomas Hoo, died on 13 February 1455, which left the matter of Mulbarton to be finally settled by those he left behind. Under the terms of a 1428 settlement, Anne stood to inherit, but her father had rescinded this arrangement when he married for a second time, perhaps in hope of the son who was never born. Under this second settlement Mulbarton should have passed to Lord Hoo's brother but, presumably with his agreement, the original arrangement was respected and on 5 August Geoffrey acquired a new Norfolk manor from the Hoo family estates.[337] The Boleyns would have to wait until after Geoffrey's death before any more of the Hoo inheritance came their way. In the meantime, it was Lord Hoo's immediate heir, his half-brother Thomas, who seems to have acted as Geoffrey's estate agent.

The younger Thomas Hoo had three half-brothers of his own, as a result of his mother's remarriage to Sir Thomas Lewknor. One, Richard Lewknor, had taken on the execution of Lord Hoo's will, but it was his brother Sir John Lewknor who urgently needed to sell some estates to secure his family's finances.[338] The assistance Hoo offered was not entirely altruistic and the complex property transactions he facilitated on behalf of his relatives were, at times, more advantageous to himself, but it was the Boleyns who came out on top. In 1455 Geoffrey acquired the Lewknor manors of Holkham and Stiffkey on the north Norfolk coast, employing his sister Cecily as one of his feoffees for Stiffkey.[339] This was followed, in 1462, by Filby, Postwick, West Lexham and Carbroke in the same county, bringing the annual value of the Boleyns' Norfolk estates to £95 6s. 8d., or over £61,000 today.[340] From Holkham in the north to Mulbarton in the south, the bull's head seal was the mark of authority throughout the county.

Thomas, as Geoffrey's eldest son, would grow to inherit a seat amongst the leading gentry of Norfolk, but what about William? With no entail upon his newly acquired estates, Geoffrey could bequeath them as he willed, and his younger son must be established upon his own secure foundations, ideally in a separate county so the brothers could establish complementary rather than competing spheres of influence.[341] Geoffrey chose Kent and began with another shrewd purchase from a family whose star was temporarily dimmed. James Fiennes, Baron Saye and Sele, had amassed vast Kentish estates through a combination of Crown grants and aggressive acquisition but after he lost his head to Cade's rebels, many of his properties were reclaimed by the Crown and even more were gradually sold off by his son William.[342] Geoffrey would make the most of what was on offer. He began in 1460, or perhaps late 1459, with the purchase of the manors of Kemsing and Sele, valued at 40 marks a year, for the sum of 1,000 marks.[343] With a purchase price twenty-five times the annual value, this was a bargain compared to Blickling, where Geoffrey's outlay amounted to more than forty-three times the estate's annual worth.

These manors, however, just provided income. William would also need a suitable home, one to which he could bring a noble wife and in which he could raise little ladies and gentlemen. Fortunately William Fiennes had another gem for sale, a sparkling jewel that would become the most famous of all the Boleyn properties: Hever Castle. With its close proximity to London and enviable position in the hunting country of the Weald, Hever had more to offer than simply not being in Norfolk. In 1461 Geoffrey sealed the purchase deeds for both Hever Castle itself and the associated manors of Hever Cobham and Hever Brockays, 120 acres of land, 50 acres of meadow, 200 acres of woodland and 40 acres of pasture.[344] The Boleyn bulls were ranging into new and unfamiliar fields.

Hever Castle, as it was when the Boleyns moved in and as it stands today, was a far smaller house than the great brick house that would emerge at Blickling, but this befitted a younger son. Built by John Cobham under a licence to crenelate of 1383, it followed a standard square courtyard plan probably similar to that Geoffrey found at Blickling, but with a much more martial and defensive aspect. In Norfolk, Dagworth would have been able to dispense with portcullis and battlements in a way that the harassed landowners of Kent could not. Through the 1360s and 1370s, the south coast had been plagued by French attacks and the violence and uncertainty gave rise to a rash of moated castles as those who could afford to hunkered down behind vast stone walls. Passing under the unusual triple portcullis into the courtyard, the Boleyns would have found their new family chambers in the west range to their left and service rooms to their right, adjoining the kitchen in the north-east corner. Ahead lay the great hall, with windows overlooking the courtyard, but improvements were needed to bring even this castle up to the level of comfort the family would have been familiar with in Milk Street. With the exterior built to defensive standards, Hever included few, if any, large external windows. All the main windows looked into the courtyard, with no more than small, inadequate openings high on the external walls. This would have made for a dark and dingy interior, so light was an immediate priority. In the great hall new, larger windows were inserted to brighten up the imposing and naturally gloomy north-facing space but it would take more than daylight to make this a cosy family home. Across the western end of the hall, a massive timber partition, carved and decorated with the image of the green man, created a smaller parlour to receive guests in a more intimate, comfortable room. With a floor added to divide this new space horizontally, another private chamber was created on the first floor, both lit by new deep bay windows and made cosy by the addition of fireplaces. In the now reduced great hall, the heating arrangements needed urgent modernisation, as Hever still retained a central hearth. It must have done more to fill the room with smoke than it did to offer warmth and it would have been unthinkable and unfamiliar to a family used to the strict chimney building standards of fire-prone London. A new chimneystack was constructed on the north wall and the hall acquired a huge, stone-arched fireplace to warm rather than fumigate the Boleyns and their guests.[345]

Around a year later, Geoffrey added one further outlying manor, with his purchase of Pashley in Sussex from the Lewknors and their feoffees, but he rarely had the leisure to make the most of his new rural lifestyle.[346] For the first few years, the demands of business and his aldermanry kept the new owner of Blickling mostly in town. His absences from the court of aldermen were no longer than around two weeks at a time but in 1454 something changed. Between February and November he only attended seven out of a total of 107 meetings of the court and some of this time may have been spent with the builders at Blickling. He and Anne were in London to host the mercers' feast in June, but if not Blickling, then business was distracting him for most of this year. During the city's troubled years of 1456–57 and in the following year of his mayoralty, the demands of city government took priority, but thereafter a new pattern of family life seems to have emerged. From August, or occasionally July, to October or November each year, London had to manage without her alderman for the ward of Bassishaw.[347] He could have been anywhere, doing anything, but it seems likely that the Boleyns chose to escape the city's overcrowded and sweaty streets to spend late summer and early autumn at Blickling or Hever, where the air was fresher and the danger of plague more distant. Over these years, Geoffrey would have become very familiar with the roads he first travelled as a young apprentice boy. Riding between Norfolk and the city, he split his time between his old life and his new, but he was not yet done with London.

By 1460, he had disposed of his very first purchase, the Thameside tenement in St Michael Queenhithe, and in January 1463 he made one final major acquisition, a house tucked away behind the Saracen's Head inn near the southern gate to Guildhall Yard. Its upper storey extended over the stables or warehouse belonging to the inn but its public face looked out over Guildhall Yard, with its own main gate and, in the previous century, at least eight windows and a double-height jetty.[348] Despite its advantages, however, it was not Milk Street and it was probably always intended as an investment rather than a home, perhaps a top-up to the future income of his heir.

Such end-of-life planning was also underway elsewhere. Back at Blickling, the builders had completed the new Boleyn chapel at the parish church of St Andrew. Light poured in through pristine stained glass where the Boleyn arms impaled those of Hoo and any parishioners who could manage Latin looked up to read of 'Geoffrey Boleyn, late lord of this manor, and Anne his wife, who made this chapel and window'.[349] The stage was set but fate had other plans. When, on Saturday, 14 June 1463, the hastily summoned scribe sat down to commit the final wishes of Geoffrey Boleyn to the page, he did so on Milk Street, not at Blickling. His instructions, which suggest a future filled with travel, where his body might be buried in London or Norfolk, depending on where death caught up with him, probably owe more to an earlier testament used as a template than they do to any hope of recovery. Three days later, Anne was a widow.[350]

As he lay dying in the summer of 1463, Geoffrey would have given directions to write both a testament, bequeathing his moveable goods, and a will disposing of his property portfolio, but only his testament survives. In 1460, as Londoners anxiously awaited their fate, he would have done the same, but in this case only his will survives. His final instructions would have included Hever, which he had not yet purchased in 1460, but even without this important acquisition, his intentions are clear and, unsurprisingly, family was his priority.[351] Thomas was bequeathed Blickling and all other lands in Norfolk, while William stood to inherit the London houses and all the manors in Kent. Both received 300 marks, while each of Geoffrey's daughters was given 1,000 marks for her dowry, but none of this would be released until they were either 25 or married with the consent of their mother, Anne, and uncle Thomas Boleyn. By raising the normal age of majority of 21 for boys and around 15 or 16 for unmarried girls and assigning a trusted band of servants and ex-apprentices to manage the money in the meantime, Geoffrey was, perhaps, betraying the meticulous control and attention to detail that had made him so successful. The guardians he appointed to manage the inheritance of his children were trusted servants or apprentices but they were nevertheless under strict instructions to swear formal guarantees before London's chamberlain and not to trade with the money. However, Geoffrey's micro-management from beyond the grave did not stop there.[352]

Traditionally, Londoners bequeathed a third of their moveable goods to their wives and a third to their children, which left one third to aid the repose of their immortal souls. Anne's portion amounted to nearly £1,500 and that of their children was around £2,550, so Geoffrey had a considerable sum available to ease his way to the pearly gates. Like other rich, dying merchants, well aware of the post-mortem perils in store for men who had spent their lives serving Mammon, Geoffrey was moved to open-handed generosity, but in a form that was his own unique creation.[353] In total he left over £1,200 for the establishment of a wide-ranging charitable fund that would be gradually dispensed to the poor and to struggling householders over the years to come. Detailed accounts left by the executors of Ralph Verney, himself one of Geoffrey's executors, reveal that years after his death this money was being used in ways he could not have imagined, including the support of a baby girl found abandoned in the street.[354]

Usually executors were expected to enact all bequests and, while Geoffrey's executors were still ultimately accountable, they were not left to shoulder the burden alone. Instead Geoffrey did something for which it is difficult to find a parallel and installed dedicated management: a trustworthy man who would run the day-to-day business of this charity, bestowing Geoffrey's specific bequests, responding to requests for alms and being paid a suitable salary for his labours. If Geoffrey's legacy was dispensed in response to small personal requests for aid, as was usual, this man would have handled thousands of such appeals every year. Little wonder, perhaps, that his executors balked at the workload, but equally unsurprising that a professional businessman wanted a dedicated money manager even after his death. Whether this meticulous control of every detail had made Geoffrey an easy husband, father or friend is another question, but it had certainly made him a successful man.

Geoffrey's final words, however, reveal more than just a need to dictate. They also suggest a certain spirituality, an interest in clerical education and even a frustrated scholar, perhaps inspired by his ever-present brother. Like a number of his fellow mercers, he rejected some of the pomp and self-aggrandisement that had attached itself to the funerals of wealthy men.[355] The candlesticks at his funeral were to be black, not gilt, a stipulation deemed so important it was repeated twice. There was to be no 'hearse', an elaborate framework used to hold tapers over a coffin, and no 'great feast', only a small dinner for his executors, his widow, brother and a few select guests. This presumably excluded any great banquet for his mercer brethren and was a marked contrast to his friend Ralph Verney, whose splendid celebration with food laid on at the Prince's Wardrobe cost a fantastical £289.[356] Geoffrey was not, however, prepared to discard the assistance of a chantry and a chantry priest to pray his soul through purgatory.

Founded with the sum of 200 marks, Geoffrey's chantry was intended to run for twenty years for the benefit of his soul, the souls of his parents Geoffrey and Alice, his first wife Dionisia and Adam Book, his probable master and stand-in father. This would have been entirely conventional had he been a merchant of more modest means, but as one of the richest men in London, he could have endowed a perpetual chantry with some of his city property and barely noticed the loss. At the same time, however, Geoffrey's contribution to the foundation of Queens' College, Cambridge, had secured prayers and remembrance for the same souls commemorated in his chantry, but in a far grander and more prestigious form.[357] Oxbridge colleges functioned like huge chantries for their founders and benefactors but their size and status made them far more enduring and this, perhaps, was Geoffrey's perpetual chantry, allowing his temporary chantry to be moulded to suit his other priorities: education and preaching.[358]

Geoffrey's chantry would employ just one chantry priest but what he lacked in quantity he made up for in quality. The successful candidate had to be university educated, a doctor, bachelor or scholar of divinity or, if needs must, a master of arts, but unlike most chantry founders, who made continued absence grounds for dismissal, Geoffrey untethered his chaplain from the church of St Lawrence Jewry. He was permitted, if not encouraged, to travel elsewhere as long as his days were spent serving the dying mercer's principal aims. If he was improving the educational standards of the clergy by taking himself off to study at university or if he was engaged in serving the laity through preaching, he was free to go. The accounts left after the death of Geoffrey's executor, Ralph Verney, confirm that payments were made from Geoffrey's estate to three Cambridge graduates, John Cok, Richard Stratberell and Edmund Crome, to 'preach about for him'.[359] Geoffrey was joining a wider national drive to revitalise the church by placing more university graduates in England's rectories and expanding quality preaching to the laity. It was probably no coincidence that this was a cause in which his brother was already actively involved.[360]

While at Oxford, Lincoln College had been founded to uphold orthodoxy, at Cambridge, Queens' sought to do the same through 'the extirpation of heresies and errors, the augmentation of the faith, the dignity of the clergy and the security of the holy mother church', and Geoffrey's brother Thomas was one of the men appointed to write the statutes of this new college.[361] By weaving sponsorship of preaching and education into his personal chantry, by directly funding the university education of his Norfolk neighbour Thomas Randolf, whose family came from Heydon, and by his investment in Queens', Geoffrey was making his own small contribution to the enduring health of the Church, but he was also making it a fundamental part of how he wished to be remembered.

The old mercer took his final breath on 17 June 1463 and was fittingly laid to rest in the chapel of St John in St Lawrence Jewry rather than at Blickling. The city had given him all the wealth and rank of which he dreamed and his bones would become London earth, not Norfolk loam. Despite an evident tendency to meticulous planning, he left no written stipulation about his tomb, although he may well have discussed this with family or even made pre-mortem arrangements himself. In the end his body was covered with a memorial brass engraved with the words 'now thus' repeated thirty-two times. Such fatalistic warnings of the inevitability of death and the vanities of life form part of a post-plague culture of preparing for a 'good death' and remembering the transience of life. *Sum quod eris* or 'I am what you will be' was more commonly used to express the same sentiment but the words of Geoffrey's epitaph would later be adopted as a motto by his grandson Thomas and engraved on his garter stall plate in St George's Chapel, Windsor.

On his brass were engraved the arms of Boleyn and Hoo, marks of his new gentility, but in the end Geoffrey himself was described not as the yeoman's son he was at birth or the Norfolk gentleman he became but as the Londoner he was for most of his life:

Here lies in ashes the body late of Geoffrey Boleyn, citizen, mercer and mayor of London, who [departed] from this … in 1463, on whose soul peace be perpetual.[362]

PART III

Sons and Daughters

1463–1505

11

'My Lady Boleyn'

Norfolk, Summer 1463

Writing in haste from Norwich, sometime after 1480, Edmund Paston could barely manage six words of polite salutation to his brother William before embarking upon the breaking news he had to impart. The twittering birds who spread county gossip had dropped a particularly juicy worm into his ear in the form of the 'wife to one Bolt, a worsted merchant' who was 'lately fallen a widow … and worth a £1,000'. She was, Edmund assured his brother, 'called a fair gentlewoman' and although thirty years of age 'had but two children' who were of no material hindrance for they 'shall be at the dead's charge'. All in all she was a fine prospect, as others would quickly realise, so Edmund planned to speak to her brother and urged William to 'for your sake see her'. The tender feelings of this unnamed lady were clearly fairly low down the list of matrimonial considerations but being viewed by a string of amorous or avaricious suitors was probably not the immediate wish of many newly bereaved widows.[363]

Like so many other potential spouses who litter the pages of the Paston correspondence, nothing was to come of the match with the widow Bolt. But as Anne laid Geoffrey to rest beneath brass in London, similar gossip was doubtless winging its way to Norfolk, setting ambitious men and sharp-elbowed mothers aflutter. With two unmarried heirs and three generously portioned daughters, not to mention Anne's own substantial wealth, the Boleyns were a marriage market bonanza.

For nearly twenty years Anne had been Geoffrey's constant companion and partner. Through career success and civic glory to legal battles and political upheaval, he came to know her better than any woman alive and as he prepared for the years she would spend without him, his plans are infused not only with care for her financial future but with unwavering trust. Anne was entitled to a dower comprising a life interest in a third of Geoffrey's freehold property and continued residence in the marital home. As the widow of a London citizen, she could also expect a share of his goods and chattels. By 1400 men largely enjoyed testamentary freedom to bequeath their goods as they saw fit but the customs of London, Wales and the archdiocese of York preserved a widow's right to between a third and a half of her husband's moveable goods as *legitim*, depending upon the existence of children and any provision made in life.[364] Geoffrey gave to Anne all of this and more.

In moveable wealth that became hers outright, Anne received 2,000 marks and half of her husband's silver plate, which, based on the valuation of similar bequests to his children, would have been worth around £160. Geoffrey also acknowledged Anne's right to all furnishings and household goods from the kitchen, parlour, hall, buttery, pantry and chambers, although he does not specify from which of the Boleyns' now numerous houses. Included among her husband's chattels were Anne's own 'apparel, ornaments and jewels', so Geoffrey specifically bequeathed these to his widow lest she be inadvertently left without ownership of the gown on her back. Taken together, these bequests probably amounted to at least the required third of Geoffrey's wealth, but he was more generous than the law demanded. She was to enjoy a right of residence, or 'free bench', in not one but two houses, Blickling and the family's 'chief dwelling house' in London, presumably the house on Milk Street. As her dower right she was entitled to a third of his landed income but she would have had no trouble in receiving this as Geoffrey placed his entire landed income at her disposal to maintain his estates and raise their children. His faith in her common sense, judgement and financial acumen was clearly absolute. Only if she remarried and so placed herself under the authority of some unknown third party were Geoffrey's other executors authorised to step in and manage the issues and profits of his lands and rents. At such a time, or when Thomas and William came of age and entered into their inheritance, Anne's dower entitlement would become a lifetime annuity of £66 13s. 4d, over £42,000 today.[365] Whatever she felt about Geoffrey as her husband, Anne cannot have been dissatisfied with the prospect of her life as his widow. She would never want for wealth, social standing or independence and it was entirely up to her whether she chose to hold on to the latter.

The unfortunate widow Bolt, upon whom Edmund Paston urged his brother to pounce, fared well in comparison to a few wealthy widows whose suitors dispatched soldiers rather than letters. In 1451 Anne's own cousin Jane Boys, the widowed daughter of Edmund Wychingham, had been violently abducted from her father's house and raped by a neighbour, Robert Langstrother, aided by as many as sixty armed men. Carried off to the nearby house of the Knights Hospitaller at Carbroke, in Norfolk, where Geoffrey had owned one of the manors, she subsequently agreed to marry Langstrother, rather than her betrothed, Richard Southwell. Debate continues over the truth behind this case. Did Jane actually consent to the abduction as a staged elopement or did she simply capitulate to the fait accompli achieved by Langstrother rather than face the shame of her defilement?[366] Such a scandal so close to home, both geographically and by blood, must have made its way to Anne's ears. Fortunately such actions were both rare and illegal, not the normal way to wed widow or maiden. Any wolves circling Anne were more likely to come bearing love tokens and marriage settlements than swords and lances. Anne, however, would not be a tit-bit for the scavengers. As she emerges from the cloak of coverture she appears as a woman more than capable of dispatching suitors with their tails between their legs.

What Anne had now in abundance, and perhaps for the first time in her life, were choices. She could decide where to make her home, in London or Norfolk. She and she alone could choose to remarry or remain a widow, and should she agree to take another man's ring, she could select the husband who suited her best. The king's right to arrange marriages for the widows of his tenants-in-chief had largely been extinguished by the prevalence of enfeoffment, and where it hadn't, licences to escape this feudal prerogative or pardons after the event were easily purchased.[367] Under London custom Anne could even stay in the city and continue to run her late husband's business affairs as a freewoman in her own right. Life was not the same for all widows. Anne's wealth gave her options that were a distant dream for many women. Bereaved and truly alone for the first time or constrained by an empty purse, some women rushed quickly into the arms of another and the familiar security of married life, but around half of England's wealthier widows, like Anne, had other ideas.[368]

Some opted to formalise their widowed status, choosing a new identity that was neither nun nor wife but encompassed both celibacy and motherhood. They took a religious vow of chastity and became vowesses, but while Anne certainly chose not to remarry, there is no evidence that she followed this path. She nevertheless embraced her widowhood, constructing a new single life for herself in Norfolk rather than London. In March 1467, after John Paston II had competed in the great royal tournament held that year at Eltham, he wrote home to his younger brother, John III, in Norfolk. The elder John, in London, had been conversing about, if not to, Anne while they were both in the city but 'upon Tuesday last past she rode home into Norfolk'.[369] Whether it was shopping, business or even the tournament itself that had drawn Anne to London, Norfolk was evidently regarded as her home. Her husband's will, however, had bequeathed her a residence in Milk Street and there was every reason to maintain a London base. The family's involvement in the city ran deep and would be neither quick nor, perhaps, advantageous to uproot. Of particular concern were the apprentices still under Geoffrey's mastership, whose future now lay in Anne's hands. The remaining term of city apprentices was inherited by their master's widow, who in some cases completed their training herself, but at the very least Anne would have been expected to ensure that Geoffrey's death did not destroy the prospects of these young men and that they had the chance to complete their apprenticeship elsewhere. In 1429, John Haccher, an apprentice ironmonger who found himself in the same position as Geoffrey's apprentices, prosecuted his master's widow, Beatrice Gosselyn, because she had dismissed the household and refused to either train him or make alternative arrangements.[370] Curiously, of the three young men still apprenticed to Geoffrey on the day he wrote his will, only one is recorded as completing his term and becoming a citizen and mercer. William Welles had started his apprenticeship around 1456 so was ready to take up the freedom by the time Geoffrey died, and he duly did so. His admission as a citizen was not recorded until 1467 but he was described as the apprentice of Geoffrey Boleyn, with no other master named, so this had probably been facilitated several years before by Anne.[371] Of his kinsman Geoffrey Welles and of Richard Sutton no record can be found and they may have left London. Even when a master's death did not interrupt their apprenticeship, some men, such as Hugh Joye, found a future elsewhere.

One of Geoffrey's former apprentices, Joye completed his term around three years before Geoffrey's death, and although there is no formal record of his entry into the mercers' company, he was described as a mercer when he provided surety for William Boleyn's inheritance. After that he disappears from London's records, probably because he found an alternative career in service with the Boleyns. By 1476 he was a man of business in the employ of Anne's son William, but before that time Anne may have had need of him.[372]

Geoffrey had instructed that his household be kept together for three months after his death but two years later his servant John Norlong chose Anne as his executor and left bequests to all the Boleyn children and many others who had been in his former master's employ.[373] This strongly suggests that Geoffrey's household was kept together far longer than the three months he had required, perhaps because his business concerns were so complex to wind up but possibly because Anne, aided by Norlong and Joye, developed mercantile ambitions of her own. In 1469 she, together with the Norfolk lawyer Richard Southwell, lent £70 to a collective of four Londoners, two merchants plus Thomas Porthaleyn, esquire, and John Shipley, gentleman, in what was probably a commercial transaction.[374] Similarly, in 1473, John Arundel of Lanhern in Cornwall registered a debt of £600 due to Anne and two of her sons-in-law for merchandise purchased in London.[375] As the widow of a citizen, she had every right to trade in the city, although she cannot have been driven to do so by financial need. Perhaps she had always been an active partner in her late husband's business and was simply continuing a way of life that was familiar and comfortable.

As both Geoffrey's widow and one of his executors, Anne would have shouldered at least part of the burden of running his estates and

fulfilling the ongoing demands of his will, but her legal and financial affairs went beyond wifely adherence to a list of instructions laid
down by a deceased spouse. She also had plans of her own. In 1463,
just eleven days after Geoffrey's death, Anne and her fellow executors
Ralph Verney, Richard Nedeham, Thomas Burgoyne and Hugh Fenne
contributed £733 6s. 8d. from his estate towards a £2,000 loan raised
in London to fund Edward IV's campaign in the north.[376] Geoffrey had
not favoured the business of financing the Crown in life but he had,
perhaps, taught Anne something about how to get what you want, and
what she wanted was her inheritance.

It may have been eighteen years since her father's death but Lord Hoo's
tangled estate and the claims of creditors had continued to limp through
the court of Chancery, leaving a trail of claim and blame in its wake.[377]
While the Sussex manors of Wartling, Bucksteep and Brookesmarle were
enmeshed in counterclaims, the manors of Luton Hoo in Bedfordshire and
Offley and Cockerne Hoo in Hertfordshire were far less controversial and
much easier pickings. They had been quite clearly settled on the second
marriage of Lord Hoo in 1445 and Anne's uncle Thomas was in possession, with the property set to descend to his male heirs.[378] Despite two
marriages, however, it looked certain that Thomas would die childless, so
Anne set out to ensure the property would come to her, rather than to her
three half-sisters. Her weapon of choice was her supply of ready cash and
Hoo's lack of the same.

Like his brother, or perhaps because of his brother, Hoo seemed
unable to keep money in his purse. When his brother's estate had
proved unable to provide for his three unmarried nieces, he refused to
abandon them to a state of impoverished spinsterhood and voluntarily
contributed 1,000 marks for their marriages.[379] It was a generous but
perhaps reckless act for a man who was constantly pursued by creditors
throughout the 1460s. In January 1471 he was again arrested in London
and was evidently in desperate need of the money his niece could provide.[380] By 1473 Anne had already furnished him with £100, which was
long overdue, but she was prepared to offer more at a price, and the
price was Luton Hoo, Offley and Cockerne Hoo. On 8 December 1473
Thomas settled the reversion of these manors on Anne and her heirs
and she consequently provided a loan of £300, ensuring that 'for the
more readier payment of the same' the issues of the manors became

hers with immediate effect.[381] Her half-sisters were left to fight for what remained.

Anne also had not forgotten the plans she and her husband had for the manor of Guton, although twelve years had elapsed since Geoffrey had first written to John Paston requesting aid with the acquisition of this part of John Fastolf's estate. As late as 1472, a deal was still on the table. Indeed the younger John Paston had it on good authority that Anne was sure to become the mistress of Guton Hall. It may have seemed certain that June but it would never come to pass.[382] Anne had no such difficulties, however, acquiring a new urban residence in Norwich.

The house on King Street, in the parish of St Julian, lay immediately to the south of the great merchant emporium now known as Dragon Hall. It had come into Anne's possession by 1474, having previously been owned by her uncle Edmund Wychingham, although Edmund had four daughters of his own, who were his co-heirs, so Anne probably bought rather than inherited the house. By the later fifteenth century Dragon Hall had reverted to a gentry town house more in keeping with the general character of King Street and Anne or her son would have found themselves with some interesting neighbours. In much changed circumstances, the Boleyns were reunited with the Briggs of Salle, who owned property on the opposite side of the street. The house to the south of the Boleyns' had been sold by Sir Miles Stapleton and further down the road the large house known as Wensum Lodge or The Music House was owned by Fastolf's executor and local JP Sir William Yelverton. He or his heirs would later sell it to Sir John Paston.[383] By the 1480s Anne was ploughing money into the improvement of Norwich Cathedral and although she is unlikely to have abandoned Blickling entirely, she perhaps preferred a busy city life amongst the gentry of Norwich as, one way or another, all her chicks spread their wings.

Thomas was not quite 17 years old and William no more than 12 when they lost their father.[384] Their sisters' ages are more uncertain as their births are not recorded but they were probably between or slightly younger than their two brothers, so most if not all of Geoffrey and Anne's children had yet to make a start on their adult lives. Under the terms of Geoffrey's will his brother Thomas and other executors had a say in arranging future marriages but the care and raising of the young Boleyns was left entirely in the hands of their mother to continue the nurture they had begun together. When Geoffrey wrote that his sons and daughters should be maintained 'in everything necessary to them according to the demand of their rank', he would have expected not only appropriate food and clothing, but also appropriate training and education.[385]

This was a process that must already have been well underway. There was every expectation that Geoffrey's children would live in a very different way from their father. While there would be common ground in financial or legal affairs, much of their time would be spent in a rural rather than an urban environment, and amongst the nobility or gentry rather than merchants and craftsmen. Although in the fifteenth century London's mercantile elite were increasingly adopting aristocratic culture, this was still a very different world.[386] The art of hunting, with its arcane rules and terminology, would be both an important recreation and a social networking opportunity. Ease and proficiency with horses and weaponry were both a marker of gentility and, given the ongoing civil wars and associated breakdown in law and order, an essential life-preserving skill. If they were to avoid looking like gauche arrivistes, Thomas and William had a lot to learn, but they would have started with the fundamentals.

Both merchants and gentry shared a common culture of literacy and litigiousness, so they would certainly have been taught to read and write, but what this would have actually meant is harder to define. Unlike today, when the two go hand in hand, skill at reading was more widespread than skill at writing, and while Anglo-Norman French had fallen out of common usage, Latin was often still the language of legal matters. London was well provisioned with grammar schools, including one at the church of St Mary le Bow, just a stone's throw from the Boleyns' first home, so Thomas and William would probably have been drilled in Latin, but true proficiency among the gentry seems to have been rare. They probably learnt enough to decipher formulaic legal documents or pronounce Latin prayers but English was the language in which they likely learnt to read and write more easily.[387]

Less scholarly pursuits were taught in a more informal way. Archery was a skill common to all classes and could easily be learnt in and around London, while the wide-ranging subject of 'courtesy', which could include everything from table manners and how to serve your social superiors to personal hygiene and walking or speaking correctly, was probably inculcated gradually in the home. Both boys and girls would have been taught singing, dancing and musical appreciation although, as today, some probably took more naturally to the playing of musical instruments than others. There came a point, however, when family and a familiar hearth could offer no more and both boys and girls were often sent to continue their education and forge useful relationships in the households of the greater gentry or aristocracy. This practice might have been particularly useful for the Boleyns, keen to form networks and friendships among their new East Anglian lords and neighbours. It is possible that by the age of 17, Thomas may already have found such a favourable position, although there is no record to confirm this or indicate who may have taken him in.

Education, however, was not just for the boys. Anne, Alice and Isabel would also have been taught to read and write, in English rather than Latin, but their likely proficiency is hard to estimate as it varied so widely amongst gentry women. While for many the experience of putting pen to parchment was one of trouble and toil with indifferent results, for a few it was a pleasure. Eleanor Hull, the daughter of a Somerset knight, for example, was skilled enough to translate a lengthy commentary on the seven penitential psalms from French to English in the middle of the fifteenth century.[388] The widespread use of secretaries, regardless of proficiency, made it perfectly possible to manage without basic literacy but the gentry lady's life centred around household management and that entailed checking accounts. It would have been both admirable and useful to be able to do this and to read other correspondence independently. Generally, however, gentry girls were probably less proficient than their brothers, simply because they had less opportunity or reason to practice. Like Thomas and William, their sisters would also have been trained in manners and courtesy and the girls might even have learnt to shoot. That Margaret, the eldest daughter of Henry VII, was proficient with a bow is clear from an account of her shooting a buck in the park at Alnwick, Northumberland, on her way to Scotland to marry James IV, while Anne Boleyn was given a bow by viscountess Lisle in 1532, although it proved too heavy for her to draw.[389]

The details remain unknown but Geoffrey and Anne would have made every effort to school their children in 'the demands of their rank' and prepare them for adult life. For Thomas and William, the form that life would take was clearly defined. They each had a path to tread that had been carefully and laboriously prepared by their father, but for Anne, Isabel and Alice, the future was filled with the unknown. With their generous dowries they had every hope of worldly success but that might not equal happiness. Where they would live, how they would live and crucially who they would live with must depend on the most important decision a medieval maiden had to make. If she was lucky, she might even get to make it for herself.

'For Nowadays Money Maketh Marriage'

Norfolk, 1449

Bruised and bleeding, 19-year-old Elizabeth Paston needed a way out. Not a climb through the window, shimmy down the roof and steal a horse escape route but a socially acceptable, dowry-preserving, family-friendly exit, and options were limited. Cut off from all contact with visitors or even household servants, communication with the outside world was tricky, and then there was the iron will and short temper of her mother, Agnes, by whom she was 'beaten once in the week or twice and sometimes twice on one day and her head broken in two or three places'.[390]

The intolerable crime that had occasioned such punishment? Elizabeth, it seems, was less than enthusiastic about a proposed marriage to the pox-scarred Stephen Scrope, nearly thirty years her senior. For help she appealed to family friend Elizabeth Clere, smuggling a message out by means of that customary literary go-between, a friar. Elizabeth was, understandably, worried for her young namesake and in June 1449 wrote to her brother John, but she was also brutally frank about the plight of this distressed damsel. There would be no handsome knight to rescue her from the maternal dragon. Marriage was her only way out and Elizabeth Clere begged John to find the young girl a better suitor than Scrope, although she acknowledged that if none could be found, the quadragenarian would have to do. If Agnes was to be believed, her daughter understood her limited choices perfectly well and had been successfully driven to accept even Scrope to get away, but as Elizabeth Clere cautioned John, 'sorrow often times causes women to beset [bestow] them otherwise than they should do'.[391]

Five years later, however, Elizabeth Paston was still at home and still feeling the sharp side of her mother's tongue, with Agnes 'never so fain to have been delivered of her as she will now'.[392] She eventually escaped to the home of Lady Pole but seems to have been no happier and not until she reached 28 was a marriage finally concluded with Robert Poynings. Elizabeth's new husband, or 'best beloved', as, in her own words, she 'must needs call him so now' was hardly her love-match but she had doubtless long given up any such girlish notions.[393]

Not all parents, however, regarded their unmarried daughters as irritants to be removed or commodities to be sold. Some mothers, whose own early careers had been decided by others, were moved to feminine solidarity with their girls. Katherine Willoughby, Duchess of Suffolk, married at 14 to her 49-year-old guardian, was describing the scars she shared with many other women when in 1550 she wrote:

> I cannot tell what more unkindness one of us might work more wickedly than to bring our children into so miserable a state [as] not to choose by their own liking such as they must profess so strait a bond and so great a love to forever.[394]

Norfolk, 1464

Fortunately for the Boleyn girls, their mother inclined more towards the doctrine of Katherine Willoughby than the Agnes Paston school of matchmaking. The 1,000 marks Geoffrey bequeathed to each of his daughters gave them every advantage, but with his characteristic enthusiasm for detail and planning, he had made efforts to determine their futures years before his death. In 1454, when his eldest daughter can have been barely out of infancy, Geoffrey sought to secure a marriage to Thomas Fastolf, the young cousin of Sir John Fastolf. The boy's wardship was a much-mangled bone of contention between the old knight and his enemies, and John Paston was also on manoeuvres on behalf of one of his daughters, so a betrothal was far from straightforward.[395] In the end neither John nor Geoffrey's matrimonial scheming came to anything, so the task of matchmaking was bequeathed to Anne. For the release of those mammoth dowries, the consent of Geoffrey's brother Thomas and his other executors was required but doubtless, if Anne approved, there would be no reason for the others not to fall into line.

The first record of a marriage amongst the Boleyn girls occurs just a year after Geoffrey's death, and with preparations evidently well underway, he may have had a hand in its negotiation. On 26 July 1464, John Methelay, a legal apprentice in the employ of Sir John Cheyne, attested that he had seen all the legal documentation prepared for the marriage of Isabel Boleyn to Cheyne's son William, and four weeks earlier William himself entered into a bond of £1,000 to be paid to Isabel's mother, Anne.[396] These were the essential financial arrangements without which no marriage between wealthy families could proceed. The Cheynes had been settled at Shurland on the Isle of Sheppey since the early fourteenth century, so Geoffrey may have come to know them when he entered the county as the new owner of Hever Castle, but they also walked common ground in the commercial world. Sir John traded grain and wool from his lands in Kent with London merchants and he, Geoffrey and Thomas Hoo were all members of the prestigious Taylors' fraternity of St John the Baptist.[397] Through his mother, Eleanor, William was first cousin to Margaret Beaufort; his father had been victualler of Calais, while the man-mountain that was his brother John was one of Edward IV's most trusted servants and his Master of the Horse, so the marriage brought excellent connections for the Boleyns.

Isabel's new family were based on the opposite side of Kent from Hever but despite the physical distance, she and her mother evidently remained close throughout their lives. When Isabel died, on 23 April 1485, a little over six weeks before her mother, she was buried not amongst her husband's family in Minster Abbey on the Isle of Sheppey but in the Boleyn chapel at Blickling. This may have been her request, but if so, she must have felt a deep desire to lie with her natal family, as transporting a body such a long distance was not routine. If she died at home in Kent, it would have involved taking a ship around the coast or across the Thames estuary or coming upriver to use one of the regular ferry crossings such as that at Gravesend or even London Bridge. It is far more likely that she was simply staying at Blickling with her mother when she died. Anne was nearing her seventh decade and Isabel may have come home to nurse or visit her, then succumbed to unexpected illness.[398]

Whatever the cause of her death, she was laid to rest under a brass made in the Norwich workshop of the glazier William Heyward. Isabel's mother, or perhaps her husband, chose an image that portrayed her as a wealthy, well-dressed and fashionable woman, wearing the latest butterfly headdress, and it proved to be a popular design. Just a few weeks earlier, in January that year, Anne Herward's relatives had chosen the same image for her memorial at Aldborough in Norfolk, and three years later Elizabeth Clere's brass at Stokesby shows her wearing a nearly identical dress, although fashions in headdresses had moved on. Some personalisation of the standard pattern was, however, possible so the space above Isabel's low neckline is filled with an enormous ostentatious necklace that, despite the limitations of the medium of brass, is clearly intended to represent a family fortune in gold and jewels.[399]

Anne and Geoffrey's daughter Anne was the next of the Boleyn girls to tie the knot, with her marriage taking place sometime before 1467. In April that year John Paston III wrote that Geoffrey's widow had been in Norwich with 'Heydon's wife and Mistress Alice both'.[400] 'Mistress Alice' was Anne's unmarried younger daughter and 'Heydon's wife' her elder child Anne, by then the wife of Henry Heydon. Henry's father, John Heydon, is first recorded as Geoffrey's legal counsel in his dispute with John Fastolf over payment for Blickling in 1452 but the connection evidently continued. His son Henry may even have spent his teenage years in the Boleyn household, as his name was entered on the 1468 pardon roll with the alias 'of Blickling', but which came first?[401] Was Henry boarded with the Boleyns because an engagement had been agreed while Anne and Henry were yet children or did the pair fall in love when thrown together under the same roof? Their marriage seems to have been a very happy one, so if it was arranged by their parents, they were incredibly fortunate.

Anne's new husband, Henry Heydon, came from a Norfolk family who had risen to prominence alongside the Boleyns but it was probably the influence of his new wife that, in 1468, prompted the purchase of the manor of West Wickham in Kent, around a day's travel north of Hever.[402] There he built Wickham Court, a fortified manor house similar to that the Boleyns found when they arrived at Hever, with the windows facing an internal courtyard. On the hill beside the house, the dilapidated church of St John the Baptist detracted from the Heydons' pristine new-build, so Henry rebuilt the church as well, writing his loyalty to the House of York in stained-glass white roses and flowering suns surrounding both the royal arms and those of Duchess Cecily. Since removed from the church to the house, these windows were just part of the decoration Henry and Anne lavished on their new home. The H and A deeply carved into the fireplace in the hall still bear witness to their union, while in the windows their initials are forever tied together with a wedding band in testament of what appears to have been an affectionate marriage.[403]

When Henry died in 1504, he provided for Anne to live a life of her choosing. She could decide to live at the family seat of Baconsthorpe or take the income that was provided and make her home elsewhere. It is not until Anne herself died, on 3 March 1510, that it becomes clear she chose, like her mother, a house of her own in Norwich.[404] Purchased from the executors of the Norwich alderman John Crome, who died in 1506, her new home in the parish of St Peter Hungate enabled her to avoid a dowager's life of lonely rural seclusion or a painful existence as an unwanted third wheel in the household of a married son and instead enjoy the city's lively gentry community.[405] She left numerous bequests to the city's religious institutions, including to her own parish church, which received alabaster images of St Erasmus and the Trinity and a carpet to lie before the altar displaying her arms and those of Henry.[406] She also left many personal items to her daughters and their families and to her god-children: silver-gilt cups and countless spoons, rich bed-hangings of red *say* or silk from her own chamber and gowns furred with mink. There was a covered bowl with the arms of her mother, which she must have inherited from Anne, but the 20s. left to a servant of her daughter Dorothy Cobham perhaps says most about her life. Just as her own mother spent her widowhood in company with her married daughters, Anne was evidently such a familiar visitor to Dorothy's home that she developed an affection for her servant.

Her family home was also apparently well furnished with domestic textiles, a private chapel and an astonishing number of books. The interest in education demonstrated in her father's will had clearly been translated into the education of not only Geoffrey's sons but also his daughters, and Anne was apparently an engaged reader. Henry's will included the division of an unspecified number of books from his chapel between his widow and his son John. These would have been in Latin but all his 'English books' were to be divided amongst his children after Anne had first chosen those she would like to keep for herself. Enough books to divide between a widow and at least seven children suggests a far from ordinary library. Sadly no titles are recorded and they are not mentioned in Anne's will but the 'psalter covered in blue velvet' that she left to her daughter Dorothy perhaps came from the Heydon chapel. She also left 10*s*. to the son of Thomas Landon in recompense for the primer she 'had of his father'. Like her husband and father-in-law, Anne was laid to rest in Norwich Cathedral, but while they were interred together in the Heydon chapel, she chose the nearby chapel of St Luke, which was closer, although only marginally, to her mother and brother William, in the chancel.[407]

The last of the Boleyn girls to find a husband was Alice, although she almost became a Paston in 1467. According to Anne's servants, her visit to Norwich in the spring of that year was entirely 'to sport her' but to one Norfolk bachelor it had a more personal significance. John Paston III was having girl trouble. Unlike his older brother, who was drawn to the glitter of London, the younger John was content with rural domesticity in Norfolk and the endless mundane headaches of estate management. All he wanted was a wife with sufficient wealth to establish their own household, but as a younger son with no prospect of inheritance, he had no bait beyond his own personal charms with which to go fishing. He was, however, rich in these less bankable assets. Blessed with talent, humour and an amiable nature, he was also particular about his appearance and regularly sought to update his wardrobe with hats or hose from London. In comparison to the pox-scarred senior citizen presented to his aunt Elizabeth, he was not an unappealing suitor, but it was Anne and her daughter Alice whom he wanted to convince. For advice he turned to his elder brother, who had something of a reputation as a courtier and 'the best chooser of a gentle-woman'. This prompted John II to test the water with Anne while she was in London but he found 'my Lady Boleyn's disposition' to be decidedly frosty. Despite employing every privy avenue of inquiry, he could 'in no wise find her agreeable that you should have her daughter' and so chose not to talk to her in person but Anne had evidently spoken to others and her words found their way to John's ears. If John and Alice could agree, she 'would not let [stop] it' but she 'would never advise her thereto in no wise'.

This was a long way from encouraging and threw all hopes onto John's ability to win Alice.

It was his first attempt at wooing a girl so his elder brother gave him some pointers. Since nothing could proceed without 'some comfort of her', charming Alice was the first hurdle. John advised his brother to 'bear yourself as lowly to the mother as you list but to the maid not too lowly, nor that you be too glad to speed nor too sorry to fail'. John, however, just didn't have the experience to play it cool. His brother's report of 'Lady Boleyn's disposition' seems to have put the fear of God into him and any real hope of romance was doomed. When report reached him, too late, that Anne had been in Norwich with her girls, he optimistically concluded that she wished him to 'have been in Norwich for to have seen her daughter'. This seems unlikely, but even had John been aware of her visit, his courage failed him. To John II's inquiry as to how he was progressing, he declared that he had not spoken to Anne 'nor not will do' until his brother came home, as promised, to act as his 'herald'.

The elder John never did come to his bashful brother's aid and no more is heard of the match. Alice was either less enthusiastic than her suitor or never had the chance to reach a conclusion on his charms or his new hose. Either way it was perhaps to her loss and certainly to John's advantage. By February 1476 and with several more failed prospects behind him, he was ruefully asking his brother to seek 'some old thrifty alewife' for him, and then he met Margery Brews and fell head over heels in love.[408] Unlike Anne or her daughter, Margery could see his charms and he must have been eternally grateful that neither Alice nor any of those other women had said yes.

Alice, on the other hand, must have been equally grateful for a mother who allowed her to say anything at all. Anne's agreement that even a marriage she evidently disapproved of should be allowed to go ahead if the couple were in love stands in stark contrast to the treatment meted out to Elizabeth Paston. Like Katherine Willoughby decades later, her actions were perhaps informed by her own experience of having her husband selected for her and so she allowed Alice a voice in her future. Unlike Agnes Paston, who seems to have found the presence of her daughter a constant source of irritation, Anne and her girls were close and she evidently enjoyed spending time with Anne even after she became 'Heydon's wife'. Lady Boleyn, perhaps, had confidence in the good sense she had instilled in her girls, while they, in turn, trusted a mother who had their best interests at heart. In this co-operative spirit, Alice found the man who would become her husband, but not until 1473 were the guardians of her dowry formally released by her husband, John Fortescue, nephew of the chief justice of the same name.[409]

Anne, however, may have wished she had looked upon John Paston more favourably, as Alice's marriage to John Fortescue took her so far away from home that she must have become a stranger to her mother. When she and John first married, he was serving as sheriff of Cornwall, so the young bride faced a journey of over 350 miles from Blickling to a county where the rugged gorse-strewn moors and sheltered coves were a stark contrast to the flat lands of East Anglia. Before too long, however, she was on the road back to London, as in 1476 John was admitted to Lincoln's Inn, having already acquired the court position of esquire of the body. Two years later he purchased the manor of Windridge near St Albans and on the death of his uncle, Sir John, he inherited the manors of Ponsbourne, Bayford and Gascelyn, in Hertfordshire, where Alice and John established a new life.[410] Alice's exact date of death is unknown but John remarried in 1495 so she must have died some years previously. The couple's younger son, Adrian, married by 1499 and Mary, probably their youngest daughter, in 1495, so it is unlikely they had any surviving children born after the middle of the 1480s, when Alice would have been not much more than 30, suggesting she may have died around the same time as her sister Isabel. There was no cosy widowhood in Norwich for these two wives but their brother Thomas would be even younger when his future was unexpectedly cut short.

'Servants and Lovers of the Duke of Gloucester'

Norfolk, June 1469

In the summer of 1469, Anne Boleyn marked six years of widowhood. Over that time life had settled into a new comfortable routine, at least three of her five children had blossomed into wives or husbands and although the eldest, Thomas, was yet resisting putting down matrimonial roots, her garden was filled with the scent of healthy new growth and latent potential. Overhead, the wide Norfolk skies contained nothing more threatening than a slowly circling falcon climbing on rising thermals but over 200 miles away to the north, storm clouds were gathering. Through April and May, Lancashire and Yorkshire had seen two separate uprisings, and although both were swiftly suppressed, the rebel leader, who went by the heroic alias of Robin of Redesdale, remained at large. Reluctantly, King Edward was forced to acknowledge the trouble in his realm but he did so with very little urgency and much attachment to a languid summer in the south.

Since Geoffrey had watched Edward receive the crown of Edward the Confessor in 1461, the king had worked hard to secure his new realm. Margaret of Anjou had fled across the Channel with her son Edward and in 1465 Henry VI had been finally run to ground after more than a year on the run between a network of safe-houses. With the ex-king in the Tower, one threat was removed, but others lay beneath the surface. In September

1464 Edward had informed a stunned meeting of his great council that he had secretly married Elizabeth Grey, widow of Sir John Grey and daughter of Richard Woodville, Lord Rivers. The 22-year-old king had followed his heart but his great revelation went down like a lead balloon with his audience at Reading Abbey. The earl of Warwick's work on a French alliance was instantly reduced to ashes and that was just the start of the earl's frustration. Over the coming years the queen's large family secured vast amounts of Crown patronage, various titles or offices of state and a clutch of marriages to the cream of England's aristocracy. Increasingly side-lined by the king he helped create, Warwick turned to Edward's younger brother George, Duke of Clarence, and fostered his insecurities. Despite a sizeable income bestowed by his brother, Clarence was living beyond his means and was painfully aware that what the king had given he could also take away. His finances could be secured by a marriage to Warwick's daughter Isabel but his brother would not hear of it. For both Warwick and Clarence, it seemed that Edward stood in their way. Co-opting local insurgency in the north was their first attempt to bring him to heel.

With the Great Wardrobe under orders to produce banners, standards, forty jackets of velvet and damask and a thousand of blue and murrey for the troops that would quell the insurgency, the royal party, including the king's brother Richard, Duke of Gloucester, and a collection of other nobles, rode out on 5 or 6 June 1469, on a leisurely progress to the north west via the south-east. On the way they planned to take in the pilgrimage centres of St Edmund at Bury and Our Lady of Walsingham, as well as the convivial hospitality offered by East Anglia's elites.[411] In Norwich the king was received with 'right good cheer' and the younger John Paston took the opportunity to display the family silver with a dinner in his mother's house, 'she being out'.[412] On the guest list were the queen's two brothers, Sir John Woodville and Anthony, Lord Scales, Sir John Howard, treasurer of the household, and 23-year-old Thomas Boleyn. John Paston wrote that they all 'held them content' with his hospitality, before turning his pen to a subject that, to follow his train of thought, may indicate something of the dinner table conversation. The king and his brother Richard had a more serious task at hand as they made their boozy pilgrimage through East Anglia: raising the men who would wear all those velvet livery jackets. Four of John Paston's circle, including William Calthorpe, had sworn to serve under Richard, while John himself had been offered service with the king. No mention was made of Thomas Boleyn, possibly because his allegiance was already well known or more likely because his oath was not yet sworn, but it seems that in the days or weeks to come Thomas too would be recruited by Richard. By 14 November Thomas Boleyn had made his way to London with the rest of the court, where he was appointed attorney to deliver formal possession of the manor of Sudeley to Richard. His fellow attorneys were William Calthorpe, certainly one of the duke's East Anglian recruits, and Thomas Parr, one of Richard's northern esquires.[413] Although Thomas's affiliation is never made explicit, the company he was keeping tells its own story. By November 1469 at the latest, Thomas Boleyn had placed his service, his loyalty and his life in Richard's hands as Edward's reign was turned upside down and back again.

The months between John Paston's dinner in June 1469 and Thomas Boleyn's reappearance in London in November saw the bonds of political society and even the royal family stretched to breaking point. In defiance of his brother, Clarence married Isabel Neville in Calais and threw in his lot with her father, Warwick. Together they crossed back over the Channel and prepared to mobilise an army that would compel Edward to see sense about the influence of the Woodvilles and their allies. Marching north out of London, Warwick and Clarence planned a rendezvous with Robin of Redesdale and his insurgents but William Herbert, the 'master-lock' of Edward's rule in Wales, was determined to deal with the rebels before Warwick and Clarence could arrive with reinforcements. Herbert's Welshmen came together with the northerners at Edgecote, north-east of Banbury, on 26 July and were slaughtered. An advance force from Warwick's main army turned the tide of battle against them and a victorious Warwick set out to settle old scores. Sir John Woodville, his father earl Rivers and William Herbert were brutally hunted down and summarily beheaded. The king himself was captured, imprisoned and then quietly released when Warwick found himself unable to wield power or keep order in his name. By the time King Edward entered London in October to an extravagant civic welcome, he had been joined by his loyal nobles and by his youngest brother, Richard, who had probably spent the intervening chaos raising further troops in East Anglia with John Howard. Gloucester's new recruits had apparently sidestepped what could have been a baptism of fire but Warwick and Clarence remained smouldering embers that threatened a far worse conflagration.[414]

Twelve months later, Edward was a dishevelled, penniless exile, washed up on the coast of the Burgundian Netherlands, staring back across the waves at the kingdom that had once been his. Further revolt had seen Warwick and Clarence chased from England with a price on their heads but an unholy alliance with Margaret of Anjou prompted their return. In a mirror-image replay of 1460, they landed at Dartmouth on 13 September 1470, seeking to restore Henry VI to the throne, and soon had 30,000 men in the field. Trapped and outnumbered, Edward had no choice but to avoid a battle he could not win. Fleeing south-east, the only route open skirted the treacherous margins of the Wash, where sea became solid ground and sea again, faithless and deadly. In the fading light not all of the men still loyally following their king made it to safe harbour at Bishop's Lynn, but once there, as many as possible were packed onto the available ships. It was perhaps as few as 700, maybe as many as 1,500, while those left behind were dismissed with instructions to make peace with Warwick but keep their true loyalties close. Either of these two groups may have included Thomas Boleyn but his true location remains unknown as there was no time for roll calls before the brothers turned their back on England and set sail for the Low Countries. Five weeks later, in sanctuary at Westminster, Elizabeth Woodville gave birth to the couple's first son, Edward, but his father faced an uphill struggle to regain a kingdom for the new Prince of Wales to inherit. In the words of Bettini, the Milanese ambassador to Louis XI, 'it is a difficult matter to go out by the door and then want to enter by the windows'.[415] Difficult but not impossible.

By 11 March, with a force backed by his Burgundian brother-in-law Charles the Bold, Edward and Richard were on their way home, sailing from Vlissingen bound for the loyal lands of Norfolk. But Edward was not the only one who thought East Anglia might make a favourable landing site. When the king's ships, fighting gale-force winds, made landfall at Cromer, the news was bad. Suspicious of their Yorkist leanings, Warwick had rounded up the leading men of the county and in their place the Lancastrian forces of John de Vere, Earl of Oxford, were waiting to spring a trap. Instead Edward slipped quietly back out to sea and into the teeth of the storm. Caught by raging seas, the fleet was scattered and when, two days later, the king's ship the *Antony* limped ashore at Ravenspur, she did so alone. The other ships, however, soon found landfall, many on the north banks of the Humber Estuary, and Edward was reunited with his brother Richard and his 300 men. Not a single vessel had been lost.

Simply getting ashore had been harder than expected, and despite their miraculous survival, Edward still had a fraction of the men needed to recover his crown. He urgently needed loyalists to bring forces to his aid but he was marching south through lands where the populace were more inclined to arm against him than for him. So, taking a leaf from the playbook of Henry Bolingbroke, who had landed at the same port in 1399 to take the throne as Henry IV, he let it be known that he had returned only to claim his patrimony as duke of York. Together with the studied neutrality of Henry Percy, Earl of Northumberland, this strategy cleared Edward's road south and emboldened his potential allies. By the time he reached St Albans, he had declared his true intent, gathered a considerable force, been reconciled with his rebellious brother Clarence and left Warwick behind, refusing to emerge from the safety of Coventry's defensive walls. Warwick would be dealt with later but, in London, Edward's approach presented the city's governors with a horrifying rerun of 1461.

Bombarded with letters from Warwick and Edward, both equally insistent that the city be true to their cause, and with Queen Margaret and her son expected to land at any moment, the mayor, John Stokton, found himself suddenly unwell and could not be prised from his sickbed. His Lancastrian-leaning replacement, Sir Thomas Cook, tested the way the wind was blowing and bolted for France, which left Geoffrey's old friend Ralph Verney holding the reins. With his long-held Yorkist sympathies, Edward's troops close at hand and the Crown, as usual, in hock to the city's merchants, there could be only one pragmatic choice. On 11 April the gates were unbarred and Edward entered London unopposed.[416] If he had not remained with Richard throughout, it was probably at this point that Thomas Boleyn rekindled his old allegiance, along with all the other men who poured into London to support their king. His whereabouts during Edward's exile is unknown and his actions cannot be plotted with any degree of certainty but his ultimate fate reveals the path he took to get there.

Edward may have left Warwick behind Coventry's city walls but the traitorous earl did not remain there long. Soon news reached London that he and his men were advancing rapidly on the city and twenty-four hours later

Edward, Richard and their allies marched out to a final reckoning. On the road heading north-west they soon ran into Warwick's outriders, who they chased back to Barnet, before the king set up camp for the night, but by this time it was quite dark and neither Edward nor Warwick realised just how close they were. Oblivious to their enemy's true position, Warwick's men worked their artillery through the night, sending round after round clear over the heads of the king's troops who, huddled and silent, muffling every chink of armour, remained undetected. By the time the sun rose on Easter Sunday, a thick fog had descended, and out of it Edward charged headlong at the man who had stolen his throne. Artillery was immediately useless, visibility was a matter of a few feet and men fought blindly, hand to hand, face to face in close, merciless butchery. In the dark the armies had drawn up in overlapping formation. On the Yorkist right flank Richard's men had the advantage as their line extended past the Lancastrian left flank, curling around to compress their opponents. On the opposite side of the field the Lancastrian earl of Oxford was enjoying the same advantage. Swinging around and piling into Hastings's men, they pursued the scattering Yorkists back towards London and it took some time for Oxford to regather his men. When he finally returned to the fray, Warwick's men mistook his star badge for the sun of York and attacked. The loss of Oxford's forces was bad but the death of his brother John Neville was the final fatal blow to Warwick's courage. Seizing a horse, he bolted for a nearby wood, where he was run down and brutally killed. 'And so King Edward got that field' of Barnet.[417]

By early afternoon the victorious Yorkists were streaming back through London's gates to the peal of church bells and welcoming crowds, but the returning men presented a shocking sight to some onlookers. Gerhard von Wesel, a Hanse merchant resident in London who had a front row seat for Edward's triumph, recounted in horror that 'those who went out with good horses and sound bodies brought home sorry nags and bandaged faces without noses and wounded bodies, God have mercy on the miserable spectacle'. The close-quarters slashing and stabbing had taken a hard toll on those toiling in the fog. While noble deaths attracted most attention, von Wesel noted that 'many of the commons were wounded and mostly in the face and in the lower part of the body'.[418] It is likely that Thomas Boleyn was somewhere among these butchered masses.

By 30 April 1471, his young life was over. He was 24 years old, barely four months short of inheriting his father's wealth, and his death seems to have been entirely unexpected. His brief will, only nineteen lines long, leaves everything to his mother and is evidently a document prepared in haste, not the careful considerations of a man suffering from long-term illness.[419] 1471 was a plague year and other sudden accident or illness cannot be ruled out but the pestilence did not take hold until August and the timing of his death is significant.[420] Occurring as it did just two weeks after Barnet, the most likely cause of Thomas's early demise was not disease but the fatal combination of infection and a Lancastrian sword. Thomas Parr, who had been attorney for Richard with Thomas in 1469, died on the battlefield, a swifter, cleaner and more kindly death than the creeping pain and pus that was probably the lot of Thomas Boleyn.[421]

Whatever the nature of Thomas's wounds, he may at first have been expected to live. Archaeological evidence has provided numerous examples of men who survived even serious injuries and the successful removal of an arrowhead from deep within the skull of a young Henry V saved the future victor of Agincourt.[422] Medieval surgeons employed a variety of strategies to heal wounds and counter infection, and while some were extraordinary, others were reasoned and effective. Without modern anaesthetics, thorough cleansing and exploration of wounds was difficult and only a small number of clean incisions would have been suitable for closure with dressings or sutures. Surgeons understood that most wounds must be left open to allow drainage, although whether pus was a necessary part of healing prompted fierce debate. Thomas would probably have had his injuries washed, usually with wine or vinegar, and covered with a dressing in which half the garden, kitchen or apothecary's shop might be included. Ingredients for dressings included spiders' webs, ground shellfish, clay, turpentine, oil, vinegar, earthworms and camphor. Rather more reasonably, honey was commonly used, and although the action of bacteria was not known or understood, the results spoke for themselves.

Despite the best efforts of surgeons, infection was hard to control without antibiotics, particularly in conditions that were far from the clinical hygiene of modern hospitals. Many must have succumbed quickly but others, like Thomas, were overwhelmed slowly as friends and relatives watched. Hit in the shoulder by a crossbow bolt at the siege of Châlus-Chabrol in 1199, Richard the Lionheart survived for eleven days before gangrene took his life.[423] A crossbow bolt was also responsible for a minor injury to the knee of Gabriel de Prolo from Cremona in the late thirteenth century. He lay at death's door for two months, with infection ravaging his body, before receiving treatment and eventually making a full recovery.[424] Thomas would not be so lucky.

The two long weeks that saw him sicken and fail offered more than enough time for the devastating news to reach his mother in Norfolk and for her to cover the 130 miles in return, driven hard by hope and fear. Neither of the two surviving copies of his will supply witness lists to confirm Anne's presence at the bedside of her dying first-born son but that she was his sole executrix and, other than the usual bequests to his parish church, his only beneficiary speaks of a mother reassuring her child that she would take care of everything.[425] By 23 April, when this document was sealed, it must have been evident that any other aid was beyond her power, but still Thomas lingered for one more week before finally breaking his mother's heart and shattering his father's plans. From the day he took his newborn son into his arms until the day he died, Thomas's father, Geoffrey, had been dreaming of his son's future life and working to make those dreams a reality. Building castles in the air and turning them into real stone and mortar. Just eight years earlier Geoffrey had dictated his final bequests, hoping to secure that golden future. Now his son's body would lie beside his beneath the cold stone floor of St Lawrence Jewry.

The death of adult children, although more common than it is today, brought no less grief, as acknowledged at the end of the century by an anonymous Oxford schoolboy. Long after the death of his brother, he wrote, his mother 'was wont to sit weeping every day' and 'there is nobody which would not be sorry if he had seen her weeping'.[426] Nevertheless, as both mother and executor, it would have fallen to Anne to arrange an appropriate funeral and tomb. Thomas was laid to rest beneath a brass, now lost, which displayed a quartered shield. In one quarter were the three bulls' heads of Boleyn but in the other three, Hoo quartered with St Omer, Wychingham and Malmaines, his armorial inheritance from four generations of Anne's family.[427] It was a choice that said as much about the mother who was grieving as it did about the son who was gone.

As an injured Thomas Boleyn and a victorious King Edward arrived back in London on Easter Sunday, Margaret of Anjou and her son Prince Edward were landing at Weymouth in Dorset. Her timing, just hours after Warwick's death, was hardly ideal but Margaret still had many supporters who would flock to her banner, so Edward could ill afford to rest on the laurels he had won at Barnet. He was soon on the road, hunting the queen as she made for Wales and her ally Jasper Tudor. At Tewkesbury Edward caught up with her and Margaret dug in, but it would be to no avail. When the two armies came together on 4 May, the Lancastrians were destroyed. Many men were drowned attempting to flee across the Severn. Others who sought sanctuary in Tewkesbury Abbey were murdered as Edward and his men stalked through the abbey precincts, but by far the most important corpse was Prince Edward of Lancaster. In the days that followed, his mother, Margaret, was captured and forced to submit to Edward. Five years later she would be ransomed to Louis XI, living out her days dependent on his charity. That left ex-King Henry. He had been returned to the Tower when Edward arrived in London in April but as long as he lived there would never be peace, and the bloodshed had to stop. On 21 May Henry VI was quietly murdered and his body placed on open display in St Paul's. Many lives had been cut short. Countless families, including the Boleyns, had lost sons and heirs but finally England had one king and one king only.

Thomas, perhaps, had inherited some of his father's ambition, mixed with a healthy dose of youthful enthusiasm for adventure, but not every son of a wealthy London merchant was on a career path to feats of arms or death in battle. Some followed in their fathers' footsteps, with families such as the Elsings, Odyhams or Claverings producing several generations of successful mercers, grocers or drapers.[428] As Geoffrey had argued so forcefully in 1460, citizens could not be compelled to fight outside their city, so the bloodshed of the later fifteenth century did not cut a swathe through the London population as it did through the nobility, gentry or the blood-soaked 'commons' whose injuries so shocked von Wesel. Thomas's life would have been very different, and almost certainly longer, had he taken up a merchant's purse instead of a sword, but his father had not dreamt of sons who would simply follow in his footsteps. This was equally true of Thomas's brother William, but the younger Boleyn was no carbon copy of his elder sibling.

Rapidly approaching his quarter century, Thomas Boleyn died unmarried. Although he was yet to come into his inheritance, he had somehow managed to acquire a house of his own, entirely independent of his parental estates and geographically removed, at Ingham near the east Norfolk coast.[429] He did not have a chance to travel far but he had taken the first steps on a path that could have ended in a successful career in noble service or the royal household. William, on the other hand, was settled into marriage by the age of 18 and apparently content to have the matter arranged by his mother. Such complementary characters could work well. While the elder of the Paston brothers, John Paston II, was dealing with legal affairs and jousting with the king in London, his younger sibling, John III, was managing domestic matters in Norfolk, but the Boleyns were not afforded such a healthy division of labour. The last day of April saw the death of William's only brother and the first day of May the start of his own initial term at Lincoln's Inn. His admission payment was not formally recorded until 1473 but the plans for his legal education had been laid when he was still the family's younger son.[430] Geoffrey may have divided his homes and estates between his two boys but the value of William's share was only around half that of his brother and the legal profession was a popular way for under-endowed younger sons to both supplement their income and advance their prospects.[431] While his older brother focused on networking with the nobility, William was expected to knuckle down to his studies, but in a stroke that need had evaporated. Instead he would have wide-ranging estates to manage and so, as his brother had six years previously, he joined the mercers' company in 1472, via patrimony, or paternal right, rather than by apprenticeship.[432] Membership conferred the legal advantages of a London citizen and would have aided both brothers in the management of their city property but Lincoln's Inn still had much to offer.

Scattered over London's western suburbs, the four Inns of Court could, by the fifteenth century, claim to be regarded as England's third university. Here the sons of knights, gentry or aspirational tenant farmers came to learn to be lawyers, a profession that offered both wealth and status. They observed cases in the king's courts, attended 'readings', or lectures, and participated in mock cases, or 'moots', on their way to becoming 'utter barristers'. Not all the inns' members were, however, such dedicated career-driven students. As Sir John Fortescue observed in the late 1460s, many sons were placed in the inns even though they were never expected 'to be trained in the science of the laws nor to live by its practices but only by their patrimonies'. A basic grounding in the law would always be useful for the defence and management of those patrimonies but the Inns of Court had more to offer than a crash course in property law. To Fortescue the inns were an 'academy of all the manners that nobles learn'. There boys learnt:

> to sing and to exercise themselves in every kind of harmonics. They are also taught there to practise dancing and all games proper for nobles, as those brought up in the king's household are accustomed to practise.[433]

The latter was key. The inns offered the same kind of education available in magnate or royal households but without the need for friends in high places.

Housed together, with common facilities for eating, drinking and making useful new acquaintances, the Inns of Court were both school and social club. William's contemporaries included Richard Southwell, later a servant of the Mowbray and Howard dukes of Norfolk, whose son Robert would become one of Henry VII's key financial officers, and there was ample opportunity for the two Norfolk men to enjoy themselves.[434] Christmas revels were held at Lincoln's Inn from at least 1444, with minstrels hired for the occasion, and the military aspirations of gentry sons were not neglected when the Inn erected scaffolds for members to view the jousts of 1467 and 1477–78. Such amusements also greatly enhanced the appeal of the inns over the more studious, theological offerings of Oxford or Cambridge, an advantage driven home by their location. Sandwiched between the bright lights of London and fashionable excesses of Edward's court at Westminster, the Inns of Court not only offered more useful training for laymen, they offered more fun. Strict rules against playing at dice or bringing in women were not written without due cause but neither were they always obediently observed.[435]

Unlike many of his fellow law students, however, William Boleyn entered this world of youthful *joie de vivre* with his conscience already constrained by marriage vows. Margaret Butler was the daughter of Thomas Butler, the third son of James Butler, fourth Earl of Ormond. The granddaughter of an earl, certainly, although in 1469, the approximate date of their marriage, it was a very distant, untouchable nobility. All the Ormond brothers had been staunch Lancastrians. The eldest and fifth earl, James, had been captured and executed after Edward IV's victory at Towton in 1461, his tar-covered head joining the ornaments on London Bridge, but the new king was not finished with the family. All three brothers were attainted in England in November 1461 and in Ireland the following year, and all their lands and titles were forfeit. It was during this period that Anne Boleyn stepped in with an eye to the future of her younger son, William.

Attainders passed by act of parliament could be reversed by act of parliament and often were. It was this possibility that made Margaret Butler an appealing daughter-in-law. Anne and Geoffrey may have become familiar with the Ormonds in London as the family maintained a close connection with St Thomas of Acre, home to the mercers. As well as claiming descent from a sister of St Thomas Becket, the Ormonds were valuable patrons of the church and the fourth countess of Ormond, Margaret's grandmother, had been buried there. When Margaret's own father, Thomas, died in 1515, he would join his mother, having bequeathed to the church his 'psalter book covered with white leather' in which he had written his name with his own hand. It was to be chained to his tomb for the better service of God 'by such persons as shall be disposed to occupy and look upon the same book'.[436] Margaret's father was quite the adopted Londoner, keeping a chamber at the hospital of St Thomas, renting a house in the parish of St Peter, Paul's Wharf, and having another in Westminster. His rural residences were principally Rochford Hall or New Hall in Essex but his elder brother James had settled at Fulbourn in Cambridgeshire and Geoffrey's bequest to Fulbourn's rector, Geoffrey Bishop, and his appointment as Bishop's feoffee may have come about through an early association with the Ormond family.[437] The eldest brother, James, also passed Christmas 1459 with Sir John Fastolf in Southwark so there was ample opportunity for the Boleyns and the Butlers to come together.[438]

The marriage settlement for William Boleyn and Margaret Butler dates to 1469, by which time they were already married. William would have been 18 or 19 but his bride was barely out of the nursery.[439] An inquisition held in October 1486, after the death of her mother, gave Margaret's age as 20 years and more, three years younger than her sister Anne.[440] This would suggest she was born around 1466 but jurors were often vague or inaccurate and in this case must have been several years astray. Margaret would give birth to her first child, Anne, on 18 November 1475, which is incompatible with a birth date of 1466 as she would have been just 9 years old.[441] Margaret must have been born before 1466 and was therefore not as young as 3 at her marriage, but there is no reason to doubt that Margaret really was married as a very young child. The marriage of infants was not uncommon, particularly among the aristocracy, and Margaret's elder sister Anne had been both married and widowed by 1469, while probably still a teenager.[442] Such marriages would be reconfirmed and consummated later, with the canonical age of consent being 14 for boys and 12 for girls, but society and careful mothers were wary of forcing very young girls into adult roles before they were ready. Noble daughters, particularly heiresses, certainly became wives and mothers at a younger age than their less affluent neighbours but evidence suggests it was unusual for child marriages to be consummated before girls were 15 or 16 at least. For the unfortunate few, however, this must have been little comfort. Margaret Beaufort's traumatic delivery of the future Henry VII at the age of 13 and the childbed death of Henry IV's daughter Blanche at her second pregnancy, aged 16, demonstrate that male expediency, particularly when money or power was involved, could trump both societal norms and the wishes of girls or their mothers.[443]

Unlike Margaret Beaufort, Margaret Boleyn's first-born did not live to adulthood. Anne was buried at Blickling under a brass that depicts her as a young woman but which records her age with poignant precision. At just three years, eleven months and thirteen days, William and Margaret laid their tiny daughter to rest and inscribed in days the grief of her teen-age mother. Margaret was to give birth to at least ten other children and probably endure many more failed pregnancies before her death in late 1539 or 1540. If she was around 15, rather than 9, when Anne was born in 1475, then she lived to be 80, not an impossible life expectancy but an unusual one.[444] The older her age at Anne's birth, the more improbable her age at death, so although not as young as 9, it is likely that Margaret became a mother while still in her early to mid-teens and with very little agency in her fate.

As her father, Thomas, was still under attainder in 1469 and therefore not in possession of his usual landed income, he offered land from Margaret's mother's inheritance, untouched by his attainder, rather than a cash dowry. The Ormonds submitted the manor of Vera Worthy in Devon with the stipulation that, when he came of age, William add lands in Kent to the value of £20 per annum.[445] As William and Margaret exchanged their wedding vows, that was the sum total of the financial benefits the

Boleyns could expect from their marriage. William was not marrying an heiress, he was marrying the chance of an heiress. Even should the attainders on the Ormond family be reversed, it was John Butler, elder brother of Margaret's father Thomas, who would succeed to the earldom and most of the family lands. John might father a son and heir, and even if he did not, Margaret and her sister Anne could yet find themselves with a baby brother who would supplant them as their father's heir. In the end none of this happened. All attainders against the Ormond family were eventually reversed. John Butler died unmarried in the Holy Land in 1476 or 1477 and despite two marriages, Margaret and Anne were Thomas's only children. When he died in 1515, the Boleyns and the St Legers, Anne Butler's marital kin, were his English heirs.[446] This great good fortune would tumble numerous properties into the laps of Margaret and her son Thomas, including Rochford Hall and New Hall in Essex and Fulbourn in Cambridgeshire, but all that lay decades ahead.[447] As far as William knew in 1469, the estates he owned were all he would ever own unless he earned more for himself.

Through his twenties and early thirties William is conspicuously inconspicuous despite excellent connections. His sister Isabel's brother-in-law John Cheyne was the king's Master of the Horse and his own uncle-in-law John, Earl of Ormond, was back in royal favour, with Edward IV allegedly describing him as 'the goodliest knight he ever beheld and the finest gentleman in all Christendom'.[448] But if William made any effort to join his relatives at court, he left no lasting impression or mark of his success. His activities appear to have been entirely financial and familial. His mother, Anne, was reprising her role as family banker and William acted with her when in 1476 she lent £100 to his father-in-law Thomas Ormond and, in 1481, twice that sum, prudently securing repayment of the former against New Hall in Essex and the latter against Swavesey in Cambridgeshire.[449] In 1476, together with his sister Alice and her husband Sir John Fortescue, he leased the convent garden of Westminster Abbey, now more familiar as Covent Garden, for an annual rent of 100s. and a measure each of the apples and pears grown within the earthen walls.[450] He also possibly dabbled in his father's trade, again in partnership with Thomas Ormond, as there are numerous bonds of debt bearing their names. Creditors through the 1470s and 1480s include several London merchants but also William Catesby, a close aide to Richard, Duke of

Gloucester, later Richard III, and John Sapcotes, Richard's esquire of the body and receiver for the duchy of Cornwall.[451] Most are for less than £40, although the £100 owed to the mercer William Purchase suggests commercial enterprise rather than household supplies. However, the debts incurred either side of August 1485 to members of King Richard's inner circle hint at a group of friends and allies that would be as defining for William as it was destructive for his brother.

'Meet for the Court and Meet for the Country'

Tower of London, 5 July 1483

The light of a waning moon slipped through deep-set windows and was lost in the flickering candlelight of the chapel of St John the Evangelist, where William Boleyn and seventeen other soon-to-be knights silently watched the candles burn down. Between knees and cold hard stone an unfamiliar hooded robe, like the clothes of someone else, emphasised the shedding of one skin and the creation of something new. He would emerge from the two-day ritual washed clean and remade as a Knight of the Bath but the whole elaborate ceremony, wrapped in symbolism, was just one component part of the magic and mythmaking of a coronation. William had been summoned by young Edward V to come and play his part but that was a month past and it had not been the 12-year-old son of Edward IV standing beside William's linen-shrouded bath, dispensing the principles of knighthood along with the bathwater. As William lowered his head in prayer, sleepless Londoners tried to push their worries aside and forget the 4,000 armed men installed to keep the city peaceful and compliant. Just yards away, behind the massive walls of the Tower, lay Edward IV's two young sons, Edward and Richard. Perhaps sleeping soundly in their beds, perhaps already dead.[452]

Face to face, eye to eye, close enough to feel breath, Richard III stood before the esquire who was about to become Sir William Boleyn. In a position designed to emphasise the personal relationship being created between the man receiving knighthood and the man conferring it, Richard placed his arms either side of his neck and 'smite the squire in the neck, saying thus "be thee a good knight"' and kissed him.[453] With new spurs on his heels and sword girt about his waist, William had moved beyond the wealth and comfort that had come easily from his father and achieved a status that Geoffrey never managed to attain, but the past was never far away. With his black robe exchanged for the blue gown of a fledgling Knight of the Bath, he joined Richard's coronation procession as it left the Tower and made its way along Cheapside, passing yards from the door of his childhood home. He rode through a city where tailors, embroiderers, carpenters and painters had been given six days to repurpose the preparations made for Edward V and where, nearly forty years before, Geoffrey had played his own small part in the coronation procession of the now deposed, exiled and recently deceased Queen Margaret of Anjou.[454] William's first experience of the warmth of royal favour came wrapped in reminders of how quickly and profoundly the weather could change, but for the moment at least, the sun of York was shining on his fortunes.

Distinct from the more prestigious Order of the Garter, which was explicitly associated with military prowess, and more impromptu knightings on the field of battle, the Knights of the Bath were often chosen on the basis of service. While sons of the nobility would qualify through blood and family loyalty, for gentry men of no particular distinction, like William, it was a personal honour and an individual reward.[455] For many this recognised financial, judicial or administrative office, and those knighted with William were largely men who had either made themselves useful as JP, sheriff or commissioner or were at least the sons of knights, but William held no such role.[456] He was not yet even on the commission of the peace for Norfolk or Kent, the entry level of local administration. Ostensibly he had spent the last decade engaged in a little light legal training at Lincoln's Inn and amassing bonds for minor debts, so how did he find himself among this select band of knightly brothers? Who was William Boleyn to Richard III?

The answer is certainly not a close confidant, yet not a stranger, not a vital cog in government and yet eminently useful. The new king must have been at least familiar with William Boleyn as in 1480, when Richard transferred lands to his college at Middleham, the charter was witnessed by Robert Chamberlain, Gloucester's steward in East Anglia; Sir James Tyrell, a known retainer; Ralph Willoughby, an esquire of the body; George Hopton, son of Richard's future treasurer of the household; and William Boleyn.[457] As with his brother Thomas, it was the company William kept that indicates his affinity, but a name on a witness list hardly warrants a knighthood. If he was regarded as someone worth cultivating and yet apparently not directly working for Richard, perhaps he was allied with someone close to the king, and high on Richard's list of indispensable allies was Sir John Howard.

Howard, who had served Edward IV militarily, diplomatically and in his native East Anglia for decades, was rewarded for supporting Richard's kingship with the dukedom of Norfolk, left vacant by the death of his cousin John Mowbray, and with his share of the Mowbray inheritance that Edward had diverted to his younger son. This alone would surely have been enough to secure his loyalty but he was also made chief steward of the duchy of Lancaster south of the Trent and was given Richard's own post as admiral of England.[458] The latter role required deputies around the country, and for the coast of Norfolk and Suffolk, Howard chose William Boleyn.[459] There are few surviving records to tell of his activity or prominence but William was evidently known and trusted by Howard. Nineteen years previously, in 1464, John Howard had himself been appointed deputy admiral for Norfolk and Suffolk, and if he remained in post throughout, William may have been Howard's own deputy, making the reshuffle of 1483 a one-rung promotion for all concerned.[460] While William was probably only in Richard's peripheral orbit, he was useful to John Howard, and that made him useful to the new king. Of the fifty men summoned for knighthood at Edward V's abortive coronation, only thirteen made the list for Richard's. William and his father-in-law, Thomas Ormond, made the cut but his friend and brother-in-law Henry Heydon and many others were ruthlessly dropped.[461]

If William had a formal role in the Howard household, it would have been during the 1470s, and unfortunately the extensive Howard household accounts that survive have a gap between 1471 and 1481, but he certainly had friends among the wider Howard family.[462] In 1465, the year John Wyndham was betrothed to Howard's daughter Margaret, he and William were involved in a joint property transaction, and over the years the Boleyn–Wyndham connection would only strengthen. The pair acted together again in 1475 and 1486, while, in 1501, Wyndham and another of John Howard's sons-in-law, Edmund Gorges, were William's feoffees. The following year Wyndham would be executed but William was one of many guarantors required for the vast sum of over £2,800 payable by his son Thomas to recover the family lands.[463] Back in the 1480s, however, William was hoping that his carefully cultivated alliances would bear fruit, and they soon did.

On 28 June, Richard issued his first commission of the peace for Norfolk, naming the bench of JPs who would administer local justice, and a little minor housekeeping was in order since the last commission in November. Robert Ratcliffe was too closely associated with the Woodvilles and John Paston III with the recently executed William, Lord Hastings, while Anthony, Earl Rivers, was also no longer in possession of his head.[464] In their place were a collection of Richard's loyalists, including Henry, Duke of Buckingham, Sir William Calthorpe, retained by Richard in 1469, Ralph Willoughby, one of William's fellow witnesses to Gloucester's charter of 1480, and John Wyndham. Conspicuous by his absence and apparently easily forgettable, William Boleyn was not included. This, however, was quickly corrected, probably as a result of William's own petition, and three weeks later a second commission was issued with just the one crucial change. In the rush to set the cogs and wheels of normal government running, Norfolk was not the only county where it took several attempts to get everything just right.[465]

Embarrassing hiccup aside, William had arrived. A seat on the bench meant standing shoulder to shoulder with families who had been leading Norfolk society for generations. While he had first come to the notice of the Crown in the last months of Edward's life, with a commission to investigate a minor family land feud, it was only with Richard's accession that his prominence was assured.[466] The new king had need of his expertise, which, remarkably for a man who grew up miles from the sea, was apparently ships and shipping. Somehow William had become a Norfolk specialist in coastal affairs. In September 1483 he was tasked with supervising Edmund Ince and John Davy, captain of the royal ship the *Carvel of Eu*, in their role as guardians of the East Anglian fishing fleet. As far as possible, the Crown wished the convoy system that protected shipping to be self-funding, so William was instructed to search out all fishermen plying the coasts and harbours of Norfolk and Suffolk and collect appropriate contributions.[467] It was a role that already fell under the purview of his office of deputy admiral and thus played to his strengths.

On paper all looked promising. Building on the alliance with Richard that had been established by his brother's service, William had formed at least a second-hand affiliation with the man who was now king, proved his usefulness and been honoured accordingly. If Geoffrey had imagined a life for his sons, this was surely it, and given time, who knew what ripe fruit of royal patronage might fall into his lap? Time, however, was not necessarily on William's side, as earning rewards and keeping them were two different things if the king you served was not secure on his throne. Faced with rebellion and haemorrhaging supporters, Richard was looking less and less like a safe bet.

In May and December 1484, as the threat from Henry Tudor grew, William was placed on commissions of array and was faced with the same dilemma his father had faced in 1460.[468] To fight for one king or the other was not only a risk to life and limb; it could be deadly for a family's future prospects. But despite his close affiliation with the new duke of Norfolk, William seems to have avoided risking life and livelihood at Bosworth, or at least avoided an attainder. While his patron John Howard fell fighting beside his king, William kept out of trouble. His peripheral relationship to Richard's rule would have helped but so too did his post of deputy admiral. The office carried wide-ranging jurisdiction over the coast and shipping, from piracy and truce-breaking at sea to the management of convoys and safe-conducts.[469] This formal jurisdiction, combined with his commission regarding the security of local shipping, made the coast his specialist subject, so in 1485 his place was probably by the sea. Throughout that summer, coastal counties were on high alert. Francis Lovell and his ships patrolled the Channel and the knights, esquires and gentlemen of England sighed at the arrival of yet more instructions to arm. In the absence of reliable intelligence on Henry Tudor's preferred landing site, credence was given to prophecy, which ambiguously foretold Milford, taken to mean the small village of Milford opposite the western tip of the Isle of Wight.[470] Prophecy was almost right. On 7 August Henry Tudor made landfall near Milford Haven in Pembrokeshire, on the opposite side of the country from Norfolk.

The news reached Richard at Nottingham four days later and messengers were dispatched the length and breadth of England with warnings of dire consequences for those who failed to turn out for their king, but many dragged their feet, and who could blame them?[471] By 19 August John Howard and his East Anglians had arrived at the assembly point at Leicester but it is unclear whether William Boleyn was among them. In the end it did not matter. With King Richard reduced to a mangled corpse, Henry VII proved willing to recruit useful men from Richard's team sheet and only twenty-eight were attainted for fighting at Bosworth.[472] Whether by keeping his head down at home or by coming through the battle unscathed, William and his family had survived yet another regime change with limbs and livelihood intact. The years spent nurturing relations with the Howard family were, in the short term, a loss chalked up to experience but there was still opportunity under a new dynasty.

Prudence and self-preservation aside, William had much in the summer of 1485 to keep him close to home, and more than enough reasons to grieve beyond the fate of his gamble on the Howards. Following hard on the heels of the death of his sister Isabel in April, the death of William's mother, Anne, on 6 June removed a constant presence and guiding hand from his shoulder.[473] With typical foresight and no little love of dynastic exhibitionism, Anne had already planned her burial place at the heart of Norwich Cathedral. In 1463, the year of Geoffrey's death, the spire of the cathedral had been struck by lightning and the resultant fire ripped through the roof and set light to woodwork, necessitating widespread rebuilding, but the remodelling of the east end, which began after 1480, also presented an opportunity. With modernised arches, some fancy vaulting and a row of blank shields around the refaced walls, the new presbytery was set to attract some serious patronage, particularly from a certain emergent family keen to make their presence concrete.[474] On both sides of the high altar and bookending the founder's tomb, it was clearly Anne's money that wrapped this most sacred space with the iconography of her natal and marital families. Hoo quartered with St Omer were her father's arms, impaling Boleyn they proclaimed her marriage to Geoffrey and with Wychingham the marriage of her parents. The arms quartered with Boleyn are the alleged Bracton arms, but with the arms of Anne's son William, there was no need for such creativity. Hoo quartered with Boleyn impaling Butler denotes William and his wife, Margaret, although their arms were probably added by William some years later. It was within the embrace of all this armorial ancestry that Anne was laid to rest, although the stone that once held her brass has since been moved to the south-east corner of the ambulatory. At the end of the seventeenth century, however, three of the original ten shields still remained to identify her and confirm that her final journey ended on the south side of the sanctuary.[475] She had died just weeks before Henry took the throne, leaving her son to steer the family's fortunes through a new Tudor Age.

While change was ubiquitous in the summer of 1485, William apparently sailed through without shipwreck. His evident usefulness and willingness to reach accommodation with the new regime meant his appointment to commissions and crucially his role as JP continued without interruption or injury to family pride. A seat on the bench was not just a defining feature of the county gentry; it was also a source of enhanced prestige, and while removals were rare, they were keenly felt both personally and practically. Sitting in quarter session, JPs heard criminal cases, dispensed justice and enjoyed powers of inquiry into everything from cloth manufacture to the detection of counterfeit coins. In an incredibly litigious period, when the property-owning classes were as often armed with lawyers as they were with a sword, membership of the commission also served to advance the interests of family or friends, while hindering opponents.[476] It also helped that the role was not particularly onerous, with only a small portion of the total bench required at each quarter session. Men such as Sir William Yelverton, and other legal professionals, claimed their 4*d*. per day for most of the days the justices were sitting, but men such as William Boleyn rarely did. Of the 255 session days between his admission to the bench in 1483 and his death in 1505, he only sat for forty, an impressive absence rate of over 84 per cent, but William was not serving because he was dedicated to the administration of justice.[477] He was there because it was his duty and because the role embodied his family's new identity. The Boleyns had come a long way since Nicholas Boleyn stood in jeopardy of his life. Now they were amongst the men who dispensed verdicts to others, the men who made the rule of kings a practical reality.

Without local agents like William Boleyn, it would have been impossible to exercise central government in the counties close to London, never mind in the more distant corners of the realm, but with rank came responsibilities beyond the confines of the courtroom. Any king, but particularly one so recently arrived on the throne as Henry VII, needed men who could handle a sword as readily as they handled the law.

In 1487 Henry faced the first challenge to his reign, in the form of the 10-year-old son of an Oxford joiner or organ-maker named Lambert Simnel. Coached to play the role of Edward, Earl of Warwick, son of George, Duke of Clarence, and backed by the earl of Lincoln, who really was the nephew of Edward IV and Richard III, the boy and the conspiracy around him had been giving Henry a headache since the turn of the year. With the aid of Margaret of York, now Duchess of Burgundy, the rebels had procured a troop of some 2,000 mercenaries, who Henry feared would soon be stepping ashore in south-east England, so on 7 April 1487 Norfolk, Suffolk and Essex were placed on high alert. Commissions of array headed by the duke of Suffolk and earl of Oxford also demanded the service of William Boleyn, John Paston and Henry Heydon, while the king made his presence felt with a personal progress through East Anglia, celebrating Easter at Norwich.[478] Although far from groundless, the immediate alarm came to nothing. Lincoln and his mercenaries spent two weeks at sea, sailing west along the Channel and rounding the perilous tip of Land's End before making landfall in Ireland to be reunited with their child-pretender. There they gathered more supporters and Simnel was crowned in Dublin with a crown hastily borrowed from a nearby statue of the Virgin Mary. When they finally touched English soil, it was on the Furness peninsula in Lancashire, 300 miles away from Norwich, but in the meantime Henry had not been sitting still. As it became clear East Anglia was not the conspirators' port of choice, he relocated to Kenilworth Castle and began to gather his army.[479]

In the days after the issue of Henry's commission, there was some doubt about the loyalty of certain Norfolk gentry. Rumour had it that John Paston was consorting with viscountess Lovell, wife of a key conspirator, while Sir Edmund Bedyngfeld wrote that William Boleyn and Henry Heydon had travelled as far as Thetford before turning back towards home. Bedyngfeld, who had been knighted with William at Richard's coronation, was convinced William and Henry would not turn out even if the king had need of them.[480] Given William's former association with the late duke of Norfolk and his paymaster Richard III, it is hardly surprising that such gossip was given credence, but it was baseless. John Paston not only arrived to fight for his king but was knighted on the field of battle, and although William is not specifically named among those who joined the king at Kenilworth, there is every reason to suppose that he and Henry Heydon did in fact get further than Thetford.[481] Henry's victory at Bosworth may have ended his service as deputy admiral but that was a minor injury. In rebellion William would have everything to lose and nothing to gain.

As he sized up his enemies across the fields outside Stoke on the morning of 16 June, Henry too stood to lose all he had so recently acquired, but the royal army surpassed that of the rebels both 'in number of soldiers and in resources' and it would take only Henry's vanguard to rout his enemies, cut down the earl of Lincoln and demote Lambert Simnel from king-pretender to kitchen turnspit.[482] Henry could sit a little more comfortably on his throne, but for the new Tudor king it was far from the end of rebellion.

Just two years after the battle of Stoke sent Simnel to the kitchens, William was again put to work raising men to deal with revolt, this time in Yorkshire.[483] On this occasion he seems to have sent six men under the command of the earl of Oxford rather than serving himself but he had certainly assuaged any lingering doubts about his loyalty. With six years of experience on the bench under his belt and sufficient seniority to command respect, in November 1489 William followed his father into the office of sheriff, not in London or his native Norfolk, but in his adoptive county of Kent.[484] As it had been for Geoffrey, the shrievalty was a double-edged sword, honourable and prestigious but also burdensome and expensive. With no official salary and few formal perquisites, the office was, like that of JP, riddled with corruption. Backhanders, bribes and abuse of power were often the only way to recover substantial expenses and tales such as the *Gest of Robyn Hode*, which vilified the self-serving sheriff, were popular because corrupt officialdom endured even as the all-powerful sheriff declined.[485] William was more fortunate than many, as he received an ad hoc reward of £100 for his service as sheriff of Kent, but the demands of county government and military service were coming thick and fast and there was little sign of any respite.[486]

While William was focused on endless writs and the pounds, shillings and pence of the Kentish shrievalty, Henry was engaged in a little continental side hustle. His backing for the teenage Anne, Duchess of Brittany, was intended to stop the duchy being swallowed whole by her neighbour, France. On that score it was a strategy doomed to failure but it was entirely successful in making England a target of French aggression, so through 1490 and 1491 William was employed in the muster of troops and deployment of beacons to defend the coast of Norfolk.[487] There was no immediate invasion but fear remained, and when Anne of Brittany and Charles VIII of France united their territories in marriage, it did nothing to make Henry or south-coast communities any less twitchy. Even more alarmingly, the arrival in France of another pretender for England's crown gave Charles the ammunition he needed to hit Henry where it hurt.

By his own later confession, Perkin Warbeck was the son of John Osbek, comptroller of the town of Tournai, but to those who believed in him, he was Richard, Duke of York, the youngest of the princes in the Tower. Whether the story was true or false, Henry knew only too well that a few determined allies and a little foreign backing could take a kingdom. If he wanted to keep his, he must sever Warbeck from the oxygen of French support.

At around 14,000 men and 700 ships, the army assembled on the south coast in the autumn of 1492 was the largest gathered for service overseas in the fifteenth century, so unsurprisingly it swept up a number of familiar names. The ubiquitous earl of Oxford held joint command with the king's uncle Jasper, Duke of Bedford, and marching up the gangplanks onto the waiting ships were Thomas Ormond, Henry Heydon and William Boleyn.[488] By 2 October the massed ranks of the English were in Calais but that was no date to be starting a military campaign, with the weather turning and winter on the way. Undeterred, the army pushed south-west to the barred gates of Boulogne, where they besieged the town and proceeded to bombard the inhabitants into submission and Charles VIII into action. His response was simply to pay the English to go away, a huge annual pension of 50,000 French crowns. It was an offer that Henry, after some deliberation, could not refuse but Charles's promise to withhold future support from Warbeck was just as valuable. Denied both a glorious victory and the spoils of war, but without a sword being drawn, William and the rest of the army traipsed back home, where the commons were counting how many taxes they still had to pay to fund Henry's *tour de Boulogne*.[489]

At least William could go home, pack his armour away and put his feet up for a while. Other than a judicial commission of oyer and terminer in 1495, the Crown would make no additional demands upon his military skills or his administrative capabilities for the next five years and he had a chance to deal with his own affairs.[490] In 1495 he sold all the family property in London, including his childhood home, bringing to an end the Boleyns' links with a city that had given them so much and of which his father had been so proud. The new owner of Milk Street was, appropriately enough, another up-and-coming mercer, Richard Lakyn, who supplied green velvet copes embroidered with portcullises and other vestments for Henry VII's chapel, as well as 240 garters for garter robes.[491] William also continued to expand the Boleyns' interests around Blickling, renting lands from the prior of Norwich on a favourable ten-year term.[492] He is recorded as owning swans on the river at Blickling, identified by his personal mark of three semi-circles, and by his death he had also acquired the Norfolk manors of Wickmere, Gowthorp and Fretenham, but before then the armour had to come back out of the coffer.[493] Henry had not seen the last of Perkin Warbeck or of rebellion, and therefore neither had William.

Ousted from French territory under the terms of the Peace of Étaples, Warbeck found backing, as had Lambert Simnel, from the hand of Margaret of York, Duchess of Burgundy, and for the next three years he remained at large, popping up for skirmishes at Deal or in Ireland, but essentially elusive until in late 1495 he turned up in Scotland. James IV proved happy to welcome him as Richard, Duke of York, to find him a noble bride, in the form of Katherine Gordon, and in September 1496, to join him in a six-day border raid on northern England. Warbeck turned back when the populace failed to rally to his standard but James burnt and pillaged his way as far as Heton Castle, 9 miles south-west of Berwick, and in retaliation Henry demanded an army even larger than that he had led into France. Destined for Scotland were 20,000 land forces and 5,000 naval, conveyed in seventy ships and paid for by a £120,000 grant of taxation ratified by parliament in January 1497. Once again the tax collectors of England were empowered to delve into the purses of everyone from peer to peasant, but when the local provost entered the small Cornish village of St Keverne on the Lizard peninsula, the unstoppable force of royal taxation met the immovable granite of Cornish resolve. Michael Joseph, a blacksmith, or *An Gof* in his native tongue, said 'no' and so did all his neighbours and all of their neighbours. Rebellion erupted out of Cornwall, gathering support from labourers, craftsmen, gentry and even Baron Audley along the road. By the end of May the rebels were at Exeter and by June at Wells, from where they turned east through Winchester and Guildford, bearing down on London with a force 10,000 strong. William was soon climbing back into his saddle.

With an army already at his back, Henry was temporarily uncertain where to point it but decided that the Scots would have to wait as the immediate threat came from the other end of his realm. By 16 June he had caught up with the rebels on the outskirts of London and was lodged at Lambeth Palace while his vast army of 25,000 men set up camp on nearby St George's Field. Yet again William Boleyn was in the field for his king but this time he was joined by his son Thomas, aged 20 and getting his first taste of army life.[494] Four miles away at Deptford the rebel camp numbered an impressive 15,000 but they were vastly and hopelessly outnumbered.

With the sun barely an hour over the horizon, on 17 June the two sides met on a plain near Blackheath and, if they were once again under the command of that East Anglian stalwart the earl of Oxford, the Boleyn men would have been in the second charge against the rebel host. It was swift, brutal and almost entirely one sided. The Cornish had been marching for weeks, were poorly armed and many lost heart when it came to the reality of facing their king on the battlefield. By the time Henry reached Blackheath from Lambeth it was all over. Thomas had seen his first blood spilt and William had seen his last.[495]

While Henry had been sorting out his Cornish troubles, he had not been getting any closer to dealing with his Warbeck problem, but as the autumn storms blew in, the king finally had the elusive pretender in his sights. On 7 September Warbeck made landfall on English soil, stepping ashore at Whitesand Bay on Cornwall's Atlantic coast, hoping to mop up residual resentment. For the second time in four months, rebellion swept out of Cornwall, but this time Henry was ready. Once again vast numbers of men were recruited but William and Henry Heydon, with an eye to the future and their own old age, opted to dispatch their sons, so it was the two cousins, Thomas Boleyn and John Heydon, who were paid wages and travel costs to bring their retinues to the king.[496] It was a changing of the guard and probably their first experience of leading men without paternal supervision but it would not prove too challenging. By the time Warbeck and his allies reached Taunton, they were dispirited and ill-prepared to face a far superior royal force. Under cover of darkness the pretender abandoned his followers and fled towards sanctuary at Beaulieu Abbey in Hampshire, from where he was efficiently extracted and forced to renounce all previous claims of royalty. It had taken six long years but Henry had finally put an end to 'Perkin's folly'.[497]

At the age of 46, William must have been more than ready to retire his sword arm from active service and bequeath those duties to his son, but age brought experience for which the king still had use. In 1499 William was appointed to the joint shrievalty of Norfolk and Suffolk, although this time there would be no gratuity of £100 and his personal balance sheet looked far less healthy. A year after the end of his tenure, he still owed £776 15*d*. to the Exchequer, and while most of the debt was cleared as payments came in, by 1502 he was still short. Such matters rarely escaped the notice of Henry VII's crack team of debt enforcers, with the result that William was bound by personal obligation to pay the outstanding sum of £20.[498] By that stage the settlement of his debt probably came out of his own pocket, and having held office twice, he was clearly ready to add 'sheriff' to the list of things from which he would like to retire. In April 1502 he secured a free pass excusing him from the shrievalty of any county, although the demands of his other legal or administrative duties continued until his death.[499] It was perhaps some recompense that the Crown also required a more congenial form of service. On the most important ceremonial occasions, the greater gentry were expected to appear, dressed to impress in velvets and silks and dripping in gold chains such as the two livery 'collars of esses' William bequeathed to his son. This nobility in numbers enabled the king to exhibit the wealth, might and grandeur of his realm and William would regularly play his part.

His first invitation to a grand court celebration came in 1494 for the creation of 3-year-old Prince Henry as duke of York and it was a glittering extravaganza. From beginning to end, the festivities covered sixteen days, from the procession through London's packed streets on 29 October, in which the young prince impressed by riding unaided, to the final day of the tournament on 13 November. Amongst a 'great press of knights and esquires' in the parliament chamber at Westminster, William listened to the bishop of Exeter read aloud the letters patent that made the infant prince a royal duke, before joining a formal procession followed by days of feasting and merry-making. With his brother-in-law and lifelong friend Henry Heydon also in attendance, William finally had a chance to forget the responsibilities of his position and enjoy the perks. These festivities, however, would pale into insignificance beside the pageantry arranged for the reception and marriage of Katherine of Aragon and Henry VII's eldest son, Prince Arthur.[500]

15

Father and Son

London, November 1501

For two long years London's traders and craftsmen had answered Henry's call to arms, taking in hand not sword or halberd but saw, hammer and paintbrush. Directed by king and council but co-ordinated by the city, they would craft both the practical necessities and the propaganda pageantry that would make Arthur's marriage to Katherine the international dynastic triumph Henry intended, and their 'to-do' list was lengthy. The six pageants alone demanded a castle with a real portcullis, a mechanical representation of the zodiac, a hand-cranked elevator system that propelled three children upward towards an image of Arthur and an endless array of red roses, carved dragons and white harts. At St Paul's and the bishop's palace, 4,300ft of plank board was employed to build a platform, rooms were refitted and a furnace and forge set up to make ironwork, while Henry blew £14,000 on jewels.[501] It was intended to be the wedding of the century and anyone who was anyone would be there.

This minutely choreographed royal extravaganza had so many moving parts that detailed written plans had to be produced, but repeated interventions by everything from the weather to capricious mariners prompted frequent revision and improvisation. Initially expected to arrive via Gravesend, Katherine was to be welcomed at the Tower by Prince Henry with a large reception committee, including William

Boleyn and a clutch of East Anglians whose presence probably owed much to the organisational input of the earl of Oxford as Lord Great Chamberlain. Katherine, however, sailed away from her homeland on 17 August 1501 and straight into the teeth of a violent summer storm that left her ships limping back to Laredo with broken masts trailing canvas and tackle. Repairs completed, they made a second attempt on the Bay of Biscay but were intercepted by the Devonian captain Stephen Brett, one of several experienced mariners sent by Henry to guide the princess safely to England. Meanwhile, the plans for Katherine's reception had been quickly revised around a landing at Southampton but Brett guided the Spaniards on the route he knew best, into his home port of Plymouth, where nothing had been prepared and the West Country gentry turned out to offer hospitality on the hoof. Katherine then made stately progress through southern England towards Lambeth. There was an impromptu and rather stilted meeting with her future husband and his impatient father in Hampshire but her official welcome had been relocated, for a second time, to St George's Field, where, four years earlier, William had camped with Henry's army. In the end it took place at Kingston, where the duke of Buckingham appeared with Prince Henry and a party of 300–400 attendants that probably included William Boleyn and the rest of the original Tower reception committee. Thereafter, and probably much to the relief of the organisers, events reverted to the pre-arranged schedule and William fell in line for Katherine's formal entry procession into London. Over London Bridge on freshly sanded streets, through cheering crowds held back by barriers, they made their way to St Paul's past six pageants of welcome laden with allegory and symbolism. While most would have understood the basic message, Tudor roses, heraldic beasts and St Catherine with her wheel being common currency, the more complex allusions must have gone right over the heads of many observers. The convoluted speeches of the actors may have clarified matters for those close enough to hear but crucially it all looked and sounded spectacular.[502]

The marriage ceremony itself was scheduled for Sunday, 14 November, and both William and his son Thomas were present in St Paul's to watch Katherine, clad in white satin, gold, pearls and precious stones, enter on the arm of 10-year-old Prince Henry to be joined in marriage to his older brother, Arthur. Thomas's name was not included in the published running order but by his own later testimony he was certainly present in the cathedral and probably throughout the festivities.[503] Over the last years of his father's life and beyond, the name of Thomas Boleyn would become ever more prominent.

Although much about the early career of William's eldest son is uncertain, he started, as his father did before him, with basic legal training. Around 1495 he enrolled at the New Inn, one of the inns of chancery, where he would have been a contemporary of Thomas More, but he elected to follow this with a courtly rather than a county career.[504]

At the death of Henry's beloved queen, Elizabeth, in 1502, an extensive list of all the officers and servants who received cloth includes neither William nor Thomas Boleyn, but by 1509 Thomas was an esquire of the body and was issued with black cloth for the king's funeral.[505] This is the first reference to Thomas holding any formal appointment at court but such success was not achieved without a consistent and long-term effort to gain the favour of the king. Perhaps his first opportunity came during Henry's summer progress through a drought-ridden East Anglia in 1498, when the court spent 22 August at 'Master Boleyn's' place at Blickling.[506] To the unnamed clerk who wrote these words on behalf of his master, John Heron, Treasurer of the Chamber, this clearly meant Master Thomas Boleyn, as William's knighthood would not have been so casually forgotten, but it was likely no coincidence that William Boleyn found himself elsewhere.[507] The decision to let Thomas, rather than his father, welcome the king to Blickling was probably a strategic one aimed at kickstarting his career, and the Boleyns were not the only family who had the same idea. The 'Master Cotton' who hosted the court on 29 August could have been the elderly Thomas Cotton, esq., of Landwade, Cambridgeshire, but it is far more likely to have been his son Robert, who, like Thomas Boleyn, was 21 in 1498 and being given a chance to shine.[508] The Boleyn heir was being primed to become the public face of the family and while some jobs, such as the shrievalty of Norfolk and Suffolk, still required the weight of William's years and experience, Thomas was given every opportunity to practise the accomplishments of nobility. Learning to lead a body of fighting men and to play the charming host were essential skills but nothing would do more to help or hinder his future prospects than his choice of wife. While William yet lived, Thomas was most certainly not in possession of a fortune, so the son had to look to his father, and William sought to revive an old relationship that had never been forgotten but had been, unavoidably, put on ice.

At Bosworth, where William's former boss, John Howard, Duke of Norfolk, was killed beside Richard, his son Thomas Howard did not escape unscathed. Seriously injured, he was captured on the battlefield and both father and son were attainted, but Howard presented the new king with a dilemma. Was the bird he had caught a useful tool fit for retraining or a beast that might turn on its master? Was he prepared to accept a master at all? The safest course was to cage him and so Thomas spent over three years immured in the Tower of London. During the revolt of Lambert Simnel and the earl of Lincoln in 1487, he was offered a chance of escape and his refusal probably helped to convince Henry he could be a loyal asset. Release finally came in January 1489, along with restoration to the earldom of Surrey and to those lands not his inheritance from his father. When rebellion erupted in Yorkshire, he travelled north with the royal army, and when Henry returned south, he was left behind as the king's lieutenant in the north, with either the opportunity to prove himself or the rope to hang himself. It quickly became apparent it would be the former as over the next ten years he demonstrated military skill, political acumen and an ability to heal the wounds of King Richard's former heartland. Gradually he recovered his father's lands until, in 1499, peace with Scotland made his presence in the north less vital and he was recalled to court, where he fell straight back into bed with the Boleyns.[509]

Surrey was growing closer to the king every day and his eldest son, Thomas, had recently married the queen's sister Anne, so a marriage into the Howard family not only spelled a return to former allegiances for the Boleyns, it also promised the kind of power and patronage that they may have been hoping for in 1483. Times had changed, however, and William was no longer a little-noticed member of the Norfolk gentry. When Surrey returned south in 1499, he found his father's former deputy installed as sheriff and Thomas Boleyn on his way to a career at court. Finally the Boleyns were poised to cash in on their Howard connections.

The prospective bride was Surrey's eldest daughter, Elizabeth Howard. When her father was imprisoned after Bosworth, she, her siblings and her mother sought refuge on the Isle of Sheppey, where an escape to France could be more easily effected, but when he was released and posted to the north, the family decamped to Sheriff Hutton Castle in Yorkshire, where Elizabeth would have spent the rest of her childhood. There they were later joined by the poet John Skelton, who probably wrote his 1,600 lines of self-congratulatory verse *The Garland of Laurel* at Sheriff Hutton around 1495. In it Skelton describes the ladies in the sewing circle of the countess of Surrey who embroider him a laurel wreath. Skelton was never going to be anything less than complimentary but the unmarried Elizabeth and her younger sister Muriel are themselves garlanded with praise. Elizabeth is a maiden of both virtue and learning whom 'Dame Nature' 'hath freshly embeautied with many a goodly sort of womanly feature' while her younger sister, on the cusp of womanhood, is all bashful blushes and 'roses red of hue with lilies white'.[510] With the two families resident hundreds of miles apart, it is unlikely Thomas Boleyn knew Elizabeth as a child, but if Skelton is to be believed, she was a beauty upon whom any suitor might 'set his whole delight'. If she truly was learned (and her mother's patronage of a poet such as Skelton would suggest so), she would have made a good match for the highly educated Thomas. Later praised by Erasmus for being outstandingly learned, Thomas's fluent Latin and excellent French would prove to be the foundation of his diplomatic career.[511]

Over the years much ink has been expended attempting to determine the birth dates of Thomas's children and, by association, the date of his marriage. Elizabeth's sister Muriel was certainly married by 1500 to John Grey, Viscount Lisle, as when the dowager viscountess Lisle wrote her will in August, she referred to 'my lady Muriel, the lady Lisle'.[512] Her elder sibling may have married before her, but possibly only shortly before, as the betrothal of both these eligible young ladies to families based in southern England was probably associated with the Howards' move south in 1499. Except for a brief period in 1495, when he attended the marriage of his son, Thomas Howard seems to have been constantly resident in the north.[513]

William Boleyn settled Elizabeth's jointure in July 1501, by which time she was already his daughter-in-law, and the timing is almost certainly related to the payment of dowry by her father over the previous months. These two sides of a marriage settlement were inextricably connected. A bride's dowry was usually provided in instalments and the settlement of jointure was dependent on the payment of all or an agreed part of these sums. In 1495, for example, Sir John Arundell married Elizabeth, the daughter of Thomas, Marquess of Dorset, and under the terms of the marriage settlement, the bride's father agreed to pay a dowry of 1,000 marks in three instalments: 200 marks before the wedding, 200 at Christmas after the jointure was settled and the balance the following May. Equally, failure to complete payment of a dowry would nullify the unfortunate bride's claim to her agreed jointure.[514] Fortunately for Elizabeth there can have been no doubt that her father was good for the money and William duly completed his side of the bargain. He settled on Elizabeth a life interest in the manors of Carbroke and Holkham in Norfolk, plus Pashley and a handful of other lands in Sussex, with immediate effect, as well as a life interest in the Kentish manors of Hever, Kemsing and Sele, although this was deferred until after his own death.[515]

As William advanced in years, he gradually withdrew from duties that would take him far from the comfort of home, and his son Thomas assumed his place. The marriage of Arthur and Katherine would be William's last recorded appearance at a state ceremonial occasion, so in July 1503, when Henry's 13-year-old daughter Margaret set out for Scotland to marry James IV, it was with Thomas Boleyn in her train. The earl of Surrey with his countess headed proceedings, accompanied by 'many ladies and gentlemen very nobly arrayed' in velvet, damask, cloth of gold and 'great chains', and amongst the 'fair company' were 'Thomas Boleyn, son and heir of Sir William Boleyn' and 'John Heydon, son and heir of Sir Harry Heydon'.[516] Given the close friendship of their fathers, these two cousins must have grown up together and were doubtless having a fine time all the way to the boar's head feast in Edinburgh.

Despite still being described by reference to his father, Thomas was moving out of William's shadow.[517] He had been married for several years and, by his own account, Elizabeth gave him a child every year in the early days of their marriage, so he was already a father several times over.[518] What Thomas and Elizabeth really needed was a home of their own but they apparently did not find it in Kent. Writing from Hever in 1538 and discussing the theft of hawks by some of his servants, Thomas declared that in the thirty-three years he had 'dwelt in this country [county]' he knew not 'of any such ill act done by any of my folks'.[519] This would date Thomas's residence in Kent to 1505, which corresponds with Elizabeth's marriage settlement. Had William intended his son and daughter-in-law to have immediate use of Hever, he surely would not have reserved it to himself for life.

In 1502, William was added to the bench of JPs in Kent, apparently suggesting that Thomas could not use Hever because his parents had moved in, perhaps with the intention of leaving the many chambers of Blickling to their son and grandchildren, but all is not as it appears.[520] Although the surviving evidence is patchy, William never claimed his 4*d.* per day for any session of the peace in Kent during the two years where payments are recorded and his name does not appear on any of the indictments sent up to King's Bench from the county.[521] When in residence in Kent, he may have been active outside the quarter sessions, particularly exercising a JP's power over riot and forced entry. His experience may have been useful as the stability of Kent was gradually eroded by the slow slide into bankruptcy of Sir Richard Guildford and the consequent encroachment of his rival Lord Bergavenny. If so then it was, perhaps, the king who placed William on the bench as a steadying hand rather than the appointment being made at William's request to reflect a change in his normal residence.[522]

In contrast to Kent, there are multiple sources of evidence showing that William was active in Norfolk to the end of his life. He was appointed to deliver or try the prisoners at Norwich gaol in November 1502, and again in February 1505, and those at East Derham in June 1504.[523] He also continued, if intermittently, to claim payment for his work as a JP in Norfolk: two days in 1501, one day in 1503 and six days in 1505, the joint busiest year of his life. One of the cases from 1505 involved a steward of the earl of Surrey and it is not impossible that he would have travelled back to Norfolk to play his part in protecting the family interest, but Howard involvement cannot account for the other five days and there is no need to do so.[524] William himself made it perfectly clear where he was living. As he lay dying, he requested that his executors provide for 'a conveyance of my said sinful body from my manor of Blickling into the said cathedral church in Norwich'.[525] But if William was at Blickling, Thomas and Elizabeth cannot have been there as well. Multigenerational households were not popular with those who had the wealth and property to avoid them, particularly when they involved two married women and a nursery of small children. With a host of servants to do the hard labour, household management for gentry women was akin to running a small business, with staff to manage, stock-flow to monitor and accounts to be kept, and it was fundamental to female identity and power. Ideally a household had one, not two, women at the helm and on her marriage Elizabeth would have expected to fulfil the role she had been trained for, not a secondary position.

It would appear, therefore, that William made no particular concession to the marriage of his eldest son. Throughout his life he must have split his time between Norfolk and Kent. The Weald offered far better hunting and the Heydons would not have seen fit to build a house down the road from Hever had William not been regularly in residence. All available evidence suggests this was a pattern he had no intention of changing just because his eldest son had married. Neither was he prepared to give up any more income than necessary. In 1536 Thomas responded to a request from Jane, widow of his son George, for an increase in her income. Her plea was granted but not without Thomas grumpily recalling that in the early years of his marriage, before his father's death, he had to make do with an income of only £50.[526] He was probably not exaggerating. Surviving rentals from the first half of the sixteenth century for the manors of Pashley, Holkham and Carbroke, which were settled on Elizabeth Howard at her marriage, list annual rents of £30 16s. 9d. but those for both Holkham and Carbroke are incomplete.[527] If allowance is made for these omissions, it is likely that the £50 income Thomas never forgot came from Elizabeth's jointure and that it was the only revenue allowed to them from the Boleyn estates. William, it seems, was a father entirely capable of putting his own interests first.

Where then, did Thomas and Elizabeth call home between their marriage and William's death? Rochford Hall in Essex did not come into Boleyn hands until the death of Thomas Ormond in 1515 and he certainly remained in residence there until the end of his life. Amongst the Ormond papers are various records of improvements carried out or supplies purchased for his household and his will refers to his goods and chattels at Rochford.[528] The two small brass crosses at Hever and Penshurst commemorating Henry and Thomas Boleyn, sons of Sir Thomas Boleyn, are not particularly enlightening. The brasses themselves must date from after Thomas's knighthood in 1509 but that does not determine the boys' dates of death, although that of Thomas at Penshurst is far more likely to have occurred after his father became keeper of Penshurst in 1522.[529] In 1506 Thomas was described as being 'late of Blickling', in theory implying that he had been resident there previously but had recently moved. However, in this case the chancery clerk inserted *nuper*, or 'late', before the name of every person not a peer, probably to cover his back should there be any challenge on the identity of the men later.[530] Whether he lived there or not, Blickling belonged to Thomas and he would always be 'of Blickling'. Many years later, when Anne Boleyn and Henry VIII's daughter Elizabeth sat upon England's throne, Mathew Parker, Archbishop of Canterbury, described himself as a 'poor countryman' of the queen's mother, implying that Anne was born, as he was, in Norfolk. But the Boleyns were forever a Norfolk family and this would have been true regardless of where Anne's mother went into labour, particularly when Parker wished to advertise a loose connection to the queen's family.[531]

A clue lies in the pardon roll of 1509. Here, Thomas was described as being of Blickling, Hever, the New Inn without Temple Bar and [Luton] Hoo, Bedfordshire, these being the residences by which he was known.[532] Those obtaining pardons made an effort to ensure this list of aliases was comprehensive so that the pardon could be employed in any future prosecution, no matter how they were identified. Fathers' names, trades and professions, job titles and official appointments were all routinely included. It would appear, therefore, that Thomas and Elizabeth lived in one of these four places in the early years of their marriage, as another residence, within the previous ten years, would probably have been mentioned. Elizabeth could hardly move into an Inn of Chancery, and had the couple rented a house in London, the city would likely have been named as a separate residence since the Inns of Court were not technically part of London.[533] If William was still using Blickling and Hever, and if Thomas was bearing the cost of a household separate from that of his father (as his complaint about having to live on only £50 would suggest), then Luton Hoo has to be considered as a possible first home for Thomas, Elizabeth and their rapidly growing family. While seemingly unwilling to disrupt his established mode of living, William was, perhaps, happy to allow use of a more distant residence in a county less central to his life.

Unfortunately there is no record of the house at Luton Hoo between 1319, when Robert Hoo leased it to his mother for £10, and the early seventeenth century, when Sir Robert Napier built a new house.[534] In 1430 Thomas Hoo was sheriff of Bedfordshire and in 1434 he swore the oath not to maintain malefactors as a resident of the county, so there must have been a suitable house at Luton Hoo at this date.[535] Seventy years later, there was apparently somewhere to unpack the linen as, whether before or after his father's death, Thomas apparently lived there, at least temporarily, before 1509. It was around 35 miles to Whitehall, no more than a full day of travel for Thomas, as he pursued his studies at the New Inn or advanced his career at court.

For William, however, there was no question that Norfolk was home. It was where his family heritage lay, it was where his mother lay and, when he himself died on 10 October 1505, it was where he chose to be laid to rest.[536] Gathered around his bedside as the priest prepared his mind and soul for death were his closest family, with his sister Anne and son-in-law John Shelton acting as witnesses and his son Thomas as an executor.[537] With concern for the widowhood of his wife, William arranged that Margaret would continue to live 'within the site or mansion of my said manor of Blickling conveniently to be chosen there and appointed at the pleasure of the same Dame Margaret'. Alternatively, she was to have her husband's 'place in Norwich to dwell in for term of her life', which would have been the house his mother acquired during her own widowhood.[538] With both freedom of choice and a particular focus on Norwich, William may have been inspired by the experience of his mother's later years, when she had access to homes in London, Norwich and at Blickling, or by the arrangements put in place by Henry Heydon for William's sister Anne the previous year.[539] Margaret's widowhood would be a long one and in her later years she was at Hever with her son, but in the early days she may have used any of these Norfolk homes, enjoying, as her sister-in-law did, freedom to choose.

Despite his long residence at Blickling, William rejected his father's chapel and chose instead to be laid to rest next to his mother in Norwich Cathedral, swayed perhaps both by the status of the site and by filial affection. His tomb was placed in an elevated position in the eastern arch on the south side of the presbytery, resting on top of the Bozoun chapel, which sits on the lower floor level of the ambulatory with its back to the presbytery.[540] Such a location seems improbable today but by 1500 the floor level of the presbytery had been raised quite considerably, and with three further steps up to the level of William's tomb, it would have sat comfortably, if very prominently, within the archway. On top of his altar tomb a 'flat stone' displayed all the familiar armorial devices of his parents and other lost shields must have displayed the Butler arms, but the inscription, recorded in 1680, was succinct and sparing:

Here lies the body of William Boleyn, knight, who died 10 October 1505, upon whose soul may God have mercy, Amen.[541]

At some point between 1799 and 1875, the presbytery floor level was lowered again, which must have resulted in the loss of the steps up to William's tomb and ultimately its removal, as well as the relocation of Anne's grave stone, but for several centuries it sat on high within the cathedral's most sacred space.[542] Contemporaries would have been quite literally unable to overlook the intended focus of their prayers and William ensured there would be plenty of these. Three priests were dedicated to the remembrance of his soul in the cathedral for twenty years but William also continued what was rapidly becoming a family tradition of endowing prayers at Cambridge. An additional priest was to perform the same twenty-year routine of masses and prayers at the university and William also followed his father's lead in funding public preaching. One of Norwich's friars, a doctor Hugh, was to 'preach the word of almighty God within the city of Norwich' for the next four years, but unlike Geoffrey, whose final wishes included vast charitable provision, William's will included almost none.[543] There are legacies for the church at Blickling, for the Norwich friars and a generous 5s. for every householder at Blickling, but little else, and an overall spend that was just pocket change compared to the sums dispensed by Geoffrey. A testator's charity, however, was never purely altruistic. It also secured vital prayers for the soul struggling through purgatory, so it is unlikely William was truly neglectful of his own post-mortem self-interest. The lengthy list of saints in the preamble to his will indicates he was nothing if not a good Catholic and as such he must surely have made prior charitable arrangements with his executors.

What William left behind was a family primed to succeed. The old Howard association that had seen the Boleyns through civil war and dynastic change had become one of blood that would help shape the lives of the next two generations. Geoffrey's interest in clerical education and the bookish interests of William's sister Anne and her husband had come to fruition in the education William provided to his son Thomas, whose diplomatic and courtly career owed much to a proficiency with French and Latin that his father must have facilitated. Anne was still a toddler in the nursery when her grandfather died but she too learnt to 'speak French well', first with Margaret of Austria and later in France, where she also acquired the continental, cosmopolitan sophistication that would help to capture a king and transport the family far away from William's county-based life-style.[544] With the exception of the Howard connection, William had not really been a change-maker. He had lived the life imagined and prepared by his father and mother, having been parachuted into the greater gentry by Geoffrey's astonishing success. In Norfolk his wealth and relationships gave him personal influence, while his offices made him an essential tool of royal government, but he perhaps lacked the inclination to take on the vast workload of royal administrators like Sir Thomas Lovell or Sir Robert Southwell and he was consequently no high flyer showered with Crown offices, sinecures or grants. Neither, however, was he a wanton spendthrift or the family fool and his steady, secure custodianship conveyed his son's patrimony in robust good health. It would be Thomas who was the natural courtier, the overachiever and, together with his daughter, the true heir to his grandfather's ambition.

Epilogue

The well-worn tale of Thomas Boleyn and his world-famous daughter has been told many times and in many ways. Despite the passage of centuries, Anne's spirit, her triumph and her brutal death have lost none of their power to capture hearts and minds. There is, however, little to be gained by re-visiting those much-thumbed pages or the well-travelled corridors of Henry's court, other than to view those years as part of a much longer story.

Through Anne's courtship, coronation and walk to the scaffold, one woman endured. Married to Geoffrey's son William while still a child, Anne's grandmother, Margaret, lived through it all, watching from the side-lines as her family rose and fell, losing sons and grandchildren before her. She was, however, probably only intermittently able to engage with either the pride or the pain. From 1519, three years before Anne made her first recorded appearance at court in the *Château Vert* pageant, Margaret was gripped by an unnamed madness. Touched with 'diverse infirmities and sicknesses', she became 'a lunatic, frenetic, insane and not of sound mind', although her illness was not constant and in her 'lucid intervals' she may have understood what was happening to her family.[545] This was the language of the civil authorities, not physicians, but the words used were precise and specific to the behaviour and temperament of the person being described. *Insanus* was a fairly neutral term and *lunaticus* indicated an illness that was cyclical, having good and bad periods, but *freneticus* denoted behaviour towards the active or violent end of the spectrum. It implied a loss of control, either physically or emotionally, and was rarely used to describe mentally ill landowners, being more often associated with violent criminals.[546] Although Margaret's age might suggest a disorder of old age, it is highly unlikely she was suffering from a degenerative condition such as dementia, given that her illness included lucid intervals and given that she lived with her symptoms for twenty years, surviving until at least her late seventies. It is more probable that she had some form of relapsing, remitting condition, of which the most common is bipolar disorder, which would also fit with the unusual use of 'frenetic' to describe her behaviour.[547] For decades Margaret would have needed care, help and understanding, and while he simultaneously managed his own career, a tetchy monarch and his daughter's rise, it was Margaret's eldest son, Thomas, who saw to her care.

Thomas and his mother had long enjoyed a close and trusting relationship. In 1515, on the death of her father, Margaret wrote to her eldest boy, relying on his judgement in the pursuit of her inheritance 'as though it were [her] own deed'. She offered to come up to London if necessary but, already in her fifties, she was not keen to 'labour so far' if Thomas could do well enough without her.[548] As her health declined, she must have become ever more reliant upon him to arrange both personal nursing and the financial management of her estates, which raised some concern as Thomas came to realise his vulnerable mother would likely outlive him. Shortly before his death, he granted her an annuity of 400 marks out of the Ormond lands in Essex, probably to ensure she was well cared for when he was no longer around.[549]

When Thomas died on 12 March 1539, Margaret lost her estate manager and so came to the attention of the Crown.[550] As she was a landowner incapable of managing her own estates, the king had an interest in both her person and her property and could take both into a form of wardship similar to that of an underage heir.[551] This prerogative right was rarely exercised when there were trusted family to assume responsibility but in September the escheator stepped in, preceded by Thomas Cromwell, exercising the king's interest. Just days after Thomas Boleyn's death, Cromwell sent agents to Hever but they were under strict instructions to assist in 'entertaining the old lady Boleyn there in best wise to her comfort'.[552] For Margaret, the sudden change in routine must have been distressing, and although efforts were made to put her at ease, it was probably all too much.

She had already lived far beyond her expected years and by 20 March 1540 she had joined her son Thomas.[553] These two deaths in quick succession would trigger a gradual break-up of the Boleyn estates that had been so carefully collected by Geoffrey and his heirs.

William and Margaret Boleyn's improbably large brood meant Thomas had three brothers, and while William was a priest, James and Edward were married men. Had the family's luck on the fertility lottery held, both might have produced an heir to the family fortune, but those charmed days were well and truly over. James died in 1561, leaving no surviving children, and Edward pre-deceased him as father to a clutch of daughters. Just as on their way up the Boleyns had benefitted from the male-line failures of other families, their lands were dispersed via heiresses or sales to enrich other gentry families or new aspirational self-starters.

Thomas did still have one surviving daughter, and Mary was his heir under common law to the unentailed lands of her father and grandmother.[554] Mary, however, was not her father's heir for any entailed lands, particularly the family's core property acquired by Geoffrey and entailed on the male line by his will. A sizeable chunk of these Norfolk manors went to George's widow, Jane, in jointure before reverting, after her death, to Thomas's brother James.[555] Over the coming years he would sell almost everything apart from Blickling as he sought to consolidate an estate around there and the family's roots in Salle.[556] Mulbarton and Holkham were sold to John and Thomas Gresham, scions of the mercer-merchant family to be reckoned with in early Tudor London. Both William Boleyn and Thomas Gresham had grown up under the same roof on London's Milk Street, as Gresham's father, Richard, leased the Boleyns' old home.[557]

In Kent, James gave the manors of Hever, Kemsing and Sele, plus £200 cash, to the king in return for Moor Hall in Salle and five other Norfolk manors, mostly in the vicinity of Salle and Blickling.[558] But James's brother William had also inherited an interest in the Boleyns' Kentish manors and he was far from satisfied with the compensation arranged by James. The result was an unpleasant court case that revealed these two brothers had once been so close they planned to share a house in Salle. But whatever affection had existed was irretrievably broken as the family that pulled together so well on their way up resorted to squabbling over fractions of manors on their way down.[559]

In 1553 James settled Hevingham, Cawston, Kerdiston and Reepham, the former Crown manors he had received in exchange for Hever, on his great-niece Princess Elizabeth, but that still left Blickling.[560] The true Boleyn heartlands could not go to a Boleyn but they would at least descend to a relative. James granted the reversion of both to John Clere, the son of his sister Alice, in return for the astonishing price of £3,000, although he would not live to enjoy his purchase. By James's death in 1561, John's son Edward Clere still had £400 to pay but that would have to be settled with James's executors. After more than a hundred years, Blickling had become Clere territory.[561]

To Eric Ives, Anne Boleyn was that rarity, 'the self-made woman' who succeeded by virtue of her own abilities rather than by wealth or family.[562] It is certainly true that Anne forged a path armed with her own personal brand of charm, intellect and acumen. No brother or father could write that future for her; it was hers and hers alone. When Anne is the beginning, middle and end of the story, her pedigree and nobility are a given, but this is a view from the sixteenth century that pre-supposes a world in which the Boleyns were naturally and inevitably creatures of the royal court. From the perspective of the fourteenth century, it is clear this was never a foregone conclusion. Without the hard work, the triumphs and even the failures of the generations who went before her, the great-great-granddaughter of Norfolk yeoman Geoffrey Boleyn would have been more at home curtseying to the king as he rode through the county on progress to Walsingham than exchanging marriage vows. Even for his son, Geoffrey, life in London could have turned out very differently. For most boys who went through apprenticeship, particularly in a lesser craft like Geoffrey, the future was one of small-scale business and perhaps a shop of their own. Only a minority of London's citizens became successful merchants and even fewer, perhaps as little as 10 per cent, were able to translate that into the landed foundations of a gentry lifestyle.[563] Even then merchant outcomes varied. There was a world of difference between buying one manor and catapulting the next generation into county leadership and the shrievalty of three counties as Geoffrey did.

Then Geoffrey's son Thomas died in the days after Barnet and the Boleyns nearly succumbed to the same fate that destroyed the ambitions of other city families. The early death of an heir spelled the end for many merchant dynasties. Richard Whittington was not blessed with one, never mind two, healthy sons and his vast wealth went to enrich city life rather than future Whittingtons. Even surviving sons and grandsons did not necessarily equal success, as demonstrated by Simon Eyre's efforts to curtail and control his profligate son from beyond the grave.[564] However, had Geoffrey's eldest boy not died, his brother William would not have been heir to all the Boleyn estates, and neither would his son. Thomas may not have been regarded as a suitable husband for Elizabeth Howard and Anne Boleyn may never have been born. Viewed from the fifteenth century, the Boleyns' financial and dynastic ascent looks far less inevitable and far more precarious.

Partly they were simply lucky. Neither Geoffrey nor William could produce sons if fate and biology were not on their side, but commercial success and trustworthy heirs were another matter. Geoffrey's wealth was of his own creation, a product of his evident talent, and his sons were not wastrels because they had been raised to pull in harness with a shared sense of purpose. There is less evidence for Geoffrey's relationship with his children but his wife, Anne, was certainly confident in the marital judgement of her girls and William remained close to his mother both in life and in death. It was such teamwork over generations, allied with good fortune, that enabled the Boleyns to gather the bricks of ambition and build them higher and faster than those around them. Money and land, legal training and education, noble or royal connections and a hard-won respect in county administration and military service all went into the construction. But the mortar in this wall was not just gold and silver in coins, but also in wedding rings, as judicious marriages to far more ancient families were touched by the shimmer of Boleyn good fortune. Neither Anne Hoo nor Margaret Butler was assured an inheritance when they married, but heiresses they would prove to be, even though the Boleyns were playing this game at a time when the odds were increasingly stacked against them. While over a third of family estates were dispersed through inheritance in the female line at the end of the fourteenth century, a century later this had fallen to less than a fifth.[565]

From fathers to sons and even daughters, what each generation of the Boleyns was looking for was nothing revolutionary. It was simply a better, easier, more respected and protected life for their children, but the pace of the family's social mobility between Geoffrey's apprenticeship in 1421 and Anne's coronation in 1533 was itself an ingredient in their success. Slower change over many generations meant more opportunities for dynastic failure. While the Boleyns were undoubtedly fuelled by ambition, it was an ambition that looked forward with hope to what they might become, not backwards with discomfort at what they had been. The fabricated arms, pedigrees or even names of the Boleyns and their upwardly mobile relations were just part of the dressing-up box of gentility, not a sign of genealogical embarrassment. Geoffrey moved back to the same few miles of Norfolk from whence he came, where his parents and grandparents would be remembered by all. It was not the move of a man who wanted to hide his origins but a sign of pride in who he was. Like other London merchants, he was proud of his success and keen to advertise his mercantile achievements in stained-glass chapel windows and monumental brasses.

It was, perhaps, this same self-confidence that allowed Anne to imagine she could be queen and to hold to her path. All she needed was the one thing that her family had been assured of for generations, a healthy son. It was a cruel fate that her life coincided with the expiry date on the Boleyns' biological good fortune. For Anne and her brother George, that gave their enemies the upper hand and wrote their violent deaths, but it had equally catastrophic implications for her family's long-term survival.

For the Boleyns, like so many other late medieval families, success was temporary. Whether through biological failure, battlefield death, execution and attainder or intractable debts, the ways up were limited but the ways down boundless. In a world where land was synonymous with power, this cycle was a brutal necessity that opened the door to new blood, but few crested its waves like the Boleyns or left behind, with the receding tide, such an enduring legacy.

Notes

Introduction: The Name of the Game

1 British Library, Royal MS 17 B XLVII, f. 160v.

2 'Donsel' means 'esquire' but, coming as it does from the papal registers of indulgences, is undoubtedly wishful thinking.

3 S.J. Payling, 'Demographic Change and Landed Society in Late Medieval England', *The Economic History Review*, New Series, 45:1 (1992), pp. 51–73. Sylvia L. Thrupp, 'The Problem of Conservatism in Fifteenth-Century England', *Speculum*, 18:3 (1943), pp. 363–68 (p. 367).

4 Christopher Dyer, *Making a Living in the Middle Ages: The People of Britain 850–1520* (New Haven & London, 2002), p. 362.

5 Peter Coss, 'An Age of Deference', in *A Social History of England 1200–1500*, ed. Rosemary Horrox & W. Mark Ormrod (Cambridge, 2006), pp. 31–73 (p. 65).

6 Sylvia L. Thrupp, *The Merchant Class of Medieval London* (Michigan, 1948), pp. 310–11.

7 Kate Mertes, 'Aristocracy', in *Fifteenth-Century Attitudes: Perceptions of Society in Late Medieval England*, ed. Rosemary Horrox (Cambridge, 1994), pp. 42–60 (pp. 49–54).

8 *Middle English Sermons*, ed. W.O. Ross, Early English Text Society, original series 209 (London, 1940), p. 237; quoted in Thrupp, *Merchant Class*, p. 288.

9 P.J. Corfield, 'Class by Name and Number in Eighteenth-Century Britain', *History*, 72:234 (1987), pp. 38–61 (p. 47).

10 Mertes, pp. 44–45.

11 Christine Carpenter, *Locality and Polity: A Study of Warwickshire Landed Society 1401–1499* (Cambridge, 1992), pp. 40–41, 56–65, 85–86.

12 Dyer, *Making a Living*, pt. 3.

13 Coss, *Deference*, pp. 63–68. Dyer, *Making a Living*, pp. 340–57.

14 Sarah Kelly Silverman, 'The 1363 English Sumptuary Law: A Comparison with Fabric Prices of the Late Fourteenth Century' (unpublished MSc thesis, Ohio State University, 2011), p. 62.

15 Peter Coss, 'Knights, Esquires and the Origin of Social Gradation in England', *Transactions of the Royal Historical Society*, 5 (1995), pp. 155–78 (pp. 177–78).

16 *Chronicon Henrici Knighton Vel Cnitthon Monachi Lycestrensis*, ed. J. Rawson Lumby, 2 vols (London, 1889–95), II, p. 299.

17 F.R.H. Du Boulay, *An Age of Ambition: English Society in the Late Middle Ages* (London, 1970).

18 Emma Lipton, *Affections of the Mind: The Politics of Sacramental Marriage in Late Medieval English Literature* (Notre Dame, IN, 2007), pp. 1–15. Fiona S. Dunlop, *The Late Medieval Interlude: The Drama of Youth and Aristocratic Masculinity* (York, 2007), pp. 34–39. Mark Addison Amos, '"For Manners Make Man": Bourdieu, de Certeau and the Common Appropriation of Noble Manners in the Book of Courtesy', in *Medieval Conduct*, ed. Kathleen Ashley & Robert L.A. Clark (Minneapolis, 2001), pp. 23–48.

19 Thrupp, *Merchant Class*, pp. 314–15.

20 Mike Savage and others, *Social Class in the 21ˢᵗ Century* (London, 2015), pp. 5–11.

Chapter 1: Meet the Boleyns

21 TNA, PROB11/5/12.

22 See Chapter 12.

23 In 1463, in a fictitious legal dispute that was really a property sale, Thomas was given as the son of Nicholas, omitting John. TNA, CP40/808, m. 156v.

24 TNA, JUST3/49/1, m. 20v.

25 Frederick C. Hamil, 'The King's Approvers: A Chapter in the History of English Criminal Law', *Speculum*, 11:2 (1936), pp. 238–58.

26 TNA, JUST3/49/1, mm. 20v, 23.

27 Eamon Duffy, *Saints, Sacrilege and Sedition: Religion and Conflict in the Tudor Reformations* (London, 2012), p. 84. W.L.E. Parsons, *Salle: The Story of a Norfolk Parish, its Church, Manors and People* (Norwich, 1937), pp. 139–40.

28 Bruce M.S. Campbell, 'Agricultural Progress in Medieval England: Some Evidence from Eastern Norfolk', *Economic History Review*, 36:1 (1983), pp. 26–46 (p. 28).

29 Bruce M.S. Campbell, 'The Land' in *A Social History of England 1200–1500*, ed. Rosemary Horrox & W. Mark Ormrod (Cambridge, 2006), pp. 179–237 (pp. 206–17). J.L. Bolton, '"The World Turned Upside Down": Plague as an Agent of Economic and Social Change' in *The Black Death in England*, ed. Mark Ormrod & Philip Lindley (Donnington, 2003), pp. 17–78 (p. 19).

30 H.E. Hallam, *Rural England 1066–1348* (Brighton, 1981), pp. 44–45.

31 Bruce M.S. Campbell, 'Population Change and the Genesis of Common Fields on a Norfolk Manor', *Economic History Review*, 33:2 (1980), pp. 174–92 (p. 177). NRO, NRS 2605/3, mm. 10v, 12–13v.

32 Campbell, 'Agricultural Progress', pp. 27–28.

33 NRO, NRS 2605/2–3.

34 Anne F. Sutton, 'The Early Linen and Worsted Industry of Norfolk and the Evolution of the London Mercers' Company', *Norfolk Archaeology*, 40 (1989), pp. 201–25 (pp. 201–05, 207–11).

35 Davis, I, p. 140.

36 Anne F. Sutton, *The Mercery of London: Trade, Goods and People 1130–1578* (London, 2005; repub 2016), p. 234. The cap-makers of London were scouring caps in the Thames in 1398, *Memorials of London and London Life*, ed. H.T. Riley (London, 1868), p. 549. Geoffrey Boleyn leased a small piece of land at Cappes Bridge in 1435, NRO, NRS 2788, 12D6, m. 43.

37 Sutton, 'Linen and Worsted', p. 205.

38 Blomefield, VIII, pp. 269–76. Parsons, *Salle*, pp. 4–18. For this period manor court records exist for Kirkhall: 1327–99, 1413–24 (too damaged to view), 1461–78; Stinton: 1344, 1422–60, 1470; and extracts from Nugoun's relating to Marshgate Green. Rentals exist for Kirkhall: 1370, 1480, 1494; Stinton: 1350, all NRO. Parsons was also able to view court entries *c.* 1400–22 but it has not been possible to identify these.

39 'Bullen' & 'Bolling', *The Oxford Dictionary of Family Names in Britain and Ireland*, ed. Patrick Hanks, Richard Coates & Peter McClure (Oxford, 2016), www. oxfordreference.com. 'Bolle', *Middle English Dictionary*, quod.lib.umich.edu/m/ middle-english-dictionary/dictionary.

40 BL, Cotton MS Nero E VII, f. 128.

41 Margaret Paston, wife of John Paston who was looking for the worsted like silk, was a Mautby before her marriage.

42 NRO, NRS 2605/1, mm. 17v–18.

43 Christopher Dyer, *Standards of Living in the Later Middle Ages: Social Change in England c.1200–1520* (Cambridge, 1989; rev. 1998), pp. 110–17.

44 NRO, NRS 2605/1, m. 20.

45 NRO, NRS 2605/2, mm. 5v, 38–39, NRS 2605/3, mm. 2, 5, 9.

46 R.S. Gottfried, *The Black Death: Natural and Human Disaster in Medieval Europe* (New York, 1983), p. 45. Bolton, 'World Turned Upside Down', pp. 22–23.

47 NRO, NRS 2605/3, m. 9.

48 NRO, NRS 2605/3, mm. 10v, 12–13v.

49 NRO, NRS 2605/3, mm. 10v, 12.

50 Frank Meeres, *How Norwich Fought Against the Plague* (Lowestoft, 2021), p. 21. Bolton, 'World Turned Upside Down', p. 23.

51 W. Hudson & J.C. Tingey, trans. & eds, *The Records of the City of Norwich*, 2 vols (Norwich, 1906–10), II, pp. 205–06.

52 NRO, NRS 2605/3, m. 19.

53 Mark Bailey, *After the Black Death: Economy, Society and the Law in Fourteenth-Century England* (Oxford, 2021), pp. 70–76, 85, 157–59.

54 Bailey, pp. 187–93. Dyer, *Making a Living*, pp. 285–90. Herbert Eiden, 'Joint Action Against "Bad" Lordship: The Peasants' Revolt in Essex and Norfolk', *History*, 83 (1998), pp. 5–30 (pp. 22–23, 28). Bolton, 'World Turned Upside Down', pp. 45–46.

55 Bailey, pp. 77–80, 206–18.

56 Caroline M. Barron, 'The "Golden Age" of Women in Medieval London' in *Reading Medieval Studies, Vol. 15, Medieval Women in Southern England* (1989), pp. 35–58 (pp. 39, 45–46). Hovland, pp. 281–83.

57 Bailey, pp. 74–75, 215. Dyer, *Making a Living*, pp. 293–97, 358–59.

58 Bailey, pp. 82–83, 142. Dyer, *Standards of Living*, pp. 158–59. Dana Ann Durkee, 'Social Mobility and the Worsted Weavers of Norwich *c.*1450–1530' (unpublished PhD thesis, Durham, 2017), pp. 89–98.

59 NRO, NRS 2605/4, m. 5.

60 NRO, NRS 2605/3, mm. 25v, 27–27v, 30, 2605/5, m. 4v. W.L.E. Parsons, 'Some Notes on the Boleyn Family', *Norfolk Archaeology*, 25:3 (1934), pp. 386–407 (p. 390).

61 TNA, JUST2/104, m. 53v.

62 Bolton, 'World Turned Upside Down', p. 27. NRO, NRS 2605/5, mm. 13, 14v.

63 'Messuage' could imply either a house and associated lands or simply the land on which a house might be built. TNA, CP25/1/167/171/1385. Dyer, *Making a Living*, pp. 293–94.

64 TNA, CP25/1/168/177/85.

65 Bailey, pp. 187–90. W.M. Ormrod, 'The Politics of Pestilence: Government in England after the Black Death' in *The Black Death in England*, ed. Mark Ormrod & Philip Lindley (Donnington, 2003), pp. 147–81 (pp. 159–67).

66 M.H. Keen, *England in the Later Middle Ages* (London, 1973, repr. 2000), pp. 267–70. R.B. Dobson, *The Peasants' Revolt of 1381*, 2nd edn (London, 1983), pp. 36–44, 123–47, 155–211.

67 Eiden, 'Joint Action', p. 23. TNA, KB27/486, m. 27v, KB27/489, mm. 48v, 51v.

68 TNA, KB9/166/1, m. 93.

69 TNA, KB9/166/1, m. 55.

70 Eiden, 'Joint Action', pp. 16–21. Andrew John Prescott, 'Judicial Records of the Rising of 1381' (unpublished PhD thesis, Bedford College, University of London, 1984), pp. 161–70.

71 Eiden, 'Joint Action', p. 23.

72 Blomefield, VIII, pp. 269–76.

73 Parsons, *Salle*, p. 7. CCR 1385–1389, p. 140.

74 CCR 1389–1392, p. 489.

75 Maryanne Kowaleski, 'A Consumer Economy', in *A Social History of England 1200–1500*, ed. Rosemary Horrox & W.M. Ormrod (Cambridge, 2006), pp. 238–59 (p. 255). *Calendar of Papal Registers Relating to Great Britain and Ireland*, ed. W.H. Bliss, J.A. Twemlow & C. Johnson, 14 vols (London, 1904), V, p. 129.

Chapter 2: 'Fair Living for a Yeoman'

76 TNA, PROB11/5/12. LBL, pp. 54, 62–63. Dyer, *Standards of Living*, pp. 160–69, 173. John Schofield, *Medieval London Houses* (New Haven & London, 1995), pp. 111–13. Nat Alcock & Dan Miles, *The Medieval Peasant House in Midland England* (Oxford, 2013), p. 5. Katherine L. French, *Household Goods and Good Households in Late Medieval London* (Philadelphia, 2021), pp. 67–68, 92–94.

77 Parsons, *Boleyn*, p. 389.

78 Parsons, *Boleyn*, pp. 389–90. Blomefield gives a date of death of 30 April 1411 but no source. Blomefield, VI, pp. 381–409.

79 NRO, NRS 2621 12C2.

80 CPR 1429–1436, p. 90.

81 Parsons, *Salle*, pp. 19–71.

82 Parsons, *Salle*, pp. 22–23. Parsons, *Boleyn*, pp. 389–90.

83 *Archdeaconry of Norwich Inventory of Church Goods temp. Edward III*, ed. Aelred Watkin, Norfolk Record Society 19, (1947), p. 77.

84 NRO, WHT 5/58/1.

85 CPR 1429–1436, p. 407. *Parliament Rolls of Medieval England*, ed. Chris Given-Wilson, Paul Brand, Seymour Phillips, Mark Ormrod, Geoffrey Martin, Anne Curry & Rosemary Horrox, 16 vols (Woodbridge, 2005), XI, pp. 149–50.

86 Bolton, 'World Turned Upside Down', pp. 35, 53.

87 *Papal Registers*, VIII, p. 516.

88 J.I. Dent, 'Boleyn Heraldry in Norwich Cathedral', *Norfolk Heraldry, The Journal of the Norfolk Heraldry Society*, I (Norwich, 1991), pp. 29–34. *The Visitation of Norfolk*, ed. Walter Rye (London, 1891), pp. 51–52.

89 *Commons 1422–1461*, IV, p. 900. Steven Gunn, *Henry VII's New Men and the Making of Tudor England* (Oxford, 2016) p. 31. 'John Writhe' & 'Sir Thomas Wriothesley', www.oxforddnb.com.

90 Colin Richmond, *The Paston Family in the Fifteenth Century: Fastolf's Will* (Cambridge, 1996), p. 12.

91 NRO, NRS 17943, 41C5. Colin Richmond, *The Paston Family in the Fifteenth Century: The First Phase* (Cambridge, 1990), pp. 120–24.

92 Blomefield, VIII, pp. 269–76.

93 Parsons, *Salle*, pp. 81–85.

94 NRO, NCC Will Register Doke, f. 224. Carol M. Meale, 'Women's Voices and Roles' in *A Companion to Medieval English Literature and Culture c. 1350–c. 1550*, ed. Peter Brown (Oxford, 2007), pp. 74–90 (pp. 83–84). Oxford, Bodleian Library, MS Bodley 758.

95 Carole Hill, *Women and Religion in Late Medieval Norwich* (Woodbridge, 2010), pp. 14–15, 162. Norman P. Tanner, *The Church in Late Medieval Norwich 1370–1532* (Toronto, 1984), pp. 64–66. Roberta Gilchrist & Marilyn Oliva, *Religious Women in Medieval East Anglia: History and Archaeology c. 1100–1500* (Norwich, 1993), pp. 71–73, 95.

96 NRO, NRS 10949, 25D6. TNA, C147/116.

97 Geoffrey and his brother Thomas not only remained close to their sister but were also intimately involved with each other and it seems unlikely, given their affection, that they had other siblings to whom they never refer.

98 A.B. Emden, *A Biographical Register of the University of Cambridge to 1500* (Cambridge, 1963), pp. 70–71. John Venn & J.A. Venn, *Alumni Cantabrigienses*, 2 vols (Cambridge, 1922), I, pt. 1, p. 174. J. Armitage Robinson, 'Thomas Boleyn Precentor of Wells', *Somersetshire Archaeological and Natural History Society*, 61 (1916), pp. 1–10.

98 Blomefield, VIII, pp. 244–48.

Chapter 3: The Golden Ticket of a London Apprenticeship

99 *The Historical Collections of a Citizen of London in the Fifteenth Century ('Gregory's Chronicle')*, ed. James Gairdner (London, 1876), pp. 128–61, www.british-history. ac.uk. *The Great Chronicle of London*, ed. A.H. Thomas & I.D. Thornley (London, 1938), p. 115. *The Brut or The Chronicles of England*, ed. Friedrich W.D. Brie (London, 1906), p. 426. Nicola Coldstream, 'The Roles of Women in Late Medieval Civic Pageantry in England' in *Reassessing the Roles of Women as 'Makers' of Medieval Art and Architecture*, ed. Therese Martin (Leiden, 2012), pp. 175–96 (p. 182). *London Bridge: Selected Accounts and Rentals 1381–1538*, ed. Vanessa Harding & Laura Wright (London, 1995), pp. 77–89.

100 Apprentices could be as young as 12 but 14 was commonly held to be an appropriate age in the fifteenth century, Stephanie R. Hovland, 'Apprenticeship in Later Medieval London *c*. 1300–*c*. 1530' (unpublished PhD thesis, Royal Holloway, University of London, 2006), pp. 51–54. Memorials, p. 239. LBK, p. 201.

101 H.S. Bennett, *The Pastons and their England: Studies in an Age of Transition* (Cambridge, 1922; reprinted 1995), pp. 153–57.

102 *Hugh Alley's Caveat: The Markets of London in 1598*, ed. Ian Archer, Caroline Barron & Vanessa Harding (London, 1988), p. 87.

103 Hovland, p. 132. For discussion of apprenticeship also see Barbara A. Hanawalt, *Growing up in Medieval London* (Oxford, 1993).

104 *Remains of the Early Popular Poetry of England*, ed. William Carew Hazlitt (London, 1864), p. 114.

105 Geoffrey never refers to him as his former master, but Adam was a prominent hatter and international merchant involved in the mercery trade, and given their evidently close relationship, this is the most likely conclusion.

106 www.englandsimmigrants.com

107 LCA, vol. 74, pt. 2, no. 3, p. 4. LCA, vol. 74, pt. 2, no. 4, pp. 92, 104, 107, 150, 153, 155.

108 LBI, p. 176. John Stow, *The Survey of London*, ed. H.B. Wheatley (London, 1987), p. 230.

109 MA, II, 743. TNA, PROB11/5/12. *A Form for the Commemoration of Benefactors to be used in the Chapel of the College of St Margaret and St Bernard, commonly called Queens' College Cambridge*, ed. George Cornelius Gorham (Cambridge, 1823), p. 2. Cambridge University, MS QC 76 'Misc A', f. 3.

110 Caroline M. Barron, 'London and the Crown 1451–61' in *The Crown and Local Communities in England and France in the Fifteenth Century*, ed. J.R.L. Highfield & Robin Jeffs (Gloucester, 1981), pp. 88–109, repub. in *Medieval London: Collected Papers of Caroline M. Barron*, ed. Martha Carlin & Joel T. Rosenthal (Kalamazoo, 2017), pp. 57–82 (p. 57).

111 Caroline M. Barron, *The Medieval Guildhall of London* (London, 1974), pp. 25–35. Christopher Wilson, 'The Original Design of the City of London Guildhall', *Journal of the British Archaeological Association*, 129 (1976), pp. 1–14.

112 LBK, p. 201.

113 LBD, pp. 195–96.

114 Hovland, pp. 212–13.

Chapter 4: Commerce and Commodities

115 The court physician John Gaddesden (1280–1361) also recommends washing either the testicles or the breasts in salt and vinegar. Henry Patrick Cholmeley, *John of Gaddesden and the Rosa Medicinae* (Oxford, 1912), p. 53.

116 Sylvia L. Thrupp, *The Merchant Class of Medieval London* (Michigan, 1948), p. 104.

117 TNA, PROB11/5/12.

118 See Chapter 5.

119 Dorothy Burwash, *English Merchant Shipping 1460–1540* (Toronto, 1947; repr. Newton Abbot, 1969), pp. 72–73, 76–77. Thomas Dhoop, 'Shipbuilding and Life Onboard', University of Southampton, Future Learn, 2017, www.futurelearn. com/info/courses/shipwrecks/0/steps/7968. For images of the spaces under the end castles and the cabins built on top for royal or noble passengers see Joe Flatman, *Ships & Shipping in Medieval Manuscripts* (London, 2009), figs. 5, 20, 82, 86–88, 149–50.

120 Sutton, *Mercery*, pp. 235–36.

121 Geoffrey's first cargos home dated 10 October–12 November 1431. LCA, vol. 74, pt. 2, no. 4, pp. 30, 40, 42.

122 Michael Limberger, 'Regional and Interregional Trading Networks and Commercial Practices at the Port of Antwerp in the Fourteenth and Fifteenth Centuries: The Testimony of Merchants and Skippers in Court Records', *Nuevo Mundo Mundos Nuevos*, Colloques, journals.openedition.org/nuevomundo/69938.

123 There is no record of Adam importing goods under his own name in 1431 although he was back in the market the following year.

124 N.J.M. Kerling, *Commercial Relations of Holland and Zeeland with England from the late Thirteenth Century to the Close of the Middle Ages* (Leiden, 1954), p. 160.

125 Limberger, 'Port of Antwerp'.

126 Probably hair combs rather than those used in cloth production as later customs rates specify decorative cases or use by barbers. LCA, vol. 74, pt. 2, no. 4, pp. 30, 40, 42. *A Tudor Book of Rates*, ed. T.S. Willan (Manchester, 1962), p. 18.

127 LCA, vol. 74, pt. 2, no. 4, pp. 103–04, 106–07, 150–51, 153, 155, 158.

128 *Studies in English Trade in the Fifteenth Century*, ed. Eileen Power & M.M. Postan (London, 1933), pp. 330–60.

129 Sutton, *Mercery*, pp. 242–50, 290.

130 J.L. Bolton, 'London Merchants and the Borromei Bank in the 1430s: The Role of Local Credit Networks', in *Fifteenth-Century X, Parliament, Personalities and Power: Papers Presented to Linda S. Clark*, ed. Hannes Kleineke (Woodbridge, 2011), pp. 53–74 (pp. 62–64). G. Biscaro, 'Il Banco Filippo Borromei e Compagni di Londra 1436–1439', *Archivio Storico Lombardo*, 4th ser., 19:38 (1913), pp. 283–386

(p. 372). F. Guidi-Bruscoli, 'London and its Merchants in the Italian Archives 1380–1530' in *Medieval Merchants and Money, Essays in Honour of James L. Bolton*, ed. Martin Allen and Matthew Davies (London, 2016), pp. 113–36, (p. 122).

131 LCA, vol. 74, pt. 2, no. 5, pp. 101, 103, 143–45. LCA, vol. 74, pt. 2, no. 6, p. 24.

132 TNA, E122/209/1, f. 52.

133 Sutton, *Mercery*, p. 291.

134 MA, I, p. 485. LBK, p. 201.

135 Sutton, *Mercery*, p.5.

136 Such as Robert Large, William Olyver and Richard Riche. LBK, p. 201. TNA, E 122/73/5, mm. 9d–10. LCA, vol. 74, pt. 2, no. 4, pp. 38–41.

137 MA, I, p. 477. LBK, p. 201.

138 Sutton, *Mercery*, pp. 246, 290. LCA, vol. 74, pt. 2, no. 8, pp. 90, 94–95.

139 *Views of the Hosts of Alien Merchants 1440–44*, ed. Helen Bradley (London, 2012), pp. 38, 93–99.

140 Cloth sale in partnership with Stephen Broun. *Views of Hosts*, p. 95. Geoffrey became so deeply involved with the Contarinis that when he called in their debts, prompting others to follow suit, the firm were bankrupted. Paula C. Clarke, 'The Commercial Activities of Geovanni Marcanova di Giacomo' in *Cittadini Veneziani del Quattrocento: I due Giovanni Marcanova Il Mercante e L'umanista*, ed. Elizabeth Barile, Paula C. Clarke & Giorgia Nordio (Venice, 2006), pp. 247–373 (pp. 335–36). In 1453, Geoffrey managed to sell 15,000lbs of pepper, which must have arrived in an Italian galley, back to a Venetian merchant. TNA, E159/235, Trinity Term 1459, mm. 42, 45. Wendy Childs, '"To oure losse and hindraunce": English Credit to Alien Merchants in the Mid-Fifteenth Century' in *Enterprise and Individuals in Fifteenth-Century England*, ed. Jennifer Kermode (Stroud, 1991), pp. 68–98 (pp. 81, 94). Sutton, *Mercery*, pp. 229, 310–11.

141 An optimistic attempt to use chapmen to retail his goods within the city was swiftly stamped out by the mercers but even after his death, debts were still being pursued that Geoffrey had accrued in partnership with a chapman from Staines. CPR 1461–1467, p. 507. TNA, C241/230/33. CPR 1446–1452, p. 9. MA, II, p. 643.

142 'Simon Eyre', www.oxforddnb.com.

143 Jim Bolton, *The Medieval English Economy 1150–1500* (London, 1980), p. 303.

144 In 1448 Geoffrey lent money to John Grene, who imported linen in 1450, and in 1457 he lent to John Neve, who imported linen and paper the same year. CCR 1441–1447, pp. 200, 476. CCR 1454–1461, pp. 199, 219. CPMR 1437–1457, pp. 173, 175, 180. LCA, vol. 74, pt. 2, no. 10, p. 210; vol. 74, pt. 2, no. 12, pp. 58, 61.

145 TNA, CP40/757, rot. 379, C241/243/28.

146 The Genoese were fined £6,000 for an attack by Genoese pirates off Malta in 1458. Childs, p. 87. R.A. Griffiths, *The Reign of King Henry VI* (Stroud, 1981), p. 795. CPR 1446–1452, pp. 472, 572. Pamela Nightingale, *A Medieval Mercantile Community: The Grocers' Company and the Politics and Trade of London 1000–1485* (New Haven & London, 1995), p. 469.

147 See below, TNA, C1/26/272.

148 LCA, vol. 74, pt. 2, no. 11, p. 86, vol. 74, pt. 2, no. 12, pp. 103, 105–06, 108–10, 113–14, 117, 119–20, 122–24, 126. In the late 1450s, Geoffrey was shipping wool

to Calais as the factor of John Brown who, with his partner John Pontrell, had been granted a licence to retain part of their subsidy payments in order to recoup a £1,500 loan. Selling that advantage to factors, such as Geoffrey, speeded up the process. Other merchants shipping under his licence included John Croke, John Tate, Robert Stowe, Thomas Danvers, William Yorke and William Haddon. TNA, C76/140 m. 14.

149 CPR 1446–1452, pp. 472, 572–73.

150 K.B. McFarlane, 'Loans to the Lancastrian Kings: The Problem of Inducement', *The Cambridge Historical Journal*, 9:1 (1947), pp. 51–68 (p. 64).

151 McFarlane, p. 62.

152 CPR 1446–1452, pp. 472, 572.

153 Even in the greatest mercantile guilds, only around 15 per cent of the membership surpassed a landed income of £20 or a post-mortem estate worth £1,000. Figures for the mercers from the tax assessment 1436, Thrupp, *Merchant Class*, p. 110. Figures for the grocers from wills dated 1386–1506, Sutton, *Mercery*, pp. 189–90.

154 TNA, PROB11/5/376.

155 CPR 1441–1446, p. 400. TNA, E159/235, Trinity Term 1459, mm. 42, 45. Sutton, *Mercery*, pp. 310–11. Childs, pp. 81, 94.

156 TNA, C1/26/272.

157 TNA, C241/254/136, C241/254/138, C241/243/24, C1/43/200.

158 Thrupp, *Merchant Class*, pp. 14–39.

Chapter 5: Enter the First Anne Boleyn

159 *Brut*, p. 489. Robert Withington, *English Pageantry: An Historical Outline*, 2 vols (Cambridge 1918–20), I, p. 148. *Chronicles of London*, ed. Charles Lethbridge Kingsford (Oxford, 1905), p. 156. Coldstream, pp. 183–84.

160 Elizabeth Norton, *The Boleyn Women* (Stroud, 2013), pp. 18–19. Lauren Mackay, *Among the Wolves of Court: The Untold Story of Thomas and George Boleyn* (London, 2018), p. 13.

161 Charles Henry Cooper, *Memorials of Cambridge*, 3 vols (Cambridge: William Metcalfe, 1860), I, pp. 297–98. Gorham, *Queens'*, p. 2. Cambridge University Archives, MS QC 76 'Misc A', ff. 3v, 5v.

162 Dionisia died before 1446, the year Geoffrey and his second wife had their first child, and Adam Book disappears from London's records after 1434.

163 Emden, pp. 70–71. Venn & Venn, I, pt. 1, p. 174.

164 Blomefield, VIII, pp. 244–48.

165 Beaufort nominated him as rector of Hackford, Norfolk, when they returned from Switzerland. *Rymer's Foedera, Vol. 10*, ed. Thomas Rymer (London, 1739–1745), pp. 575–94, www.british-history.ac.uk. Blomefield, VIII, pp. 223–26. Emden, pp. 70–71. Venn & Venn, I, pt. 1, p. 174.

166 GEC, VI (1926), p. 562. William Durrant Cooper, 'The Families of Braose of Chesworth and Hoo', *Sussex Archaeological Collections*, 8 (1856), pp. 13–131 (p. 110).

167 William Dugdale, *The Baronage of England* (London, 1675–76), pp. 233–34. GEC, VI (1926), pp. 561–67. Durrant Cooper, pp. 110–18.

168 Anne married Roger Copley and Elizabeth married Thomas Massingberd. *The House of Commons 1422–1461*, ed. Linda Clark, 7 vols (Cambridge, 2020), IV, p. 963. Thrupp, pp. 263–65, 361, 374.

169 *Commons 1422–1461*, IV, p. 961. TNA, CP25/1/293/71/308.

170 *Commons 1422–1461*, IV, p. 967. Nicholas Harris Nicolas, *Testamenta Vetusta*, 2 vols (London: Nichols & Son, 1826), I, pp. 272–74. TNA, C141/6/23.

171 CPR 1441–1446, p. 81. TNA, C1/44/185–8.

172 Thomas Hoo's step-mother Elizabeth Etchingham married, as her second husband, Sir Thomas Lewknor and Richard was their son. Durrant Cooper, pp. 130–31. *Regestrum Thome Bourgchier Cantuariensis Archiepiscopi 1454–86*, ed. F.R.H. du Boulay (Oxford, 1957), p. 173. *Commons 1422–1461*, IV, p. 963, V, p. 247.

173 TNA C140/10/21. Anne's age is given as 'thirty years and more' at her father's death in 1455, C139/156/11.

174 Their mother was Elizabeth Darcy, née Wentworth, a lady in waiting to Catherine of Aragon. Barbara J. Harris, *English Aristocratic Women 1450–1550* (Oxford, 2002), p. 91.

175 Emden, pp. 70–71. *A History of the County of Middlesex, Vol. 12, Chelsea*, ed. Patricia E.C. Croot (London, 2004), pp. 238–250, www.british-history.ac.uk. Armitage Robinson, 'Thomas Boleyn Precentor of Wells', pp. 1–10 (p. 7).

176 Shannon McSheffrey, *Marriage, Sex and Civic Culture in Late Medieval London* (Philadelphia, 2006), pp. 43–45.

177 Henrietta Leyser, *Medieval Women: A Social History of Women in England 450–1500* (London, 1995), p. 109.

178 McSheffrey, p. 45.

179 Thomas Hoo made Mulbarton his main residence in the early 1420s and Anne was born around 1425, *Commons 1422–1461*, IV, p. 959.

180 D.J. Keene & Vanessa Harding, *Historical Gazetteer of London Before the Great Fire Cheapside: Parishes of All Hallows Honey Lane, St Martin Pomary, St Mary Le Bow, St Mary Colechurch and St Pancras Soper Lane* (London, 1987), 104/23, www.british-history.ac.uk.

181 LMA, MS CLA/023/DW/01/278 (1). John Schofield, Patrick Allen & Colin Taylor, 'Medieval Buildings and Property Development in the Area of Cheapside', *Transactions of the London and Middlesex Archaeological Society*, 41 (1990), pp. 39–237 (pp. 87–88, 105). Schofield, *London Houses*, p. 166.

182 Schofield, *London Houses*, pp. 106, 118–28.

183 French, *Household Goods*, p. 93.

184 Thrupp, *Merchant Class*, pp. 140–42. French, *Household Goods*, pp. 43–74, 80–81.

185 Thrupp, *Merchant Class*, p. 371. 'Sir Ralph Verney', www.oxforddnb.com. *Letters and Papers of the Verney Family*, ed. John Bruce (London, 1853), pp. xvi–xvii. *Commons 1422–1461*, VII, p. 306.

186 TNA, PROB11/6/7. Caroline M. Barron, *London in the Later Middle Ages: Government and People 1200–1500* (Oxford, 2004), p. 169. Caroline M. Barron, 'The People of the Parish: The Close of St Bartholomew's Hospital in Fifteenth-Century London' in *The Urban Church in Late Medieval England*, ed. David Harry & Christian

Steer (Donington, 2019), pp. 353–79 (p. 377). E.A. Webb, 'The parish: Inhabitants', in *The Records of St. Bartholomew's Priory and St. Bartholomew the Great, West Smithfield, Vol. 2* (Oxford, 1921), pp. 248–291, www.british-history.ac.uk. *Commons 1422–1461*, III, p. 655.

187 In 1453 Geoffrey and Lok lent money to another mercer, William Wydnesson. In 1450 Lok chose Geoffrey to be a trustee of his property in Fulham and Geoffrey returned the favour for the purchase of his grand mansion in London. CPMR 1437–1457, p. 180. LMA, MS CLA/023/DW/01/192 (23). TNA, CP25/1/152/93/150, PROB 11/5/16. Thrupp, *Merchant Class*, p. 353.

188 LBK, pp. 300, 307.

189 *Commons 1422–1461*, V, p. 607.

190 MA, I, pp. 485, 565, II, 589. TNA, PROB11/5/12. John Lewys, who became Geoffrey's apprentice in 1442–43, remained as his servant and was remembered in his will.

191 Barbara A. Hanawalt, *The Wealth of Wives: Women, Law and Economy in Late Medieval London* (Oxford, 2007), p. 136. *Harrison's Description of England*, ed. Frederick J. Furnival, New Shakespeare Society Publications, 3 vols (London, 1877), I, lxiii.

Chapter 6: 'A Multitude of Riff Raff'

192 Rachel Podd, 'Reconsidering Maternal Mortality in Medieval England: Aristocratic Women *c.* 1236–1503', *Continuity and Change*, 35 (2020), pp. 115–37.

193 Richard Page wrote to Sir William Stonor that he prayed God would send Lady Stonor 'a good time and a good deliverance'. Harris, *Aristocratic Women*, p. 101.

194 'Bone lace' was woven using threads wound onto multiple bobbins ,which may themselves have been made of bone. Catherine Amoroso Leslie, *Needlework through History: An Encyclopedia* (London, 2007), pp. 22–23.

195 TNA, C131/274. Katherine French, 'The Material Culture of Childbirth in Late Medieval London and its Suburbs', *Journal of Women's History*, 28:2 (2016), pp. 126–48 (p. 132).

196 French, *Childbirth*, p. 136.

197 French, *Childbirth*, pp. 133–34. Nicholas Orme, *Medieval Children* (New Haven & London, 2003), p. 16.

198 Geoffrey's inquisition post mortem gives Thomas's age in 1463 as 17 (although the London jurors said 18) and the returns for Sussex and Norfolk specify a birthday of 7 September. A birth date of 7 September 1446 would correlate with his failure to claim his patrimony. Under the terms of his father's will Thomas could not enter his inheritance until he was 25 or married, so not until 7 September 1471, but he was dead by June. Thomas shares his birthday with his great-grandniece Elizabeth I. TNA, C140/10/21, PROB11/6/33. LBL, p. 110.

199 Stow, p. 230.

200 Leyser, p. 129.

201 Leyser, p. 130. Harris, *Aristocratic Women*, p. 106. French, *Childbirth*, p. 139.

202 See Chapter 10.

203 Griffiths, pp. 515–29, 676–84. R. Virgoe, 'The Death of William de la Pole, Duke of Suffolk', *Bulletin of the John Rylands Library*, 47 (1965), pp. 489–502 (pp. 491–94).

204 GEC, VI, p. 563.

205 Griffiths, p. 639.

206 Griffiths, p. 625.

207 'Gregory's Chronicle', pp. 177–96, www.british-history.ac.uk.

208 Anne's inquisition post mortem, held on 25 July 1485, gives William's age as 'thirty-four years and more'. The inquisition post mortem for her uncle Thomas Hoo, esq., held on 28 October 1487, gives William's age as 'thirty-six years and more'. Both statements would be accurate if William was born between 29 October 1450 and 25 July 1451. William acknowledged satisfaction for his patrimony on 9 March 1473 but had probably received it sometime before. He was not yet 25 but Geoffrey's will allowed his sons to inherit when they were either 25 or married, and William had been married since 1469. TNA, C141/6/23. *Calendar of Inquisitions Post Mortem Henry VII*, no ed., 3 vols (London, 1898–1955), I, 138. LBL, p. 110. Berkeley Castle Muniments, MS BCM/H/1/3/1–2.

209 Griffiths, pp. 615, 619.

210 For Cade's Revolt see Montgomery Bohna, 'Armed Force and Civic Legitimacy in Jack Cade's Revolt 1450', *English Historical Review*, 118:477 (2003), pp. 563–82 (p. 563). Dan Jones, *The Hollow Crown: The Wars of the Roses and the Rise of the Tudors* (London, 2014), pp. 111–18. Griffiths, pp. 610–28. *Three Fifteenth-Century Chronicles with Historical Memoranda by John Stowe*, ed. James Gairdner (London, 1880), pp. 58–78, www.british-history.ac.uk. 'Bale's Chronicle' in *Six Town Chronicles of England*, ed. Ralph Flenley (Oxford, 1911), pp. 132–34.

211 Jones, pp. 125–26.

212 Griffiths, p. 305.

213 Griffiths, pp. 308, 641–42. *English Historical Literature in the Fifteenth Century*, ed. Charles Lethbridge Kingsford (Oxford, 1913), pp. 364–65.

214 'Gregory's Chronicle', pp. 177–96, www.british-history.ac.uk.

Chapter 7: Common Council to House of Commons

215 Sutton, *Mercery*, pp. 478–80, 487–88.

216 Sutton, *Mercery*, p. 172. MA, I, p. 561.

217 Barron, *Later Middle Ages*, pp. 138, 160.

218 Barron, *Medieval Guildhall*, p. 25.

219 CPR 1441–1446, pp. 65–66.

220 Seventeen years later, as Burton prepared for death, he would entrust the supervision of his will to his former fellow warden, LMA, MS 9171/5, ff. 303–04.

221 Sutton, *Mercery*, pp. 172–73.

222 MA, I, pp. 573–77.

223 LMA, MS COL/CC/01/01/4, ff. 90v, 95, 97v. LBK, p. 308.

224 Thrupp, p. 265.

225 LBK, p. 315.

226 Caroline Barron, 'Telling the Time in Chaucer's London' in *'A Verray Parfit Praktisour': Essays Presented to Carole Rawcliffe*, ed. Linda Clark & Elizabeth Danbury (Woodbridge, 2017), pp. 141–152 (p. 146).

227 Barron, *Later Middle Ages*, pp. 159–60, 342. *Munimenta Gildhallae Londoniensis, Liber Albus, Liber Custumarum et Liber Horn*, ed. Henry Thomas Riley, 3 vols (London, 1862), III, pp. 3–5. LBD, pp. 206–07.

228 Mercers' Accounts, II, p. 633.

229 Barron, *Later Middle Ages*, pp. 160–68, 357.

230 LMA, MS COL/CC/01/01/5, f. 4v.

231 LBK, p. 101. Reginald R. Sharpe, *London and the Kingdom*, 3 vols (London, 1894–95), I, pp. 273–74.

232 Jennifer Caddick, 'The Painted Chamber at Westminster and the Openings of Parliament 1399–1484', *Parliamentary History*, 38:1 (2019), pp. 17–33 (pp. 18, 22–24).

233 Parliament Rolls, XII, pp. 33–40.

234 Barron, *Later Middle Ages*, pp. 136–46.

235 'MS Rawlinson B 355' in Flenley, *Six Town Chronicles*, p. 106. Griffiths, p. 615.

236 Griffiths, p. 615. Alfred B. Beaven, *The Aldermen of the City of London*, 2 vols (London, 1913), I, p. 175.

237 LMA, MS COL/CC/01/01/5, f. 43. Beaumond was always the bridesmaid and never the bride, being nominated for aldermanic office seven times and never selected. When he wrote his will he described himself as being 'in lot and scot', i.e. being ready to serve in every office becoming a good citizen and paying his dues. Beaven, I, pp. 47, 130, 145, 153, 174, 199, 206. *Calendar of Wills Proved and Enrolled in the Court of Husting London 1258–1688*, ed. Reginald R. Sharpe, 2 vols (London, 1890), II, p. 533.

238 Beaven, I, pp. 2, 47, 82, 130, 137, 153, 168, 174, II, p. 15.

239 LMA, MS COL/CC/01/01/5, f. 65v.

240 Beaven, I, pp. 90, 122, 137, II, p. 221.

Chapter 8: 'The Rising and Wanton Rule'

241 LMA, MS COL/CC/01/01/5, ff. 79–82v.

242 LMA, MS COL/CC/01/01/5, ff. 78v–80v.

243 Attendance lists compiled by Caroline M. Barron.

244 *Commons 1422–1461*, III, p. 407. MA, II, p. 737.

245 MA, II, p. 755.

246 Sutton, *Mercery*, pp. 178, 182. MA, II, pp. 741, 749, 751.

247 'Bale's Chronicle' in Flenley, *Six Town Chronicles*, p. 140.

248 Griffiths, p. 715.

249 LMA, MS COL/CC/01/01/5, f. 132v.

250 Barron, 'London and the Crown' p. 64. LMA, MS COL/CC/01/01/5, f. 150.

251 Griffiths, pp. 715–26. Jones, pp. 137–41.

252 See Chapter 10.

253 In 1348 and 1520 there were around 100 liverymen and although this number may have declined in the middle of the fifteenth century, along with the general population, when invited guests were added the party would have remained sizeable. Sutton, *Mercery*, pp. 92, 458.

254 *Acts of Court of the Mercers' Company 1453–1527*, ed. Laetitia Lyell & Frank D. Watney (Cambridge, 1936), p. 42. Sutton, *Mercery*, pp. 556–57.

255 These can still be seen on the tomb of the Dacre family at Herstmonceux church, to whom they were sold following the dissolution of the abbey. George Elliot, 'A Monumental Palimpsest: The Dacre Tomb in Herstmonceux Church', *Sussex Archaeological Collections*, 148 (2010), pp. 129–44. Durrant Cooper, p. 118.

256 Griffiths, pp. 741–46. Jones, pp. 142–51. C.A.J. Armstrong, 'Politics and the Battle of St Albans 1455', *Bulletin of the Institute of Historical Research*, 33 (1960), pp. 1–72.

257 'Gregory's Chronicle', pp. 196–210, www.british-history.ac.uk.

258 'Bale's Chronicle' in Flenley, *Six Town Chronicles*, pp. 142–43. Griffiths, p. 746. Jones, pp. 150–51.

259 Riley, *Memorials*, p. 636.

260 LBH, p. 277.

261 LMA, MS COL/CC/01/01/005, f. 267.

262 *Munimentia Gildhallae Londoniensis: Liber Albus*, ed. Henry Thomas Riley (Cambridge, 1859), p. 23. Barbara A. Hanawalt, *Ceremony and Civility: Civic Culture in Late Medieval London* (Oxford, 2017), pp. 59–62. Barron, *Later Middle Ages*, pp. 145–51. LBK, pp. 371–72.

263 LMA, MS COL/CC/01/01/005, ff. 253v, 264v.

264 TNA, PROB11/5/139.

265 For this section I am indebted to the work of J.L. Bolton, 'The City and the Crown 1456–61', *London Journal*, 12:1 (1986), pp. 11–24. Griffiths, pp. 791–92. 'Bale's Chronicle' in Flenley, *Six Town Chronicles*, pp. 143–44. Kingsford, *Chronicles of London*, pp. 165–67. LMA, MS COL/CC/01/01/006, ff. 1–1v, 27. [very badly damaged].

266 Kingsford, *Chronicles of London*, p. 167.

267 LMA, MS COL/CC/01/01/006, f. 125v.

268 Griffiths, pp. 791–92. Bolton, 'City & Crown', pp. 14–15. Kingsford, *Chronicles of London*, p. 167. LBK, pp. 385–90.

269 Bolton, 'City & Crown', pp. 11–24.

270 Modern analysis has demonstrated that the balance of trade was very much in England's favour and revealed the bullion shortage to have been a Europe-wide phenomenon. Bolton, *Medieval English Economy*, pp. 313–14. *The Libelle of Englyshe Polycye*, ed. G. Warner (Oxford, 1926), p. 18.

271 Between September 1449 and the summer of 1455, total alien exports of wool through London, Southampton and Sandwich combined was 4,410 sacks. By the period March 1455 to November 1457, this had actually only increased slightly, to 5,062 sacks. T.H. Lloyd, *The English Wool Trade in the Middle Ages* (Cambridge, 1977), p. 276.

272 Griffiths, pp. 731, 756. Bolton, 'City & Crown', p. 16. Lloyd, pp. 275–76. W.I. Haward, 'The Relations Between the Lancastrian Government and the Merchants of the Staple from 1449 to 1461', in *Studies in English Trade in the Fifteenth Century*, ed. Eileen Power & M.M. Postan (London, 1933), pp. 293–320. G.L. Harriss, 'The Struggle for Calais: An Aspect of the Rivalry Between Lancaster and York', *English Historical Review*, 75 (1960), pp. 30–53.

273 LMA, MS COL/CC/01/01/006, ff. 1–1v.

274 Bolton, 'City & Crown', p. 14.

275 Commons 1422–1461, III, p. 656.

276 MA, II, p. 741.

277 *Commons 1422–1461*, III, p. 408. Richmond, *Paston Family: First Phase*, p. 210. CPR 1446–1452, p. 231.

278 *Commons 1422–1461*, III, p. 408, VI, p. 631. For credit prosecution see Chapter 4.

279 Nightingale, *Grocers' Company*, pp. 509–10.

280 TNA, C66/493, m. 23.

281 Bolton, 'City & Crown', p. 21. LMA, MS COL/CC/01/01/005, f. 152.

Chapter 9: 'Our Honourable and Worthy Mayor'

282 An armed skirmish between the young duke of Somerset and Salisbury's son Sir John Neville on Cheapside was only narrowly avoided. Griffiths, p. 800. Kingsford, *Chronicles of London*, p. 167.

283 LBK, p. 392. COL/CC/01/01/006, f. 180v.

284 LBD, pp. 34–35.

285 Hanawalt, *Ceremony & Civility*, pp. 62–64. Riley, *Liber Albus*, pp. 23–24.

286 MA, II, p. 829.

287 Hanawalt, *Ceremony & Civility*, pp. 62–65. Riley, *Liber Albus*, pp. 23–24. Barron, *Later Middle Ages*, pp. 147, 151–53.

288 Barron, *Later Middle Ages* p. 153.

289 Beaven, II, pp. 7, 10, 11. LMA, MS COL/CC/01/01/6, f. 184v.

290 Hanawalt, *Ceremony & Civility*, pp. 75–76. Betty R. Masters, 'The Mayor's Household before 1600' in *Studies in London History Presented to Philip Edmund Jones*, ed. A.E.J. Hollaender & William Kellaway (London, 1969), pp. 95–114.

291 Griffiths, pp. 804–05. 'Bale's Chronicle' in Flenley, *Six Town Chronicles*, p. 145.

292 Griffiths, pp. 805–06. Kingsford, *Chronicles of London*, p. 168.

293 'MS Rawlinson B 355' in Flenley, *Six Town Chronicles*, p. 111–12. Kingsford, *Chronicles of London*, p. 168. *Brut*, p. 525. Griffiths, p. 806. Barron, 'London and the Crown', p. 65. M.I. Peake, 'London and the Wars of the Roses' (unpublished MA thesis, London, 1925), appendix viii. LMA, MS COL/CC/01/01/006, f. 192.

294 Jones, p. 163. John Stow, *Annales of England to 1603*, (no pub., 1603), pp. 668–69

295 'Bale's Chronicle' in Flenley, *Six Town Chronicles*, p. 146.

296 LBK, p. 395.

297 Griffiths, pp. 817–22. Jones, pp. 165–71.

298 Barron, 'London and the Crown', p. 65.

299 Barron, 'London and the Crown', p. 65.

300 Barron, *Later Middle Ages*, pp. 17–18. Sharpe, *London and the Kingdom*, I, pp. 297–98.

301 LBK, pp. 402–03. LMA, MS COL/CC/01/01/6, f. 227.

302 *Commons 1422–1461*, III, pp. 655–56.

303 Barron, 'London and the Crown', pp. 65–66. LBK, pp. 402–03. LMA, MS COL/CC/01/01/6, f. 196v

304 Peake, p. 133. Cora L. Scofield, *The Life and Reign of Edward the Fourth: King of England and of France and Lord of Ireland*, 2 vols (London, 1923; repub. 2016), I, p. 55.

305 LMA, MS COL/CC/01/01/6, f. 197v

306 TNA, E315/30/18.

307 LMA, MS COL/CC/01/01/6, ff. 237, 238

308 *An English Chronicle of the Reigns of Richard II, Henry IV, Henry V and Henry VI*, ed. John Silvester Davies, Camden Society LXIV (London, 1856), p. 94. LMA, MS COL/CC/01/01/6, f. 239.

309 LMA, MS COL/CC/01/01/6, f. 239v.

310 Sharpe, *London and the Kingdom*, pp. 298–301. Barron, 'London and the Crown', pp. 66–67.

311 Acts of Court of the Mercers' Company, p. 54.

312 Peake, p. 147. LMA, MS COL/CC/01/01/006, f. 254.

313 Barron, 'London and the Crown', p. 68. Griffiths, pp. 869–70. Jones, pp. 185–88. *Brut*, pp. 530–31.

314 Durrant Cooper, pp. 123–24. Josiah C. Wedgwood & Anne D. Holt, *History of Parliament: Biographies of the Members of the Commons House 1439–1509* (London, 1936), p. 466. John Whethampstede, *Registrum Abbatiae Johannis Whethamstede Abbatis Monasterii Sancti Albani*, ed. Henry Thomas Riley, Rolls Series vols 28:6a–b (London, 1872), I, pp. 392–93.

315 Calendar of State Papers and Manuscripts in the Archives and Collections of Milan 1385–1618, ed. Allen B. Hinds (London, 1912), pp. 48–49.

316 Barron, 'London and the Crown', p. 69.

317 Barron, 'London and the Crown', pp. 66–69. Peake, pp. 137–43. Griffiths, pp. 873–74. Jones, pp. 194–202. 'MS Gough London 10' in Flenley, *Six Town Chronicles*, pp. 161–62.

Chapter 10: Blickling or Bust

318 Davis, I, pp. 246–47. Dated by Davis as 1452 but re-dated by Richmond as 1451. C. Richmond, *The Paston Family in the Fifteenth Century: Endings* (Manchester, 2000), p. 106.

319 LMA, MS CLA/023/DW/01/171 (5).

320 LBK, p. 100. *Calendar of Hustings Wills*, II, p. 452. LMA, MS DL/C/B/004/MS09171/004, ff. 73.

321 Richmond, *Paston Family: First Phase*, pp. 123–34.

322 TNA, PROB11/3/544. Caroline M. Barron, 'Beatrice Melreth: A London Gentlewoman and her Books', in *Reading and Writing in Medieval England: Essays in Honor of Mary C. Erler*, ed. Martin Chase & Maryanne Kowaleski (Woodbridge, 2019), pp. 39–55.

323 TNA, C140/10/21, PROB 11/3/544. LMA, MS CLA/023/DW/01/177 (8).

324 Both Melreth's will and Geoffrey's purchase deeds do not number the properties in Lad Lane and Milk Street. They are simply described as being contained within the parish of St Lawrence Jewry, but according to the will Geoffrey wrote in 1460 and the inquisition taken at his death, he owned property in the adjoining parish of St Michael Wood Street, allegedly also acquired from Melreth's executors. As there is no record of any other purchase or of Melreth owning any other property, it seems likely that the tenements in Lad Lane actually crossed the parish boundary that divided this street. TNA, E315/30/18, C140/10/21, PROB11/3/544. LMA, MS CLA/023/DW/01/177 (8).

325 Schofield et al., 'Cheapside', pp. 131–47.

326 The sale had taken place by 1449 but it is not clear whether the lands were sold by Geoffrey II or by his father before his death. NRO, NRS 2788, 12D6, mm. 72–75v.

327 Davis, II, p. 224.

328 Anthony Robert Smith, 'Aspects of the Career of Sir John Fastolf' (unpublished DPhil thesis, University of Oxford, 1982) pp. 164–66. Helen Castor, *Blood and Roses* (London, 2004), p. 104. Griffiths, pp. 460–61.

329 Blomefield, VI, pp. 381–409. 'Sir Nicholas Dagworth', in *The House of Commons 1386–1421*, www.historyofparliamentonline.org.

330 Elizabeth Griffiths, 'The Boleyns at Blickling 1450–1560', *Norfolk Archaeology*, 45 (2009), pp. 453–68 (pp. 459–60).

331 Davis, II, p. 224.

332 TNA, C1/18/67. *Report on the Manuscripts of the Marquess of Lothian Preserved at Blickling Hall, Norfolk*, no ed., Historical Manuscripts Commission (1905), pp. 29–30. NRO, NRS 14730, 29D4.

333 NRO, NRS 10949 25D6, NRS 10848 A-B 25D4.

334 *The Itinerary of John Leland in or about the years 1535–1543*, ed. Lucy Toulmin Smith, 5 vols (London, 1908), II, p. 9.

335 Caroline Stanley-Millson & John Newman, 'Blickling Hall: The Building of a Jacobean Mansion', *Architectural History*, 29 (1986), pp. 1–42 (p. 5). Simon Thurley, 'Tudor Ambition: Houses of the Boleyn Family', Gresham College Lecture, 16 September 2020.

336 Despite Fastolf's willingness to sell and Geoffrey's willingness to buy, the two would do no further business after Blickling. In 1452 Agnes Paston heard a rumour that Fastolf had sold Heylsdon to Geoffrey but she also freely admitted that her informant, John Dam, had been wrong on other occasions and in this case he seems to have been equally mistaken. Davis, I, 38. In 1460, Geoffrey claimed that Fastolf had agreed to sell him Guton in 1451 but he had evidently been unable to conclude any such deal in the intervening nine years. Davis, II, p. 224.

337 TNA, C141/6/23, CP25/1/293/71/308.

338 Malcolm Mercer, 'Driven to Rebellion? Sir John Lewknor, Dynastic Loyalty and Debt', *Sussex Archaeological Collections*, 137 (1999), pp. 153–59 (pp. 154–56). *Commons 1422–1461*, V, pp. 247–51.

339 TNA, C146/240, C146/2709, C147/116. CPR 1452–1461, pp. 215–16.

340 *Abstracts of Feet of Fines Relating of Wiltshire*, ed. J.L. Kirby, Wiltshire Record Society vol. 41 (Devizes, 1986), p. 127. CPR 1461–1467, p. 141. CCR 1461–1468, pp. 206–07, 382–85. TNA, C1/40/47. *Commons 1422–1461*, IV, p. 970. TNA, C140/10/21.

341 No final will relating to the disposal of his estates survives for Geoffrey but there is an earlier one, written in 1460, which confirms his intention to leave his Norfolk lands to Thomas and his Kent lands to William. TNA, E315/30/18.

342 'James Fiennes, 1st Barron Saye and Sele', www.oxforddnb.com. The Fiennes family also had a connection to the Hoo family. Joan Brenchesley (née Batisford), the sister of James's mother, Elizabeth, in her will of 1453 described Thomas Hoo, esq., as her nephew. Canterbury Cathedral Archives, CCA-DCc-ChAnt/W/214, printed in *Sussex Archaeological Collections relating to the History and Antiquities of the County*, no ed., Sussex Archaeological Society, 53 (Lewes, 1910), p. 80.

343 The final payment was made in November 1460 but Geoffrey was already in possession when he wrote his will in February. TNA, E315/30/18. CCR 1461–1468, p. 133.

344 TNA, C146/137, C146/862, C146/1784, C146/2624, C146/5972.

345 Simon Thurley, 'Hever Castle' (unpublished report, 2020).

346 TNA, CP25/1/241/92/4, CP25/1/170/192/11.

347 Attendance lists compiled by Caroline M. Barron.

348 TNA, E315/30/18. LMA, MS CLA/023/DW/01/192 (23). *London Assize of Nuisance 1301–1431*, ed. Helena M. Chew & William Kellaway, London Record Society 10 (London, 1973), p. 121. David Bowsher, Tony Dyson, Nick Holder & Isca Howell, eds, *The London Guildhall: An Archaeological History of a Neighbourhood from Early Medieval to Modern Times*, 2 vols (London, MOLAS, 2007), I, pp. 179, 217–22.

349 Blomefield, VI, pp. 381–409.

350 TNA, C140/10/21.

351 TNA, E315/30/18, PROB11/5/12.

352 Kim M. Phillips, *Medieval Maidens: Young Women and Gender in England 1270–1540* (Manchester, 2003), pp. 32–34. Joel Rosenthal, 'Social Memory, Literacy and Piety in Fifteenth-Century Proofs of Age', in *Reading and Writing in Medieval England: Essays in Honor of Mary C. Erler*, ed. Martin Chase & Maryanne Kowaleski (Woodbridge, 2019), pp. 81–99 (p. 83).

353 Eamon Duffy, *The Stripping of the Altars*, 2nd edn (New Haven & London, 2005), pp. 338–56. Clive Burgess, 'Making Mammon Serve God: Merchant Piety' in *The Medieval Merchant: Proceedings of the 2012 Harlaxton Symposium*, ed. Caroline M. Barron & Anne F. Sutton, Harlaxton Medieval Studies XXIV (Donington, 2014), pp. 183–207.

354 TNA, C1/230/53, f. 4.

355 Sutton, *Mercery*, p. 171.

356 Sutton, *Mercery*, pp. 171–72.

357 Gorham, *Queens'*, p. 2. Cambridge University Archives, MS QC 76 'Misc A', ff. 3v, 5v.

358 His bequest of £100 for a new rood loft at St Lawrence Jewry also specified that existing chantries were to be maintained, suggesting an awareness of the risks of chantry failure.

359 TNA, C1/230/53, f. 4. A Cambridge Alumni Database, venn.lib.cam.ac.uk.

360 R.M. Ball, 'The Opponents of Bishop Pecok', *Journal of Ecclesiastical History*, 48:2 (1997), pp. 230–62.

361 Sheila Lindenbaum, 'London After Arundel: Learned Rectors and the Strategies of Orthodox Reform' in *After Arundel: Religious Writing in Fifteenth-Century England*, ed. Vincent Gillespie & Kantik Ghosh (Turnhout, Belgium, 2011), pp. 187–208 (p. 187). Ball, p. 252. W.G. Searle, *History of The Queens' College of St Margaret and St Bernard in the University of Cambridge 1446–1560* (Cambridge, 1867), p. 32.

362 J. Weever, *Ancient Funeral Monuments within the United Monarchy of Great Britain* (London 1631), p. 398. John Stow, *The Survey of London: containing the original, antique, increase and more modern estate of the said famous city, with additions by Anthony Munday* (London, 1618), p. 496. College of Arms, Hutton's Church Notes for London, p. 45.

Chapter 11: 'My Lady Boleyn'

363 Davis, I, p. 639.

364 Barron, 'Golden Age', pp. 35–58. Harris, *Aristocratic Women*, pp. 18, 22.

365 TNA, PROB11/5/12, E315/30/18.

366 Shannon McSheffrey & Julia Pope, 'Ravishment, Legal Narratives and Chivalric Culture in Fifteenth-Century England', *Journal of British Studies*, 48:4 (2009), pp. 818–36.

367 Harris, *Aristocratic Women*, p. 161.

368 Joel T. Rosenthal, 'Fifteenth-Century Widows and Widowhood: Bereavement, Reintegration and Life Choices' in *Wife and Widow in Medieval England*, ed. Sue Sheridan Walker (Michigan, 1993), pp. 33–58 (p. 37).

369 Davis, I, p. 396.

370 Barron, 'Golden Age', p. 45.

371 'William Welles', www.londonroll.org.

372 LBL, p. 62. TNA, SP46/183/fo51.

373 TNA, PROB11/5/206.

374 TNA, C241/254/55.

375 Archives and Cornish Studies Service, MS AR/2/1235, no. 9.

376 TNA, E403/830 mm. 1–2.

377 TNA, C1/2/82–85, C1/41/239–44. *Commons 1422–1461*, IV, pp. 963–64, 967.

378 TNA, CP25/1/293/71/308.

379 TNA, C1/44/185–88. CCR 1468–1476, p. 266. Mavis E. Mate, *Daughters, Wives and Widows after the Black Death: Women in Sussex 1350–1535* (Woodbridge, 1998), pp. 32–33. *Commons 1422–1461*, IV, p. 967.

380 *Commons 1422–1461*, IV, pp. 968–69.

381 *Inquisitions Post Mortem Henry VII*, I, pp. 68, 93. TNA, C241/254/105, C147/115.
382 Davis, I, pp. 573–75, II, p. 224.
383 Andy Shelley, *Dragon Hall, King Street, Norwich: Excavation and Survey of a Late Medieval Merchant's Trading Complex*, East Anglian Archaeology Report 112 (Norwich, 2005), pp. 60–61. Blomefield, IV, pp. 64–84; VIII, pp. 269–76.
384 Thomas was 17 on 7 September after his father's death and William was probably 12, but if born in late June or early July could still have been 11. Calculations based on dates in inquisitions post mortem for Geoffrey and Anne Boleyn, Thomas Hoo Esq., TNA, C140/10/21, C141/6/23, C142/3/75.
385 TNA, E315/30/18.
386 Caroline M. Barron, 'Chivalry, Pageantry and Merchant Culture in Medieval London', in *Heraldry, Pageantry and Social Display in Medieval England*, ed. Peter Coss & Maurice Keen (Woodbridge, 2002), pp. 219–41.
387 On the education of the gentry, aristocracy and mercantile classes, see: Nicholas Orme, 'Education and Recreation' and Alison Truelove, 'Literacy' in *Gentry Culture in Late Medieval England*, ed. Raluca Radulescu and Alison Truelove (Manchester, 2005). Nicholas Orme, *From Childhood to Chivalry: The Education of the English Kings and Aristocracy 1066–1530* (London & New York, 1984). Caroline M. Barron, 'The Expansion of Education in Fifteenth-Century London' in *The Cloister and the World: Essays in Medieval History in Honour of Barbara Harvey*, ed. John Blair & Brian Golding (Oxford, 1996), pp. 219–45.
388 Orme, *Childhood to Chivalry*, p. 127.
389 Orme, 'Education', p. 77. Eric Ives, *The Life and Death of Anne Boleyn* (Oxford, 2004), p. 156.

Chapter 12: 'For Nowadays Money Maketh Marriage'

390 Davis, II, 32.
391 Davis, II, pp. 31–33.
392 Davis, I, pp. 253–54.
393 Davis, I, pp. 41–42, 206–07. Castor, *Blood & Roses*, pp. 96, 110–11. Diane Watt, *Medieval Women's Writing: Works by and for Women in England 1100–1500* (Cambridge, 2007), pp. 123–24.
394 Harris, *Aristocratic Women*, p. 58.
395 Davis, II, p. 106. Jonathan Rose, 'Litigation and Political Conflict in Fifteenth-Century East Anglia: Conspiracy and Attaint Actions and Sir John Fastolf', *Journal of Legal History*, 27:1 (2006), pp. 53–80 (pp. 54–55). Castor, *Blood & Roses*, p. 110.
396 TNA, C146/1529, SP46/183/fo39.
397 *Commons 1422–1461*, III, p. 857. *Memorials of the Guild of Merchant Taylors of the Fraternity of St. John the Baptist in the City of London*, ed. C.M. Clode (London, 1875), pp. 155–58, 617–50.
398 For William Cheyne see: Marcus Herbert, 'The Minster Yorkist: An Armoured Effigy in the Abbey Church of the Blessed Virgin Mary and St Sexburgha, Minster, Isle of Sheppey, Kent', *The Ricardian*, 21 (2011), pp. 1–22 (pp. 7–14). *Commons*

1422–1461, III, p. 857. Francis Cheyne turned 18 on 25 July 1499. *Inquisitions Post Mortem Henry VII*, II, pp. 72–73, 166–67, 186–87.

399 David King, 'The Indent of John Aylward: Glass and Brass at East Harling', *Monumental Brass Society Transactions*, 18:3 (2011), pp. 251–67 (p. 261). Monumental Brass Society, Portfolio of Brasses, Edmund Clere and his wife Elizabeth, www.mbs-brasses.co.uk/index-of-brasses/edmund-clere-and-his-wife.

400 Davis, I, pp. 534–35.

401 NRO, NRS 14730, 29D4. TNA, C67/46, m. 16.

402 CCR 1468–1476, p. 82.

403 Mother Mary Gregory, 'Wickham Court and the Heydons', *Archaeologia Cantiana*, 78 (1963), pp. 1–21. *Commons 1422–1461*, IV, pp. 899–909. 'Sir Henry Heydon', www.oxforddnb.com.

404 TNA, E150/468/3.

405 TNA, PROB11/14/336, PROB11/16/733, PROB11/15/290.

406 St Erasmus is a slightly unusual choice but his aid was often sought for help with both abdominal pain and for childbirth, so this may indicate either her last illness or her many pregnancies.

407 TNA, PROB11/14/336, PROB11/16/733.

408 Davis, I, pp. 396–97, 534–35. Castor, *Blood & Roses*, pp. 187–88, 271–72. Bennett, *Pastons*, pp. 39–41.

409 LBL, p. 110. It has been suggested that their eldest son, John, was born as early as 1469, on the basis that he was termed an 'esquire' in 1490 and therefore probably of age, but this John Fortescue was the son of Martin Fortescue, so is evidently not the same man. CCR 1485–1500, p. 142.

410 For John Fortescue see: William Arthur Shaw, *The Knights of England* (London, 1906), p. 22. Wedgwood, *Commons Biographies*, p. 349. *Commons 1422–1461*, IV, p. 435. Thomas Fortescue, *A History of the Family of Fortescue in all its Branches* (London, 1880), pp. 236–47. *A History of the County of Hertford*, ed. William Page, 3 vols (London, 1912), II, pp. 392–405, III, pp. 91–111, 419–23, www.british-history.ac.uk. 'Sir Adrian Fortescue', www.oxforddnb.com. CCR 1476–1485, p. 113.

Chapter 13: 'Servants and Lovers of the Duke of Gloucester'

411 Thomas Penn, *The Brothers York: An English Tragedy* (London, 2019), pp. 208–09.

412 Davis, I, p. 545.

413 CCR 1468–1476, p. 102. BL, MS Cotton Julius B XII, ff. 122–23.

414 Rosemary Horrox, *Richard III: A Study in Service* (Cambridge, 1989), pp. 31–32, 78. Scofield, *Edward IV*, I, pp. 491–504. Penn, *The Brothers York*, pp. 209–221. Lynda Pidgeon, 'Antony Wydevile, Lord Scales and Earl Rivers: Family, Friends and Affinity, part 1', *The Ricardian*, 15 (2005), pp. 1–19.

415 Scofield, *Edward IV*, I, pp. 509–39, 545–46. Penn, *The Brothers York*, pp. 225–68. *Calendar of State Papers Milan 1385–1618*, p. 210.

416 Scofield, *Edward IV*, I, 566–76. Penn, *The Brothers York*, pp. 269–76. *Commons 1422–1461*, VII, p. 309.

417 'Warkworth's Chronicle' and 'The History of the Arrival of King Edward IV' in *The Contemporary English Chronicles of the Wars of the Roses*, ed. Dan Embree & M. Teresa Tavormina (Woodbridge, 2019), pp. 124, 172–74. Scofield, *Edward IV*, I, pp. 576–80. Penn, *The Brothers York*, pp. 277–80.

418 Hannes Kleineke, 'Gerhard von Wesel's Newsletter from England 17 April 1471', *The Ricardian*, 16 (2006), pp. 66–83 (pp. 81–82).

419 TNA, PROB11/6/33.

420 Gottfried, p. 133.

421 Charles Ross, 'Some Servants and Lovers of Richard in his Youth', *The Ricardian*, 4 (1976), pp. 2–4.

422 Including a 50-year-old soldier who received and survived a large gash to his face long before he met his death at the Battle of Towton. Robert C. Woosnam-Savage & Kelly DeVries, 'Battle Trauma in Medieval Warfare: Wounds, Weapons and Armour' and Michael Livingston, '"The Depth of Six Inches": Prince Hal's Head-Wound at the Battle of Shrewsbury', in *Wounds and Wound Repair in Medieval Culture*, ed. Larissa Tracy & Kelly DeVries (Leiden & Boston, 2016), pp. 27–56 and pp. 215–31 (p. 47).

423 Jean Flori, *Richard the Lionheart: King and Knight*, trans. Jean Birrell (Edinburgh, 1999), pp. 198–200.

424 Brian Burfield, *Medieval Military Medicine: From the Vikings to the High Middle Ages* (Barnsley, 2022), pp. 43–58, 107–10. Jon Clasper, 'The Management of Military Wounds in the Middle Ages', in *Wounds in the Middle Ages*, ed. Anne Kirkham & Cordelia Warr (Farnham, 2014), pp. 17–39. Ilana Krug, 'The Wounded Soldier: Honey and Late Medieval Military Medicine', in *Wounds and Wound Repair in Medieval Culture*, ed. Larissa Tracy & Kelly DeVries (Leiden & Boston, 2016), pp. 194–214.

425 TNA, PROB11/6/33, PROB11/6/94.

426 *A Fifteenth-Century School Book*, ed. William Nelson (Oxford, 1956), p. 17.

427 Durrant Cooper, pp. 109, 122, 131. Stow, *The Survey of London*, with additions by Munday, p. 496. College of Arms, Hutton's Church Notes for London, p. 45.

428 Thrupp, p. 223.

429 TNA, PROB11/6/33.

430 Sir John Baker, *The Men of Court 1440 to 1550: A Prosopography of the Inns of Court and Chancery and of the Courts of Law*, 2 vols (London, 2012), I, p. 333. *The Records of the Honourable Society of Lincoln's Inn: Admissions*, no ed., 4 vols (London, 1896–1981), I, p. 18.

431 TNA, C140/10/21.

432 'Thomas Boleyn', www.londonroll.org. Mercers' Company, MS John Coke, 'The Names of the Brethren of the Mercery', see 'William Boleyn', medievallondoners.ace.fordham.edu.

433 Sir John Fortescue, *De Laudibus Legum Anglie*, ed. S.B. Chrimes (Cambridge, 1942), pp. 116–19.

434 *Men of Court*, II, 1433.

435 Orme, *Childhood to Chivalry*, pp. 74–80.

436 TNA, PROB11/18/184.

437 Cambridgeshire and Huntingdonshire Archives, MSS P75/25/21–24. TNA, PROB11/5/12.

438 GEC, X, pp. 126–42. 'James Butler, Fourth Earl of Ormond' and 'James Butler, First Earl of Wiltshire and Fifth Earl of Ormond', www.oxforddnb.com.

439 Berkeley Castle Muniments, MSS BCM/H/1/3/1–2.

440 TNA, C142/1/158–60.

441 Date calculated from the brass of Anne Boleyn at Blickling. Blomefield, VI, pp. 381–409.

442 Her first husband, Ambrose Cresacre, died in 1469. TNA, PROB11/5/436.

443 Phillips, *Medieval Maidens*, pp. 36–43.

444 In a sample of 434 male peers, only 11 per cent lived to be over 70 and only 5 per cent over 75, although a few did survive into their eighties. Joel T. Rosenthal, 'Medieval Longevity and the Secular Peerage 1350–1500', *Population Studies*, 27:2 (1973), pp. 287–93.

445 Berkeley Castle Muniments, MSS BCM/H/1/3/1–2.

446 GEC, X, pp. 126–42.

447 LP, II, 1470.

448 GEC, X, p. 130.

449 TNA, C146/1955, C146/2550, E40/7701. Anne also lent £25 to Thomas Ormond independently. SP 46/183/fo53.

450 'The Bedford Estate: Covent Garden and the seven acres in Long Acre', in *Survey of London, Vol. 36, Covent Garden*, ed. F.H.W. Sheppard (London, 1970), pp. 19–21.

451 TNA, SP46/183/fo45, 52, 66, 72, C 146/1022, 2032, 4769, 4804, 6086, 9262, C 47/10/28/14, 19, 23. Horrox, *Richard III*, pp. 104, 147, 222, 259–60, 262. 'William Catesby', www.oxforddnb.com.

Chapter 14: 'Meet for the Court and Meet for the Country'

452 Fionn Pilbrow, 'The Knights of the Bath: Dubbing to Knighthood in Lancastrian and Yorkist England', in *Heraldry, Pageantry and Social Display in Medieval England*, ed. Maurice Keen & Peter Coss (Woodbridge, 2002), pp. 195–218 (p. 205). LPRH, I, p. 391. Penn, *The Brothers York*, pp. 493–94.

453 *The Coronation of Richard III: The Extant Documents*, ed. Anne F. Sutton & P.W. Hammond (Gloucester, 1983), pp. 273–74, 313. LPRH, I, pp. 390–91. Pilbrow, pp. 195–218. BL, Harley MS 41, ff. 19–24v.

454 Penn, *The Brothers York*, p. 492. 'Margaret of Anjou', www.oxforddnb.com.

455 Pilbrow, pp. 210–13.

456 *Coronation Richard III*, pp. 304, 309, 312, 318, 323, 326, 339, 367, 392, 411–12.

457 North Yorkshire County Record Office, ZRC 17502. Horrox, *Richard III*, pp. 77–79.

458 'John Howard, First Duke of Norfolk', www.oxforddnb.com.

459 Blomefield says the commission dated 21 August 1483 was made by John Mowbray, Duke of Norfolk and Lord High Admiral, but Mowbray was

neither admiral nor alive, having died in 1476, and Howard was the new duke. Blomefield, IV, pt. 2, pp. 1–46.

460 Anne Crawford, 'The Career of John Howard, Duke of Norfolk 1420–1485' (unpublished PhD thesis, Bedford College, University of London, 1975), p. 71.

461 *Harleian 433*, III, pp. 11–12.

462 *The Household Books of John Howard, Duke of Norfolk, 1462–1471, 1481–1483*, ed. Anne Crawford (Stroud, 1992).

463 NRO, WKC 3/2, 399X4, WKC 1/307, 392X6, WKC 1/220, 392X1. Crawford, p. 102. CCR 1500–1509, pp. 63, 125. BL, Add MS 21480, ff. 45v–46, www.tudorchamberbooks.org. 'Thomas Wyndham', www.oxforddnb.com.

464 Horrox, *Richard III*, p. 141. CPR 1476–1485, p. 566.

465 In Kent, Richard Lee was apparently deleted by mistake from the first commission and it took two further commissions in July to reinstate him and to add two further names, Horrox, *Richard III*, pp. 141–42.

466 CPR 1476–1485, p. 343.

467 CPR 1476–1485, p. 466. Horrox, *Richard III*, p. 244. N.A.M. Rodger, *The Safeguard of the Sea: A Naval History of Great Britain 660–1649* (London, 2004), p. 157.

468 CPR 1476–1485, pp. 397, 490.

469 Anne F. Sutton, 'The Admiralty and Constableship of England in the Later Fifteenth Century: The Operation and Development of these Offices, 1462–85, under Richard, Duke of Gloucester and King of England' in *Courts of Chivalry and Admiralty in Later Medieval Europe*, ed. Anthony Musson & Nigel Ramsay (Woodbridge, 2018), pp. 187–214. Davis, I, pp. 667–68, II, pp. 459–60. CPR 1476–1485, p. 520. Crawford, p. 71.

470 *The Crowland Chronicle Continuations 1459–1486*, ed. Nicholas Pronay & John Cox (London, 1986), p. 177. *Harleian 433*, II, p. 229.

471 Crowland Chronicle Continuations, pp. 177–79.

472 Penn, *The Brothers York*, pp. 553–64. *Parliament Rolls*, XV, pp. 107–08.

473 TNA, C141/6/23.

474 Ethelreda Sansbury, *An Historical Guide to Norwich Cathedral* (Norwich, 1986), pp. 22–23. *Norwich Cathedral: Church, City and Diocese 1096–1996*, ed. Ian Atherton, Eric Fernie, Christopher Harper-Bill & Hassell Smith (London, 1996), pp. 193–96.

475 Arms of Hoo, Wychingham, St Omer, St Leger and Felton. Thomas Browne, *Repertorium: or some account of the tombs and monuments in the cathedral church of Norwich, begun by Sir Thomas Browne and continued from the year 1680 to this present time* (London, 1712), p. 15. Blomefield, IV, pt. 2, pp. 1–46.

476 J.R. Lander, *English Justices of the Peace 1461–1509* (Gloucester, 1989), pp. 1–48.

477 TNA, E372/329, pp. 331–5, 337–50.

478 CPR 1485–1494, p. 179.

479 Nathen Amin, *Henry VII and the Tudor Pretenders, Simnel, Warbeck and Warwick* (Stroud, 2020), pp. 73–106.

480 Davis, II, p. 452.

481 Polydore Vergil, *The Anglica Historia of Polydore Vergil A.D. 1485–1537*, trans. D. Hay (London, 1950), pp. 21–27. Shaw, *Knights of England*, pp. 24–26. Amin, pp. 116–17.

482 Amin, pp. 121–29. Vergil, p. 25.

483 Davis, I, pp. 658–59. Michael J. Bennett, 'Henry VII and the Northern Rising of 1489', *English Historical Review*, 105 (1990), pp. 34–59.

484 CFR 1485–1509, p. 132.

485 Lander, pp. 93–98, 165–66. Richard Gorski, 'Justice and Injustice? England's Local Officials in the Later Middle Ages' in *Outlaws in Medieval and Early Modern England: Crime, Government and Society c. 1066–c. 1600*, ed. John C. Appleby & Paul Dalton (Farnham, 2009), pp. 55–74. Peter Fleming, 'Politics' in *Gentry Culture in Late Medieval England*, ed. Raluca Radulescu & Alison Truelove (Manchester, 2005), pp. 50–62. Helen M. Jewell, *English Local Administration in the Middle Ages* (Newton Abbot, 1972), pp. 182–200.

486 *Materials for a History of the Reign of Henry VII*, ed. William Campbell, 2 vols (London, 1877), II, p. 562.

487 CPR 1485–1494, pp. 349, 357. John M. Curren, '"The King's Army into the Partes of Bretaigne": Henry VII and the Breton Wars 1489–1491', *War in History*, 7:4 (2000), pp. 379–412.

488 Vergil, pp. 51–53.

489 Thomas Penn, *Winter King: The Dawn of Tudor England* (London, 2012), pp. 23–25. Amin, pp. 140–69.

490 CPR 1494–1509, p. 31.

491 William employed the legal expedient of a writ of right patent (*breve de recto patens*) whereby the land was 'recovered' by Robert Rede and Thomas Kebill as the alleged lawful owners before being conveyed to Lakyn at William's request. The intention was to head off any future claims under the entail in Geoffrey's will. LMA, MSS CLA/023/PL/01/170, m. 9, CLA/023/DW/01/223, (1)(2)(23). 'Richard Lakyn', medievallondoners.ace.fordham.edu. Sutton, *Mercery*, pp. 204, 540–41.

492 NRO, DCN 44/13/3.

493 N.F. Ticehurst, 'The Mute Swan in Kent' *Archaeologia Cantiana*, 47 (1935), pp. 55–70 (p. 69). TNA, PROB11/14/790. Gowthorp was previously held by a similar set of feoffees from whom William acquired Blickling. Blomefield, V, pp. 49–54.

494 Vergil, pp. 93–97.

495 Penn, *Winter King*, pp. 29–31. Amin, pp. 173–245. I. Arthurson, 'The Rising of 1497: A Revolt of the Peasantry?' in *People, Politics and Community in the Later Middle Ages,* ed. Joel Rosenthal & Colin Richmond (Gloucester, 1987), pp. 1–18. *Great Chronicle*, pp. 276–77.

496 £15 3s. 4d. to John Heydon and £11 6s. 3d. to Thomas Boleyn, TNA, E36/126, ff. 27, 29.

497 Amin, pp. 245–75. *Great Chronicle*, pp. 281–83.

498 CFR 1485–1509, p. 295. TNA, E372/346. E101/415/3, f. 212v, E101/413/2/3, f. 13v, www.tudorchamberbooks.org.

499 CPR 1494–1509, p. 273.

500 LPRH, I, pp. 388–404.

Chapter 15: Father and Son

501 Sean Cunningham, *Prince Arthur: The Tudor King Who Never Was* (Stroud, 2016), pp. 131–43. *Great Chronicle*, pp. 297–312.

502 All refs. see, LPRH, I, pp. 404–17. *Miscellaneous State Papers from 1501 to 1726*, ed. P. Yorke, Earl of Hardwicke, 2 vols (London, 1778), I, pp. 1–20. *The Receyt of the Ladie Kateryne*, ed. G. Kipling, Early English Text, Society, 296 (Oxford, 1990), pp. 4–51. Cunningham, pp. 122–60.

503 LP, IV, 2581.

504 *Men of Court*, I, p. 332. 'Sir Thomas More', www.oxforddnb.com.

505 LP, I, p. 13. TNA, LC2/1, ff. 59–79v.

506 TNA, E101/414/16, f. 37v, www.tudorchamberbooks.org. *Excerpta Historica or Illustrations of English History*, ed. S. Bentley (London, 1833), p. 119. Raphael Holinshed, *Chronicles of England, Scotland and Ireland*, 6 vols (London, 1808), III, p. 520.

507 Mackay, p. 25.

508 TNA, E101/414/16, f. 37v, www.tudorchamberbooks.org. A.F. Wareham & A.P.M. Wright, *A History of the County of Cambridge and the Isle of Ely*, Vol. 10 (London, 2002), pp. 470–72. *Inquisitions Post Mortem Henry VII*, II, pp. 197–223.

509 'Thomas Howard, Second Duke of Norfolk', www.oxforddnb.com. Bennett, 'Rising of 1489', pp. 34–59. Susan Elizabeth Vokes, 'The Early Career of Thomas, Lord Howard, Earl of Surrey and Third Duke of Norfolk, 1474–*c.* 1525' (unpublished PhD thesis, University of Hull, 1988), pp. 13–19, 22–25.

510 M.J. Tucker, 'The Ladies in Skelton's Garland of Laurel', *Renaissance Quarterly*, 22:4 (1969), pp. 333–45. *The Poetical Works of John Skelton*, ed. Alexander Dyce, 2 vols (London 1843, repub. New York, 1965), I, pp. 396–97.

511 Mackay, pp. 49, 171, 189.

512 Tucker, p. 335. *Sede Vacante Wills: A Calendar of Wills Proved before the Commissary of the Prior and Chapter of Christ Church, Canterbury during Vacancies in the Primacy*, ed. C.E. Woodruff, Kent Archaeological Society, 3 (Canterbury, 1914), p. 137.

513 Melvin J. Tucker, The Life of Thomas Howard, Earl of Surrey and Second Duke of Norfolk (London, 1964), p. 72.

514 Harris, *Aristocratic Women*, pp. 22–24, 49–50.

515 CCR 1500–1509, pp. 63–64.

516 Account of John Younge, Somerset Herald in John Leland, *Antiquarii de Rebus Britannicis Collectanea*, ed. Thomas Hearne, 6 vols (London, 1774), IV, pp. 265–300. *The Manuscripts of his Grace the Duke of Rutland G.C.B., preserved at Belvoir Castle*, Historical Manuscripts Commission, 12th Report, Appendix IV (London, 1888), p. 18.

517 In May 1503 he was described simply as 'Sir William Boleyn's son', BL, Add MS 59899, f. 22, www.tudorchamberbooks.org.

518 LP, XI, p. 13.

519 LP, XIII, pt. 1, p. 345. TNA, SP1/132, ff. 34–34v.

520 CPR 1494–1509, p. 645.

521 TNA, E372/347–50, KB9/425–37.

522 'Sir Richard Guildford', www.oxforddnb.com. Wedgwood, *Commons Biographies*, pp. 435–37. Lander, pp. 124–29, 139–44.

523 CPR 1494–1509, pp. 322, 361, 408.

524 TNA, E372/345–48, 350, KB9/437, m. 13.

525 TNA, PROB11/14/790.

526 LP, XI, p. 13.

527 Pashley 1517, £15 5s. 1d., lists both demesne rents and rents of assize. Carbroke 1540–41, £11 2s. 9d., lists former demesne lands only. Holkham, 1514, £4 8s. 11d. (including rents decayed by this date), does not specify demesne or wider manor but it was valued at £10 in 1463 so this likely represents only a fraction of its true value. For comparison Pashley was valued at £6 13s. 4d. in 1463. East Sussex and Brighton and Hove Record Office, MSS AMS 5692/7, AMS 7002/4/2/4/3. TNA, LR2/220, ff. 270–74, C140/10/21. Holkham Hall, MS Davidson 227.

528 TNA, SP46/183/fo180, fo189, fo196, SC12/1/12, C47/10/28/29, SC6/HENVIII/919–21, PROB11/18/184.

529 LP, IV, ccxlvi, 525, 673, 696, 880. TNA, SP1/102, f. 139.

530 TNA, C54/370A, m. 14.

531 *Correspondence of Mathew Parker D.D. Archbishop of Canterbury*, ed. John Bruce (Cambridge, 1853), p. 400.

532 LP, I, p. 238.

533 For example, 'William Goche of London, Brome, Norfolk and Clifford's Inn' or 'Thomas Pekham of Wroteham, Kent, London, Barnard Inn in Holborn, Middlesex and Lamehithe, Surrey', LP, I, pp. 238, 249.

534 *A History of the County of Bedford*, Vol. 2, ed. William Page (London, 1908), pp. 348–75, www.british-history.ac.uk.

535 CPR 1429–1436, p. 373. *Commons 1422–1461*, IV, p. 959.

536 Browne, *Repertorium*, p. 14.

537 William's other executors were Thomas, Earl of Ormond and Sir Robert Southwell. TNA, PROB11/14/790.

538 This seems to say 'plate' rather than 'place' but this must be an error, c and t being very similar. TNA, PROB11/14/790.

539 PROB11/14/336, PROB11/16/733.

540 John Adey Repton, *Norwich Cathedral at the end of the Eighteenth Century, with descriptive notes by William Wilkins*, ed. S. Rowland Pierce (Farnborough, 1965), pl. 2. Section of the Cathedral Church in Norwich, by William Wilkins, Jnr, 1784, property of Norwich Cathedral.

541 Browne, *Repertorium*, pp. 14–15. Blomefield, IV, pt. 2, pp. 1–46.

542 Blomefield, IV, pt. 2, pp. 1–46. Anne's stone may have temporarily been placed on top of the tomb of her son before being removed to the ambulatory. Henry Harrod, *Gleanings among the Castles and Convents of Norfolk* (Norwich, 1857), p. 295. I am grateful for the advice and assistance of Dr Gundun Warren, Librarian and Curator at Norwich Cathedral.

543 TNA, PROB11/14/790.

544 Corpus Christi College, Cambridge, MS 119, f. 21. Translated in Philip W. Sergeant, *The Youth of Anne Boleyn* (London, 1923), pp. 17–18.

Epilogue

545 TNA, E150/87/6.

546 Wendy J. Turner, *Care and Custody of the Mentally Ill, Incompetent and Disabled in Medieval England* (Turnhout, Belgium, 2013), pp. 66–81. Wendy J. Turner, 'Defining Mental Afflictions in Medieval English Administrative Records' in *Disability and Medieval Law: History, Literature, Society*, ed. Cory James Rushton (Cambridge, 2013), pp. 134–56.

547 A form of schizophrenia is also possible, although bipolar disorder is the more common disease. I am most grateful to Prof. Tom Dening, Head of the Centre for Dementia at the University of Nottingham, for his advice on potential diagnoses.

548 LP, I, pt. 2, p. 977.

549 LP, XIV, pt. 1, p. 398.

550 Death date from inquisition post mortem TNA, E150/639/4, E150/493/4.

551 Margaret McGlynn, 'Idiots, Lunatics and the Royal Prerogative in Early Tudor England', *Journal of Legal History*, 26:1 (2005), pp. 1–20.

552 LP, XIV, pt. 1, pp. 239–40.

553 LP, XV, pp. 286–87.

554 TNA, SP1/102, ff. 139–40, CP25/2/4/21/33HENVIIITRIN, 48, CP25/2/4/21/34HENVIIITRIN, 73. LP, XV, pp. 286–87, XVI, p. 382, XVII, pp. 210–11, XVIII, pt. 1, p. 365. Kent Archives, U1450/T6/89. Edward Hasted, *The History and Topographical Survey of the County of Kent*, 12 vols (Canterbury, 1797), III, pp. 126–45. A.P.M. Wright & C.P. Lewis, *A History of the County of Cambridge and the Isle of Ely*, Vol. 9 (London, 1989), pp. 381–86. Wareham & Wright, *County of Cambridge*, Vol. 10, pp. 136–43.

555 Blickling, Calthorpe, Filby, Stiffkey, Postwick and the Ormond manor of Swavesey, Cambs, which reverted to Mary. LP, XIV, pt. 1, p. 403. LP, XV, p. 117.

556 For sales see Blomefield: West Lexham, Hook Hall in Calthorp, Filby, Carbroke, Stiffkey, Postwick. CPR 1547–1548, p. 337. The issues of Gowthorp were reserved for twenty years by William's will, then it went to Edward, who immediately sold it in 1525. TNA, PROB11/14/790. Blomefield, V, pp. 49–54.

557 Sutton, *Mercery*, pp. 540–41. 'Sir Thomas Gresham', www.oxforddnb.com. Blomefield, V, pp. 75–83, IX, pp. 231–44.

558 Egmere, Hevingham, Cawston, Kerdiston & Reepham. TNA, E305/2/A33. LP, XV, p. 174.

559 TNA, E150/1224/7, C1/1493/28–29, C4/43/72, E305/2/A33. LP, XV, pp. 174, 295.

560 CPR 1553–1554, p. 361.

561 Parsons, *Salle*, p. 17. CPR 1553–1554, p. 362. TNA, PROB11/44/387.

562 Ives, p. 195

563 Thrupp, *Merchant Class*, pp. 283–84.

564 'Richard [Dick] Whittington' and 'Simon Eyre', www.oxforddnb.com.

565 Payling, pp. 51–73 (p. 55).

Select Bibliography

Online Sources

Articles & Biographies of MPs 1386–1421 (www.historyofparliamentonline.org)
Calendar of Close Rolls (www.archive.org & www.hathitrust.org)
Calendar of Fine Rolls (www.archive.org & www.hathitrust.org)
Calendar of Patent Rolls (www.archive.org & www.hathitrust.org)
A Cambridge Alumni Database (venn.lib.cam.ac.uk)
Chamber Account Books of Henry VII & Henry VIII (www.tudorchamberbooks.org)
England's Immigrants Database (www.englandsimmigrants.com)
Letters & Papers of the Reign of Henry VIII (www.british-history.ac.uk)
London Apprenticeship Records (www.londonroll.org)
The London Customs Accounts, ed. Stuart Jenks (www.hansischergeschichtsverein.de/london-customs-accounts)
Medieval Londoners Database (medievallondoners.ace.fordham.edu)
The Oxford Dictionary of National Biography (www.oxforddnb.com)
Victoria County History (www.british-history.ac.uk)

Manuscript Sources

British Library:
Cotton MS Julius B XII
Cotton MS Nero E VII
Harley MS 41
Royal MS 17 B XLVII

London Metropolitan Archives:
CLA/023/DW/01 Court of Husting: Deeds and Wills
COL/CC/01/01/004–6 Common Council: Journals
DL/C/B/004/MS09171 Commissary Court: Register of Wills

The National Archives:
C1 Early Chancery Proceedings
C47/10/28 Chancery Miscellanea: Ireland
C66 Patent Rolls
C76 Treaty Rolls
C131 Chancery: Extents for Debt
C139–141 Chancery: Inquisitions Post Mortem
C146–147 Chancery: Ancient Deeds
C241 Chancery: Certificates of Statute Merchant & Statute Staple
CP25/1 Feet of Fines
CP40 Common Pleas: Plea Rolls
E122/209 Particulars of Customs Accounts: Southampton
E159 Exchequer: Memoranda Rolls
E315/30/18 Court of Augmentations, Predecessors and Successors
PROB11 Prerogative Court of Canterbury Wills
SC6 Special Collections: Ministers' Accounts
SC12 Special Collections: Rentals and Surveys
SP46/183 Ormond Papers

Norfolk Record Office:
DCN 44/13/3
MS 13034, 31D10
NCC Will Register Doke & Brosyard
NRS 2605/1–2, 12B3 & 2605/3–5, 12B4
NRS 2606, 12B5
NRS 2621, 12C2
NRS 2788, 12D6
NRS 10848A–B, 25D4
NRS 10949, 25D6
NRS 14730, 29D4
NRS 17943, 41C5
WHT 5/58/1
WKC 1/220, 392X1
WKC 1/307, 392X6
WKC 3/2, 399X4

Other Archives:
Berkeley Castle Muniments, BCM/H/1/3/1–2
Cambridge University, MS QC 76 'Misc A'
Cambridgeshire and Huntingdonshire Archives, MSS P75/25/21–24

Canterbury Cathedral Archives, CCA-DCc-ChAnt/W/214
College of Arms, Hutton's Church Notes for London
Kent Archives, U1450/T6/89
North Yorkshire County Record Office, ZRC 17502

Published Primary Sources

Bradley, Helen, ed., *Views of the Hosts of Alien Merchants 1440–44* (London, 2012)

Brewer, J.S., J. Gairdner & R.H. Brodie, eds, *Letters and Papers, Foreign and Domestic, of the Reign of Henry VIII*, 21 vols (London, 1862–1932)

Brie, Friedrich W.D., ed., *The Brut or The Chronicles of England* (London, 1906)

Calendar of Inquisitions Post Mortem Henry VII, no ed., 3 vols (London, 1898–1955)

Campbell, William, ed., *Materials for a History of the Reign of Henry VII*, 2 vols (London, 1877)

Davis, Norman, ed., *Paston Letters and Papers of the Fifteenth Century*, 2 vols (Oxford, 1971)

Embree, Dan & M. Teresa Tavormina, eds, *The Contemporary English Chronicles of the Wars of the Roses* (Woodbridge, 2019)

Flenley, Ralph, ed., *Six Town Chronicles of England* (Oxford, 1911)

Gairdner, James, ed., *The Historical Collections of a Citizen of London in the Fifteenth Century (Gregory's Chronicle)* (London, 1876)

Gairdner, James, ed., *Letters and Papers Illustrative of the Reigns of Richard III and Henry VII*, 2 vols (London, 1861–63)

Given-Wilson, Chris, Paul Brand, Seymour Phillips, Mark Ormrod, Geoffrey Martin, Anne Curry & Rosemary Horrox, eds, *Parliament Rolls of Medieval England*, 16 vols (Woodbridge, 2005)

Gorham, George Cornelius, ed., *A Form for the Commemoration of Benefactors to be used in the Chapel of the College of St Margaret and St Bernard, commonly called Queens' College Cambridge* (Cambridge, 1823)

Horrox, Rosemary & P.W. Hammond, eds, *British Library Harleian Manuscript 433*, 4 vols (Gloucester, 1979–83)

Jefferson, Lisa, ed., *The Medieval Account Books of the Mercers of London: An Edition and Translation*, 2 vols (Farnham, 2009)

Kingsford, Charles Lethbridge, ed., *Chronicles of London* (Oxford, 1905)

Kipling, G., ed., *The Receyt of the Ladie Kateryne* (Oxford, 1990)

Lyell, Laetitia & Frank D. Watney, eds, *Acts of Court of the Mercers' Company 1453–1527* (Cambridge, 1936)

Pronay, Nicholas & John Cox, eds, *The Crowland Chronicle Continuations 1459–1486* (London, 1986)

The Records of the Honourable Society of Lincoln's Inn: Admissions, no ed., 4 vols (London, 1896–1981)

Riley, Henry Thomas, ed., *Memorials of London and London Life* (London, 1868)

Riley, Henry Thomas, ed., *Munimenta Gildhallae Londoniensis, Liber Albus, Liber Custumarum et Liber Horn*, 3 vols (London, 1862)

Rye, Walter, ed., *The Visitation of Norfolk* (London, 1891)

Sharpe, Reginald R., ed., *Calendar of Letter Books of the City of London: Letter Books A–L* (London, 1899–1912)

Smith, Lucy Toulmin, ed., *The Itinerary of John Leland in or about the years 1535–1543*, 5 vols (London, 1908)

Stow, John, *The Survey of London* (London, 1987)

Stow, John, *The Survey of London: containing the original, antique, increase and more modern estate of the said famous city, with additions by Anthony Munday* (London, 1618)

Sutton, Anne F. & P.W. Hammond, eds, *The Coronation of Richard III: The Extant Documents* (Gloucester, 1983)

Thomas, A.H. & I.D. Thornley, eds, *The Great Chronicle of London* (London, 1938)

Thomas, A.H., & Philip E. Jones, eds, *Calendar of Plea & Memoranda Rolls of the City of London 1323–1482*, 6 vols (Cambridge, 1926–61)

Vergil, Polydore, *The Anglica Historia of Polydore Vergil A.D. 1485–1537*, trans. D. Hay (London, 1950)

Yorke, P., Earl of Hardwicke, ed., *Miscellaneous State Papers from 1501 to 1726*, 2 vols (London, 1778)

Secondary Sources

Addison Amos, Mark, '"For Manners Make Man": Bourdieu, de Certeau and the Common Appropriation of Noble Manners in the Book of Courtesy', in *Medieval Conduct*, ed. Kathleen Ashley & Robert L.A. Clark (Minneapolis, 2001), pp. 23–48

Allen, Martin & Matthew Davies, eds, *Medieval Merchants and Money, Essays in Honour of James L. Bolton* (London, 2016)

Amin, Nathen, *Henry VII and the Tudor Pretenders, Simnel, Warbeck and Warwick* (Stroud, 2020)

Arthurson, I., 'The Rising of 1497: A Revolt of the Peasantry?' in *People, Politics and Community in the Later Middle Ages,* ed. Joel Rosenthal & Colin Richmond (Gloucester, 1987), pp. 1–18

Atherton, Ian, Eric Fernie, Christopher Harper-Bill & Hassell Smith, eds, *Norwich Cathedral: City, Church and Diocese 1096–1996* (London, 1996)

Bailey, Mark, *After the Black Death: Economy, Society and the Law in Fourteenth-Century England* (Oxford, 2021)

Baker, Sir John, *The Men of Court 1440 to 1550: A Prosopography of the Inns of Court and Chancery and of the Courts of Law*, 2 vols (London, 2012)

Ball, R.M., 'The Opponents of Bishop Pecok', *Journal of Ecclesiastical History*, 48:2 (1997), pp. 230–62

Barron, Caroline M., 'London and the Crown 1451–61' in *The Crown and Local Communities in England and France in the Fifteenth Century*, ed. J.R.L. Highfield & Robin Jeffs (Gloucester, 1981), pp. 88–109, repub. in *Medieval London: Collected Papers of Caroline M. Barron*, ed. Martha Carlin & Joel T. Rosenthal (Kalamazoo, 2017), pp. 57–82

Barron, Caroline M., *London in the Later Middle Ages: Government and People 1200–1500* (Oxford, 2004)

Barron, Caroline M., *The Medieval Guildhall of London* (London, 1974)

Beaven, Alfred B., *The Aldermen of the City of London*, 2 vols (London, 1913)

Bennett, H.S., *The Pastons and their England: Studies in an Age of Transition* (Cambridge, 1922; reprinted 1995)

Bennett, Michael J., 'Henry VII and the Northern Rising of 1489', *English Historical Review*, 105 (1990), pp. 34–59

Blomefield, Francis, *An Essay Towards A Topographical History of the County of Norfolk*, 11 vols (London, 1805–10)

Bolton, J.L., 'The City and the Crown 1456–61', *London Journal*, 12:1 (1986), pp. 11–24

Bolton, J.L., *The Medieval English Economy 1150–1500* (London, 1980)

Bolton, J.L., '"The World Turned Upside Down": Plague as an Agent of Economic and Social Change' in *The Black Death in England*, ed. Mark Ormrod & Philip Lindley (Donnington, 2003), pp. 17–78

Bowsher, David, Tony Dyson, Nick Holder & Isca Howell, eds, *The London Guildhall: An Archaeological History of a Neighbourhood from Early Medieval to Modern Times*, 2 vols (London: MOLAS, 2007)

Browne, Thomas, *Repertorium: or some account of the tombs and monuments in the cathedral church of Norwich begun by Sir Thomas Browne and continued from the year 1680 to this present time* (London, 1712)

Castor, Helen, *Blood and Roses* (London, 2004)

Childs, Wendy, '"To oure losse and hindraunce": English Credit to Alien Merchants in the Mid-Fifteenth Century' in *Enterprise and Individuals in Fifteenth-Century England*, ed. Jennifer Kermode (Stroud, 1991), pp. 68–98

Clark, Linda, ed., *The House of Commons 1422–1461*, 7 vols (Cambridge, 2020)

Cockayne, George Edward, ed., *The Complete Peerage of England, Scotland, Ireland, Great Britain and the United Kingdom*, 13 vols (Gloucester, 1910–59)

Coldstream, Nicola, 'The Roles of Women in Late Medieval Civic Pageantry in England' in *Reassessing the Roles of Women as 'Makers' of Medieval Art and Architecture*, ed. Therese Martin (Leiden, 2012), pp. 175–96

Cooper, William Durrant, 'The Families of Braose of Chesworth and Hoo', *Sussex Archaeological Collections*, 8 (1856), pp, 13–131

Cunningham, Sean, *Prince Arthur: The Tudor King Who Never Was* (Stroud, 2016)

Du Boulay, F.R.H., *An Age of Ambition: English Society in the Late Middle Ages* (London, 1970)

Duffy, Eamon, *Saints, Sacrilege and Sedition: Religion and Conflict in the Tudor Reformations* (London, 2012)

Dyer, Christopher, *Making a Living in the Middle Ages: The People of Britain 850–1520* (New Haven & London, 2002)

Dyer, Christopher, *Standards of Living in the Later Middle Ages: Social Change in England c. 1200–1520* (Cambridge, 1989; rev. 1998)

Eiden, Herbert, 'Joint Action Against "Bad" Lordship: The Peasants' Revolt in Essex and Norfolk', *History*, 83 (1998), pp. 5–30

Emden, A.B., *A Biographical Register of the University of Cambridge to 1500*
    (Cambridge, 1963)
French, Katherine, 'The Material Culture of Childbirth in Late Medieval London and its
    Suburbs', *Journal of Women's History*, 28:2 (2016), pp. 126–48
Gottfried, Robert S., *The Black Death: Natural and Human Disaster in Medieval Europe*
    (New York, 1985)
Gregory, Mother Mary, 'Wickham Court and the Heydons', *Archaeologia Cantiana*, 78
    (1963), pp.1–21
Griffiths, Elizabeth, 'The Boleyns at Blickling 1450–1560', *Norfolk Archaeology*, 45
    (2009), pp. 453–68
Griffiths, R.A., *The Reign of King Henry VI* (Stroud, 1981)
Gunn, Steven, *Henry VII's New Men and the Making of Tudor England* (Oxford, 2016)
Hanawalt, Barbara A., *Ceremony and Civility: Civic Culture in Late Medieval London*
    (Oxford, 2017)
Hanawalt, Barbara A., *Growing up in Medieval London* (Oxford, 1993)
Hanawalt, Barbara A., *The Wealth of Wives: Women, Law and Economy in Late Medieval
    London* (Oxford, 2007)
Harris, Barbara J., *English Aristocratic Women 1450–1550* (Oxford, 2002)
Harriss, G.L., 'The Struggle for Calais: An Aspect of the Rivalry Between Lancaster and
    York', *English Historical Review*, 75 (1960), pp. 30–53
Harrod, Henry, *Gleanings among the Castles and Convents of Norfolk* (Norwich, 1857)
Haward, W.I., 'The Relations Between the Lancastrian Government and the Merchants
    of the Staple from 1449 to 1461', in *Studies in English Trade in the Fifteenth Century*,
    ed. Eileen Power & M.M. Postan (London, 1933), pp. 293–320
Hill, Carole, *Women and Religion in Late Medieval Norwich* (Woodbridge, 2010)
Horrox, Rosemary, *Richard III: A Study in Service* (Cambridge, 1991)
Horrox, Rosemary & W. Mark Ormrod, eds, *A Social History of England 1200–1500*
    (Cambridge, 2006)
Ives, Eric, *The Life and Death of Anne Boleyn* (Oxford, 2004)
Jewell, Helen M., *English Local Administration in the Middle Ages* (Newton Abbot, 1972)
Jones, Dan, *The Hollow Crown: The Wars of the Roses and the Rise of the Tudors*
    (London, 2014)
Keene, D.J. & Vanessa Harding, *Historical Gazetteer of London Before the Great Fire
    Cheapside: Parishes of All Hallows Honey Lane, St Martin Pomary, St Mary le Bow,
    St Mary Colechurch and St Pancras Soper Lane* (London, 1987)
Lander, J.R., *English Justices of the Peace 1461–1509* (Gloucester, 1989)
Leyser, Henrietta, *Medieval Women: A Social History of Women in England 450–1500*
    (London, 1995)
Lloyd, T.H., *The English Wool Trade in the Middle Ages* (Cambridge, 1977)
Mackay, Lauren, *Among the Wolves of Court: The Untold Story of Thomas and George Boleyn*
    (London, 2018)
McFarlane, K.B., 'Loans to the Lancastrian Kings: The Problem of Inducement', *The
    Cambridge Historical Journal*, 9:1 (1947), pp. 51–68
McSheffrey, Shannon, *Marriage, Sex and Civic Culture in Late Medieval London*
    (Philadelphia, 2006)

Mercer, Malcolm, 'Driven to Rebellion? Sir John Lewknor, Dynastic Loyalty and Debt',
  Sussex Archaeological Collections, 137 (1999), pp. 153–59

Mertes, Kate, 'Aristocracy', in *Fifteenth-Century Attitudes: Perceptions of Society in Late
  Medieval England*, ed. Rosemary Horrox (Cambridge, 1994), pp. 42–60

Nightingale, Pamela, *A Medieval Mercantile Community: The Grocers' Company and the
  Politics and Trade of London 1000–1485* (New Haven & London, 1995)

Norton, Elizabeth, *The Boleyn Women* (Stroud, 2013)

Orme, Nicholas, *From Childhood to Chivalry: The Education of the English Kings and
  Aristocracy 1066–1530* (London & New York, 1984)

Orme, Nicholas, *Medieval Children* (New Haven & London, 2003)

Parsons, W.L.E., *Salle: The Story of a Norfolk Parish, its Church, Manors and People*
  (Norwich, 1937)

Parsons, W.L.E., 'Some Notes on the Boleyn Family', *Norfolk Archaeology*, 25:3 (1934),
  pp. 386–407

Payling, S.J., 'Social Mobility, Demographic Change and Landed Society in Late
  Medieval England', *Economic History Review*, 45 (1992), pp. 51–73

Penn, Thomas, *The Brothers York: An English Tragedy* (London, 2019)

Penn, Thomas, *Winter King: The Dawn of Tudor England* (London, 2012)

Pilbrow, Fionn, 'The Knights of the Bath: Dubbing to Knighthood in Lancastrian and
  Yorkist England', in *Heraldry, Pageantry and Social Display in Medieval England*, ed.
  Maurice Keen & Peter Coss (Woodbridge, 2002)

Power, Eileen & M.M. Postan, eds, *Studies in English Trade in the Fifteenth Century*
  (London, 1933)

Radulescu, Raluca & Alison Truelove, eds, *Gentry Culture in Late Medieval England*
  (Manchester, 2005)

Roskell, J.S., L. Clark & C. Rawcliffe, eds, *The House of Commons 1386–1421*
  (Woodbridge, 1993)

Schofield, John, *Medieval London Houses* (New Haven & London, 1995)

Schofield, John, Patrick Allen & Colin Taylor, 'Medieval Buildings and Property
  Development in the Area of Cheapside', *Transactions of the London and Middlesex
  Archaeological Society*, 41 (1990), pp. 39–237

Scofield, Cora L., *The Life and Reign of Edward the Fourth: King of England and of France and
  Lord of Ireland*, 2 vols (London, 1923; repub. 2016)

Sharpe, Reginald R., *London and the Kingdom*, 3 vols (London, 1894–95)

Shaw, William Arthur, *The Knights of England* (London, 1906)

Shelley, Andy, *Dragon Hall, King Street, Norwich: Excavation and Survey of a Late Medieval
  Merchant's Trading Complex*, East Anglian Archaeology Report 112 (Norwich, 2005)

Stanley-Millson, Caroline & John Newman, 'Blickling Hall: The Building of a Jacobean
  Mansion', *Architectural History*, 29 (1986), pp. 1–42

Sutton, Anne F., *The Mercery of London: Trade, Goods and People 1130–1578* (London, 2005;
  repub. 2016)

Thrupp, Sylvia L., *The Merchant Class of Medieval London* (Michigan, 1948)

Venn, John and J.A. Venn, *Alumni Cantabrigienses*, 2 vols (Cambridge, 1922)

Wedgwood, Josiah C. & Anne D. Holt, *History of Parliament: Biographies of the Members of
  the Commons House 1439–1509* (London, 1936)

Unpublished Works

Crawford, Anne, 'The Career of John Howard, Duke of Norfolk 1420–1485' (unpublished PhD thesis, Bedford College, University of London, 1975)

Hovland, Stephanie R., 'Apprenticeship in Later Medieval London *c.* 1300–*c.* 1530' (unpublished PhD thesis, Royal Holloway, University of London, 2006)

Peake, M.I., 'London and the Wars of the Roses' (unpublished MA thesis, University of London, 1925)

Prescott, Andrew John, 'Judicial Records of the Rising of 1381' (unpublished PhD thesis, Bedford College, University of London, 1984)

Thurley, Simon, 'Hever Castle' (unpublished report, 2020)

Vokes, Susan Elizabeth, 'The Early Career of Thomas, Lord Howard, Earl of Surrey and Third Duke of Norfolk, 1474–*c.* 1525' (unpublished PhD thesis, University of Hull, 1988)

Index